Marriage Bureau
The True Story That Revolutionised Dating

written by
Mary Oliver & Mary **Benedetta**

with additional material and photographs by
Richard Kurti

Marriage Bureau
First published in 1942
This edited edition published in 2021 by
B7 Enterprises Limited
Unit 2, Whitegates, Berries Road
Cookham, Berkshire, SL6 9SD
www.b7media.com

Print and digital editions distributed by
Andrews UK Limited
www.andrewsuk.com

Hardback ISBN: 9781914169250
Paperback ISBN: 9781906577704
eBook ISBNs: 9781914169267 & 9781914169274

Contents

Photo Credits

Preface: The Dating Game

I t was pure chance that led me to discover this forgotten gem. I was doing some research for a screenplay about a royal chef, when I came across a simple footnote: 'On 17 April 1939, two 25 year old women opened Britain's first marriage bureau in Bond Street.'

Immediately I was intrigued. When it was clear that the world was slipping towards a cataclysmic conflict, why on earth would two young women set up a business devoted to love and marriage?

Digging deeper, I discovered that one of the women, Mary Oliver, had written a book about it in 1942. It was only published once, possibly due to the wartime rationing of paper, before vanishing altogether, but I managed to get hold of a copy.

From the moment I turned the first page, I was hooked. This was a million miles from the stiff *Brief Encounter* world I had expected. Mary's voice was modern and blistering. Any woman who in 1942 can write *"so few wives have the intelligence to imagine that perhaps the most devoted husbands may not want to see too much of them,"* deserves an audience. Somehow I had to bring this book back to life.

In order to do that I needed to find out who owned the rights. I started on google, expanded my search through libraries and records offices, spent many days phoning lists of people who shared a surname, and finally, after 18 months, discovered seven people across two continents who, unbeknown to them, now owned the rights to the book. It was a fascinating journey, and along the way I discovered many things about Mary Oliver that showed just how ahead of her time she was.

Nowadays we take dating for granted; with online dating, virtual flirting, speed-dating, slow-dating, dinner-dating and singles' nights geared towards all ages, religions and sexual orientations, there's never been a better time to look for love. But if you wind the clock back to 1939, you find yourself in a very different world...

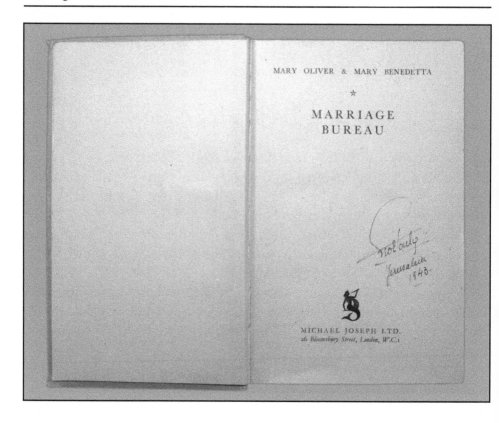

MARY OLIVER & MARY BENEDETTA

*

MARRIAGE
BUREAU

MICHAEL JOSEPH LTD.
26 Bloomsbury Street, London, W.C.1

The horrors of WWI and the Spanish flu pandemic had left Britain with an excess of nearly two million women; hard on the heels of war, the Great Depression caused huge social upheaval, disrupting whole communities and traditional ways of meeting the opposite sex. At the same time, expectations were rising; women who had worked in factories during the war had their horizons expanded, and now they had the vote as well, they set their sights higher in all aspects of life and love.

It was this yearning for something more that 25 year old Mary Oliver sensed when she set up the Bureau with just a few pounds in her pocket.

'A simple, quiet, rather demure young girl, with an intelligent, pretty face and gravely sympathetic dark-brown eyes,' is how her co-author describes Mary.

'Flamboyant.' 'Tough.' 'Sharp.' 'A loner.' 'Self-sufficient.' 'Single-minded.' 'Streetwise.' 'Dogmatic.' 'Formidable,' is how people who met Mary Oliver remember her. She was the child her parents always worried about. In 1935 they thought they'd married her off to a respectable civil servant in colonial

India. But just as everyone breathed a sigh of relief, Mary decided she didn't like the man after all and sold the wedding presents to buy a ticket back to England.

Thank goodness she dumped the dull fiancé, because it was on that steamship that she had her revolutionary idea: *to set up the UK's first ever marriage bureau.*

Chapter I

An unfortunate experiment – How Mary Oliver thought of the Marriage Bureau and why she started it – Journey to India with a one-way ticket – What happened in India – Plans to start the Marriage Bureau – Looking for an office.

Somebody had left the gate open. I noticed it because it was one of those single iron gates that had dropped on its hinges and you could never shut it casually. You had to coax it over hummocks in the gravel path and I remembered doing this when I went out.

I wondered vaguely who had come to call. Probably it was one of my mother's usual country visitors, and I didn't give it another thought, as today I was feeling particularly happy and carefree.

I had been for a walk in the rain, rejoicing secretly, while my feet seemed to float over the clogging mud paths, and I wanted to sing stupid songs to the two spaniels who were flurrying in and out of the dripping hedges. Nobody knew what those last three weeks had been like, or what a release I was now celebrating.

What did it matter if it was a gloomy day? I looked across the lawn at the square-towered village church, and its wet grey walls; at the mulberry tree in the middle of the lawn standing like an old man in a heavy damp cloak, and the dark group of yew trees at the end of the path. And I took hold of a branch of rhododendrons and shook it light-heartedly as I went past, so that the overloaded raindrops showered on my mackintosh. Nothing could possibly be sombre for me that afternoon.

The short garden path belonged to my home in Cambridgeshire, a simple farmhouse that had stood there for five hundred years. Still in my gayest mood on this summer afternoon, I opened the front door into the wide stone hall ... and heard something that made me stop quite still.

Suddenly I realised the awfulness of what had happened. My gay mood vanished before the mockery of the disaster I had done so much to avert.

*The farmhouse where Mary Oliver grew up, with
the mulberry tree and church beyond*

I dragged off my Wellington boots and stood them in a corner on the stone floor away from the rug. I was staring at the familiar copper log box, and listening to the slow tick of the grandfather clock. It seemed hours instead of seconds before the voices spoke again and made me more certain of what I dreaded to believe.

The farmhouse where Mary Oliver grew up, with the mulberry tree and church beyond.

For the past three weeks I had sat in that hall, listening for footsteps outside. Whenever they came, I darted towards the door, and as the maid appeared from the back of the hall, I had to look as if I just happened to be going out at that particular moment. Each time I had somehow manoeuvred my visitor away again, and decoyed him out of earshot towards the gate.

There was the same vigil on the telephone. For three weeks I had never dared to bathe properly, but made a cautious splashing in the bath, while I kept my dressing-gown near to hand, ready for the headlong rush to reach the telephone before anyone else. Sometimes I was beaten – usually by my schoolboy brother who so inconveniently was home for the holidays.

Mealtimes were an ordeal of anxiety. Often just as I was lulled into a false sense of security, enjoying my soup and thinking the whole thing was safely over, my mother would say: "Mr— rang you up." She always said it without comment, but in a way that made me feel she wanted him explained. Or my father would suddenly come out of a reverie about the cows and horses to give me a message from yet another caller on the telephone that they had never heard of before. I used to think how scandalised they would have been had I told them I had never heard of them either.

How could I ever tell my family that I had put an advertisement in a matrimonial weekly?

I did it because I was planning to start a Marriage Bureau, and I wanted to find out how the matrimonial papers worked, so that I could follow my own lines with the bureau and be sure I wasn't copying anything that already existed. What better way to find out than to become a client?

So I paid £5 and advertised for a husband. But in my zeal over the experiment I never gave a thought to the consequences. And these took the awkward shape of a continuous flow of would-be husbands who made surprise attacks on my home. Bus drivers, commercial travellers, city clerks, sanitary inspectors and railwaymen either rang up or arrived unheralded on the doorstep in alarmingly quick succession.

Of course, I hadn't told my family about the advertisement because they would be horrified, and I dared not mention the Marriage Bureau in case they disapproved and tried to frustrate my precious plan.

So for those nightmare weeks I had been afraid to leave the house in case I was not there when any of my 'suitors' arrived.

Finally, after three weeks there was a heaven-sent lull for two whole days, so I decided the attack was over and I could safely venture out. But it was an untimely confidence had led me out on that walk.

Now I tried to summon my courage by persuading myself that this might be a perfectly ordinary caller after all, and seizing the handle of the door I walked in bravely.

My mother was sitting in a large arm-chair by the fireplace, looking dignified but slightly bewildered. Opposite her was a nondescript little man in a black suit, with a face the colour of old paper. I remember thinking he looked like an undertaker. He was sitting so much on the edge of the low easy-chair that his knees were almost on the floor, and he was clinging with both hands to a thick gold watch-chain that hung across his waistcoat.

It seemed an eternity while I waited in the doorway and said nothing. Even the dogs seemed to sense the awkward situation – they just stood disconsolately on each side of me, still panting, their wet coats beginning to steam in the warmth of the room.

"Here *is* my daughter," said my mother. "This is Mr Wheeler, Mary."

Again the tone of voice that expected an explanation.

"Oh," I said quickly. "How do you do? Did you have a good journey?"

I tried my best to sound as though I had asked him down for the day.

"Pleased to meet you. Yes, thank you, miss; I came down by the Green Line."

The little man swivelled round and tried to stand, but his legs were so crumpled up under his knees he only got into a crouching attitude. I could imagine him in the same attitude on a bowling green.

"Was it crowded?" I asked the question while I was playing for time, wondering what had passed between him and my mother before I came in.

"Not so bad."

This was awful, because now I must say something else. I had hoped he would ramble on while I tried to assess the amount of damage that had already been done. I could only think of things to say that would hardly fit when I was supposed to know he was coming down.

Obviously he had cut out the advertisement and kept it in his pocket till he had a free day. How many more had done the same thing? There might be fifty parchment-faced men still running round with the cutting in their pockets and I mightn't be safe for months.

"Come and see the garden," I invited suddenly, forgetting that it was pouring with rain.

Once I got him outside I could tell him I was 'suited,' which was how I put off all the others, but I couldn't do that in front of my mother.

On the way to the front door I gave him an airy description of my walk to cover our retreat, as I was terrified he would start talking about the advertisement before we were out of earshot.

Outside I shut the front door carefully and began leading him towards the gate. But parchment-face had seen the church and stood gazing at it from the porch.

"Ah," he said pontifically, "to have the church so near your home."

I supposed he was thinking of our wedding, and hastily tried to change the subject. "That mulberry tree is very old," I announced bleakly.

Then I saw him scanning the ancient tombstones in the small graveyard.

"To think," he said, "All their relatives died long ago, and there's nobody to put flowers on their graves."

So he *was* an undertaker.

"But now that's unnecessary," he continued. "If they was to have everlasting flowers those graves would never look forgotten. Immortal flowers for people who've gone to the immortal life."

"You're interested in graves?"

"I live off them."

Then it crossed my mind he might be a grave-digger.

"I've plenty put by for when I can't carry on. Twelve-roomed house – holidays abroad – a tidy bit of life insurance when I die."

He removed a hand from his watch-chain to wave it expansively. "All done by flowers."

"Flowers?" I murmured vaguely.

"Wax flowers – put under glass so no dust can't get at 'em. Complete with an R.I.P. message."

The graveyard where Mary dealt with the wax flower man

So that was it. Parchment-face had made a small fortune in artificial wreaths in glass cases and wanted a wife to share it with him.

If I had not been so anxious over his conversation with my mother in the drawing-room I might have burst out laughing. Besides, there was still the matter of telling him that I was suited.

When the flower-man had gone I purposely went back to the drawing-room to write a letter. If there was going to be an inquest over him it had better happen now rather than at the dinner-table with all the family present. But I wasn't going to lead into it myself.

My mother was just leaving the room when I came in.

"I do wish," she said casually, "that you wouldn't let travelling salesmen get hold of your name and come all the way down here."

Inwardly I breathed a sigh of relief; whether by accident or not, the little wreath-maker had kept my secret gallantly.

Of course, this was all partly my own fault, as in my advertisement I had only stated that I wanted a husband who was not fat. But even if I had given more particulars, it was far from certain that the right people would come along. The matrimonial paper was a medium for people who wished to advertise for a husband or wife, but how much better it would be if there were an organisation that could arrange the actual match-making and see that only suitable people met each other.

This was my idea for the Marriage Bureau. I would make each prospective bride and bridegroom fill in a detailed form, both about themselves and about the kind of person they wanted to marry. Whenever it was possible, I would try to see clients in person, so that from my own observation I could add details to their cards which would be of value in helping us to choose the right kind of person for them to meet.

In this way I hoped to pair people off who shared the same tastes, religion, social status and income; and whose marriage, therefore, would start with a firm basis of equality and common interest.

I decided to start in London because it was most central and would be convenient for people coming home on leave from abroad. I wanted the Bureau to cover all walks of life.

And after all, London was rather like a marriage market anyway, with parents spending fortunes to display their daughters impressively before supposedly eligible young men. Surely the whole thing might be done more satisfactorily, and infinitely more cheaply, through a Marriage Bureau.

In the ordinary way nobody knows all the practical details about their prospective husband or wife before they meet them. The most important step in life is usually left to chance. Young men wander aimlessly through life, hoping that by some happy coincidence they will meet the girl of their dreams. And girls sit waiting for 'Mr Right' (that nostalgic person invented by our parents) who probably does not come along anyway. Then there is human nature's awkward trick of falling in love first and considering whether the match is suitable afterwards. Luck plays too large a part in this serious business of marriage.

It was with all these thoughts that I decided on this strange career of finding other people's happiness.

The idea first came to me when I was coming home from India, where I had stayed with an uncle on holiday. There, as so often happens, I had got engaged to a most eligible man in the district. He was older than I was, but I soon discovered that he had set ideas about the uses and purposes of a wife, and I was to be moulded along these lines. Instead of our laughing and having fun together and sharing interests, he spent most of our time together lecturing me on how I was to behave when we were married. Finally, on the eve of the dreaded and expensive wedding, I broke off the engagement, sold my wedding presents and bought a ticket home.

On the voyage I thought of all the eligible young men in places like India who want to get married and hurriedly propose to the first presentable girl they meet, who might be utterly unsuitable; and I thought of all the attractive girls in England waiting for husbands. All this ill-adjustment seemed such a waste. It was a pity there could not be some medium for bringing the right people together.

When I reached home I had exactly £15. And as £5 went on the advertisement in the matrimonial paper, I only had a capital of £10 with which to start the Bureau.

The first thing I did was to go to Scotland Yard and find out whether I would be breaking the law in any way. But the Scotland Yard officials could find no objection when I told them how I wanted to run it, nor any record of another Marriage Bureau, so I felt free to start.

I had planned the business in my cabin on the voyage home, and all I had to do now was to look for an office.

Mr. Roy H. S. Oliver

requests the pleasure of

.... company

at the wedding of his niece

Miss Audrey M. Parsons

&

Mr. J. A. Oliver

at All Saints Church Cinnamara

on Tuesday February 19th. 1935 at

12-30 and afterwards to

luncheon at Jorhat Club.

R. S. V. P.
Meleng Estate,
Nakachari P. O.
Assam.

Faded invitation to Mary's wedding that never was

'Comfortable office facilities, 12/6 per week.'

My eyes were fixed on a small-print announcement in the advertising column of the morning newspaper, and I went on staring at it until my breakfast coffee was stone cold. It sounded just what I wanted, and the rent was far more commensurate with my £10 capital than anything else I had come across. I decided to go up to London that morning.

The address was in a big West End thoroughfare near Piccadilly Circus. What in the world could be more central and convenient? I almost sang when I arrived at the entrance to the imposing modern block of offices.

"Will you please show me the empty office on the fourth floor?"

The uniformed lift attendant looked at me in surprise, and my heart sank as for a moment I fancied somebody else must have snapped it up already. Then he saw the newspaper cutting I was still holding in my hand. He nodded and beckoned me into the lift.

I thought at first I must have come through the wrong door. It was a large room, full of odd-looking men sitting at their desks in bowler hats which they had not bothered to take off. One was lying back in his chair with his feet on his desk, talking loudly down the telephone. Most of them were making notes or ringing people up, while a few just sat and stared gloomily at the others. There were several hangers-on who lolled round in overcoats with bulging pockets, and the room seemed to be littered with all kinds of samples from stockings to toothpaste.

It took me several seconds to realise they were all carrying on different businesses, (they seemed to be mainly bookies and people who send round free samples) and there was one empty desk which some of the hangers-on were using as a seat.

Then it dawned on me that the 'comfortable office facilities' meant a desk among this extraordinary assembly, without any privacy at all. I pictured my Marriage Bureau clients coming to discuss their private lives, and being leered at by the brotherhood of bowler hats.

Without a word I made my escape. When I got outside the door I found I was holding a free sample of face powder, but I was so astonished over the whole thing I never noticed it being put into my hand.

I met Heather Jenner in Ceylon and she was on the boat coming home with me. Whenever I asked her to be my partner in the Marriage Bureau (which I did several times), she thought it was all a joke, and that it would never come off anyway. Now that I was looking for an office she joined in and helped me search – though still not yet believing I was serious.

In choosing an office for our purpose we had to think of various items of importance. We could not have one where there would be a tittering lift-boy who might giggle cheekily when he was showing up some of the clients. And we could not have a commissionaire standing outside the building because people might be shy of going in when he was there. Also we had to be somewhere that allowed us to have a signboard outside.

We went to quite a number of house-agents, but directly we told them we wanted the office to start a Marriage Bureau they said they had nothing on their books. I don't know quite what they thought the Bureau was going to be, but we might just as well have announced that we wanted to start a gambling den.

Then I remembered something which gave me a little more hope. A year before I went to India I had been to look at an office in a Bond Street attic. Not that I had any idea then of starting the Bureau. It was like a new form of window-shopping that I used to indulge in when I was bored – looking at

Heather Jenner and Mary Oliver

offices in case I could ever have one of my own, though I had not the vaguest notion what I would do in it.

Now I wondered suddenly whether that Bond Street attic was still to let, and stopping to find Heather, I went along to see. When we found the board still up I felt it must be my destiny, and after fetching the key from the hairdresser on the ground floor, we ran up the stairs and unlocked the shaky little door.

There were two desks, two exciting swivel chairs (I didn't know they were out of order), a telephone, and a brown linoleum floor with dark ink-stains. We stood there thinking it over, and the more we thought the more decided we became.

After all, we could not be very ambitious with a capital of only £10. The rent was 25 shillings for one room and a lavatory perched high up in the roof space. This included lighting, heating and furniture.

Perhaps it was my delight over finding an office that at last infected Heather with enthusiasm for the Marriage Bureau. Anyway, directly she saw I was quite serious about it she agreed to set out with me on our strange career, sharing all the hard work and responsibilities that it would involve.

Chapter II

The first client – How the Bureau works – Trying to find the first client a bride – A man of position makes a happy marriage – The first client gets married – Glamorising a church mouse.

"Who do you know *socially*?"

"Nobody."

"Oh, but I saw your picture in the *Bystander*."

He was tall, dark and very good-looking. His suit was well cut and the figure in the suit moved with assurance. For a moment I thought our first client at the Marriage Bureau was going to be everything a girl could wish. I might even have liked his voice, but I was so disconcerted by his way of opening the conversation that I hardly noticed it.

I had expected the first interview with the first client to be very difficult – I was prepared for frankness or shyness, and I had rehearsed many imaginary conversations, but I had never conceived the one that took place – *who did I know of social importance?*

My reply was involuntary as I really didn't see why I should parade my few titled friends to impress this young man from Calcutta.

Fortunately I managed to pull myself together enough to add that we *did* have some girls of very good family waiting for husbands.

Actually we had no wives to offer him at all, so I tried to describe them as vaguely as I could, while Heather kicked the telephone bell underneath her desk (we discovered we could make it ring that way) and answered fictitious calls from dazzling young women.

The client's manner to us was as though he was buying cheese that he had already failed to get at a more expensive shop. I felt acutely conscious of my overalls and the paint in my hair, while he stared curiously at the pots of paint we had not even had time to push into the corner. It was our very first day in the office, and we were painting it ourselves (primrose, because we thought it was spring-like and romantic) and we never expected anyone would come near us for days.

Sometimes he stared at Heather, who is very striking with her fair good looks and tall smart carriage, but I am afraid he was only assessing the number of times she might or might not have appeared in the *Tatler*.

As soon as I could, I handed him a form to fill in and got him off the dangerous subject of brides who didn't exist. In it he had to state his requirements as to his wife's height, religion, figure, income and so on, and various details about himself including whether he had been married before and whether he had any encumbrances.

These forms sometimes arrive with rather curious entries, especially when they are sent in by post. Amongst other things clients have to fill in particulars about their hobbies and interests. One woman filled hers in as 'Sex.'

Some of the men give a touchingly full picture of the wife they have been dreaming about and could never find. Like a young officer with a generous four-figure income, and glamorous hobbies like polo and big-game hunting, who said he wanted somebody slim, with essentially good breeding and charming manners, good legs, lovely hands, a good complexion and a nice voice. The same day we received a form from an industrial chemist who only wanted somebody with 'good teeth and a straight nose.'

'Calcutta' filled in his form with alacrity. While he flourished his pen, he told me that was in jute, his income was about £800 a year and he wanted to 'marry into Society' and take his glittering society wife back to India with him.

He kept on referring to 'one's friends in Calcutta' who would be so hurt if he did not make a 'good' marriage. His main ambition in life seemed to be to get his photograph in the *Tatler*, *Sketch* or *Bystander*, and marrying a title seemed to be the obvious way to arrive at that gratifying achievement.

When he left I felt rather sick and very dispirited about our prospects of ever finding him a suitable wife. But he had paid his registration fee of £5 5s and we had put him on the books, so we just had to go on giving him introductions till he found his soul-mate, because that was the arrangement. When a marriage took place, if it ever did, he would have to pay us £21.

We felt almost dishonest at taking £5 when our capital was only £10. But we were soon to find it was very hard-earned.

That day several girls came in from varied walks of life, most of them very nervous but only at first. They soon got over it when they were telling us about their ideal husbands. If they were reasonably attractive we put them on the books and took their registration fee. Otherwise we told them that we could not accept their names until we had some people who might suit them.

Among our first day's would-be brides we had a girl who had an interesting family tree and worked in a beauty salon (not the one beneath our office). So to show Calcutta how prompt we were, we introduced them.

I deposited her at the Ritz at half-past twelve, feeling very proud of her because she certainly matched him in looks, and then left them alone together to have lunch.

Heather and I were so excited over what we believed was going to be our first match that we could hardly contain ourselves through the afternoon till we had news of how the meeting went off.

What we had entirely forgotten was that the girl with the aristocratic family had to work all day for her living, and had no time for promiscuous publicity on the race-meetings page of the *Tatler*.

He came in next day, and while he announced condescendingly that she was certainly well born, he took exception to her working in the beauty parlour. "One's friends in Calcutta, you know, wouldn't have liked it. Of course, if she had *owned* the beauty parlour and it had been in Bond Street, things might have been different."

The girl's report was equally discouraging. She rang up and said he was frightful. Nobody, in fact, took a very good view of him, and the rapturous faces I had hoped to see never came along.

Then one day he asked me out to dine with him. As I like to know as much about my clients as possible, I accepted willingly. To my dismay he was even more pompous in the restaurant than he was in our office. By the time we got to the second course every waiter in sight had been called 'Boy' and told how the standard of English cooking had gone down since he was last home on leave. "Why, the jolly old Taj was better than this."

It was so painful I tried to talk him out of the whole idea of marriage, but without much effect.

When we started the Marriage Bureau we had no typewriter, so we had to answer all our correspondence by hand. By the end of the first week it had become overwhelming and we had to hire a secretary; after another week its proportions grew *so* enormous we were obliged to install a second secretary.

By the time we had been going for a month we were getting an average of 300 letters a day, and the Marriage Bureau was well launched. So with renewed confidence we moved into a large first-floor office with an outer office and a waiting room.

The office in New Bond Street as it looks today

We tried to make our new office a much more attractive setting for the opening chapter of anyone's romance, and I think we succeeded. It had silver walls, mauve chiffon curtains, a soft carpet and vases of lilies; except for our desks it looked more like a drawing-room.

The waiting-room, and the fact that our own office where we interviewed people had a separate exit, were things that added greatly to our peace of mind as it meant there was no chance of embarrassing accidental encounters on the stairs.

Soon after we moved, a very distinguished and extremely pleasant man arrived as a prospective client. He was good-looking with a very nice expression and equally nice manners. Recently he had retired from one of the Services, and now held a responsible job for the Government somewhere out of London.

Meanwhile he was spending a pleasant, quiet life in the country, with plenty of fishing and shooting, but he wanted an attractive, well-bred wife to share it with and to be a good hostess in his home.

He had written us sensible, intelligent and quite amusing letters about the people we had suggested, and he had been corresponding with them and looking at their photographs. Now he had chosen the girl he wanted to meet, for they had already taken a liking to each other in their letters, and he had come to see us to have a talk before he took her out.

From those letters he wrote we had really got to know him quite well. He had been stationed in India most of his life, in places where he met very few people. On his leaves, although he went about a great deal, he had never happened to meet the type of person he had set his heart on for a wife.

Now that he was settled in England, retired from the army and working in a job which did not keep him fully occupied, he was feeling lonely and wanted to get married.

"I don't wish to get married just for the sake of being married," he told us, "I would rather remain single than make a regrettable mistake, for I've no use for a loveless marriage."

He also said, "Frankly I'm not keen to marry someone who's too well off. I've been more of less hard-up all my life and I'm used to it, and it wouldn't be fair to marry someone whose tastes I couldn't live up to."

This was when he eschewed meeting a beautiful peeress with a good deal of money who did not mind whether her husband had money or not, as long as he was a type to be proud of. But we were glad when he did this because we are always on our guard against fortune hunters.

When he was talking to us, he made us feel like connoisseurs in some exquisite work of art for which we were helping him to search the world. We knew that he was a man who would regard his wife as something so rare and precious that he would always be good to her and he deserved somebody especially adorable and worth such treasured keeping.

That we found just such an exquisite creature for him was one of the happenings that made the whole enterprise seem worthwhile. For the girl he had chosen to meet that day was all he had hoped for, and they were married not long afterwards. They still write to us telling us how ideally happy they are.

And all the time, it turns out they had met once before in India and liked each other then. He spoke to her for five minutes at a party and had been kicking himself ever since for not having tried to follow her up.

By now Calcutta was nearing the end of his leave and was getting impatient, for he still had not found a wife. We were just growing exasperated and thinking we would have to ship him back alone, when in walked the solution. She was rather bulgy, she wore putty-coloured clothes, and had a putty complexion; rather like a cold pudding with eyes like currants that someone had pressed too far into its surface.

But she was the daughter of a peeress, and she wanted to marry someone who would take her out to the colonies. She never said why she wanted to go there, but perhaps I was too distracted to ask her, for when she opened her bag to take out her handkerchief several picture press cuttings fluttered casually to the floor.

I stooped to pick them up and looked at them on the way, as I believe she really intended me to do. It was too good to be true – there she was, with all her bulges, standing broadside to the camera in a page from the *Tatler*. There were others of her, generally with a tin, collecting for charity, and never looking particularly glamorous. But she was there – definitely – in the *Tatler*.

She had no money, and she did not seem to have any particular gift which might replace this contingency, but we knew that did not matter. There was quite a chance she would qualify for 'one's friends in Calcutta.'

And she did. They got engaged in about three days, and I never heard a murmur of complaint about the bulges or the putty.

But there was still one last fence before the wedding. Calcutta's mother was a landlady in Scotland, where she lived in comparative comfort and prosperity. She, poor soul, had to be sacrificed on the altar of 'one's friends,' and before the wedding could be announced in *The Times* she was banished to one room in Cannes, where she would both add glamour to the announcement and not be expected to turn up at the wedding.

How her son managed it I don't know, but her exile was effected in about ten days and the wedding took place directly she was safely out of the way.

We often wonder how they are getting on. And whether the wife ever feels awkward when he talks about 'one's friends at Londonderry House,'(one of the landmarks of colonial Calcutta). For this, I learned from someone who knew him in India, was his watchword there although he had never been inside Londonderry House in his life. Anyway, they seemed delighted with each other when they left.

In a sense, though a travesty of it, these two were a fulfilment of the reason I first started the Marriage Bureau when I was coming home from India.

But there is another side of our work besides the actual match-making, which to me is just as gratifying. I discovered it soon after we first opened.

She was thirty-four and she wore a putty-coloured coat. I don't know why so many unattractive women wear putty, but they do. She had a hat like one in a cartoon in *Punch* magazine, and underneath it a face that had no sort of visible attraction beyond a reasonably clear skin. She wore glasses, quite presentable up-to-date glasses, but on her they made one think of Dorothy Parker's line, 'men seldom make passes at girls who wear glasses,' because her whole appearance was so mouse-like and ordinary. As she walked into the room, and she did not walk badly, we had a view of legs in putty-coloured woollen stockings, and shoes that came out in long thin points – just the kind of English shoes that Americans laugh at so justifiably.

From her few shy scraps of information it was easy to picture her setting. She lived in a village in Somerset, a typical English village with a church, a post-office, an inn and some retired elderly inhabitants. Her days were spent doing 'social work,' visiting the chronic invalids, arranging the flowers in the sanctuary and having passions for the vicar.

Before her lay the rest of her life along the same dull narrow channel, with no delicious turning that would suddenly whisk her out into some gay adventure. She was locked in a prison of her own making because she lacked the initiative to turn the key and walk out of it.

Then by pure chance, she saw a newspaper column about the Marriage Bureau—

"Mrs Fane, the doctor's wife, had given me some flowers from her garden that she thought could go round the font. She'd wrapped them up in a newspaper, and when I was undoing them in the vestry I couldn't help it but I'm afraid I caught sight of the column about you. And I thought perhaps..."

I realised I would have to come to the rescue with a rush, because she was suffused with a deep blush which covered the whole of her face and neck. "So you came to us because you would rather like to get married, and you just don't get a chance of meeting anybody where you live? Well, that's exactly what we're here for, so we'll see what can be done. I expect you've got some idea of the type of man that appeals to you. And you know whether you like living in the country, in Town or abroad. Are you fond of children? Would you mind taking on a widower with a ready-made family, or would you rather meet a bachelor? I do like to know all these little things because they help me so much. Also I'd like you to fill in this form, giving me a few more details about yourself."

There is usually a psychological moment in the first interview when we have to be very quick off the mark to make people feel they are not doing anything mad and extraordinary in coming to the Marriage Bureau.

Somerset was suddenly appalled at what she had done. Mentally she had split in two – one half of her had taken this dazzling plunge, while the other was shocked at her daring. It was up to me to reconcile the two.

When she first walked into the room she seemed a hopeless proposition, and merely that very sad object, a young and unattractive spinster. But while she was talking I was wondering whether I could not somehow re-create her and make her into the person she wanted to be. After all she *had* got a good clear skin and she spoke in a rather sweet, appealing little voice. In some way she *was* appealing. Surely, if one could pick out that appeal, strip away all that concealed it, and present it in a re-created human being, this would be a really satisfactory achievement. I decided to try.

By now her blushes had receded, she was relaxed from her tension like a dormouse uncurled in the first Spring sunshine, and was waiting as a delighted audience for the next act in her own enthralling drama. She had given me her complete trust and confidence, and become what a surgeon with a difficult operation to perform would call 'a good patient.'

"To begin with, I don't think you make the best of yourself." I said it quite kindly and uncritically. "I would like to show you what an attractive person you really are."

Straight away, before the shocked half could gain possession of her once more, I whisked her off to choose some underclothes. Not to an austere shop that would register ill-concealed distaste at the kind of things I believed she might be wearing, but to one in the purlieus round Piccadilly Circus that sold pretty things and yet was used to replacing strange relics without a sign of astonishment.

While she was still in a rather dazed condition at what she had done, we undressed her ... a process that was full of strange revelations.

It is hard to believe, but she had two petticoats both gathered round a tape at her waist. She wore the kind of stays the Government now say are holding up aircraft production. She had thick dark wool knickers with elastic round the waist and legs, and one of those things our grandmothers wore called a camisole, which could add any amount of matronly years to the prettiest young bosom.

Hidden beneath all these atrocities she really had a very neat little figure, and it was easy to fit her with a few dainty underclothes. The saleswoman and I exchanged a wink behind the fitting-room door, and the wardrobe belonging to her former life went into a West End dustbin.

Next I took her to get a good tailor-made suit and an attractive dress, coat and hat, smart shoes and several pairs of silk stockings. While the tailor-made was being altered I took her to the hairdresser.

It would have been easy to spend a fortune, but she only had £300 a year from a legacy, and maybe she was going to need a little spending money in the next few weeks, so I somehow managed to get the whole transformation done for £20. When she looked in the glass she was so delighted with herself that I do not think she would have cared whether it had cost her £20 or £200.

Now that she was re-created I was so pleased with the result I felt the rest would be easy going. We had even arranged for her to have a holiday in Town, away from the elderly aunt whose house she shared in Somerset. I was really very proud of her.

But I had not taken into consideration a whole mass of inhibitions that were still to be contended with, or the violent swing-over that would follow their collapse.

I had sent her out with a retired civil servant who we felt was a kind, unselfish, reliable person who would give her confidence in the male sex straight away.

Next morning the telephone rang.

"Can I come and see you?" she pleaded.

"Well, is it very important? Can't you tell me over the 'phone, because I'm frantically busy."

"No, it's so awful I can't possibly tell you on the telephone."

"Very well then, come round in half an hour."

I put down the receiver, feeling very apprehensive. Had I made a frightful mistake in sending her out with that man, whom I really thought any mother would have willingly trusted with her youngest daughter?

She came in like a ruffled chicken.

"He kissed me," she announced dramatically. "In the taxi going home."

"Well, why did you let him kiss you if you didn't want him to?"

Her face settled when she saw I did not regard it as a very startling event.

"Should one let a man kiss you the first day he meets you?"

The interview was growing difficult.

"Well, it really all depends on the man, and how much you like him. But if I were you I wouldn't let him kiss you the first time. Perhaps later if you really like him an awful lot, but not unless you do."

"How do you approach a man?" she asked suddenly, as though she were enquiring how to put a halter on a horse that was loose in a field.

"You don't."

She looked incredulous.

"No. You see," I went on, feeling the conversation was getting harder still, "it's the man's job to approach you and he doesn't like his job taken away from him."

How could I ever begin to teach her all the things that others know by instinct; the intricacies of genuine feminine naïveté; how the most elusive and detached were the most sought after?

Her very eagerness to attract was going to send her three steps back every time she took one forward. I had visions of her when she was married – waiting hand and foot on her spoilt lord, trying so desperately hard to please that he would despise her efforts, not exactly knowing why. It would be pathetic, like all the work she put into the sanctuary flowers only to spend the whole service hoping the vicar noticed them.

But that was far ahead, and we had not even found her a husband yet. I was afraid the next part of her story would be slow and disappointing, and that she would end up returning to the Somerset village, resigned to the fate from which she had risen in such daring revolt.

I couldn't have been more wrong. Instead she made the most startling progress, and my little sanctuary mouse underwent such a terrifying change that I began to think my re-creation had gone ahead of me most alarmingly.

It did end by her going back to Somerset for a while, but only to allow her finances to recover from her holiday in Town. She was still corresponding with someone very profusely, and using our office as a forwarding address (I think because she was frightened of the aunt).

Meanwhile, besides the civil servant, she had run through an M.P., a bookseller, a farmer, a naval officer and a textile manufacturer in the space of about five months. Only this time it was always the men who fell back from her unabashed advances.

One day a letter from her arrived at the office, to be forwarded to the young man she was writing to. We noticed that she had forgotten to close it down: it was very overladen, and as I picked it up a snapshot tumbled out. I looked at it. There was my sanctuary mouse, standing full view in a pair of very short scanty knickers and the barest little bust bodice, like an acrobatic dancer in a theatrical revue.

Feeling rather as if I were dreaming, I pushed it back into the envelope and in doing so I caught sight of a second snapshot – the same, only back view.

The end of the story was that she did marry the young man who had the letter with the snapshots, and the last we heard was that they were very happy.

And while I still take a special interest in grooming drab young women, I have learned that they may have to be curbed directly they get into their new disguise, for it goes to their heads like wine.

Chapter III

Problems of the Marriage Bureau – The missionaries – Mothers and daughters – Banker who put in his will that his daughters were to join the Bureau when he died – A father puts his three sons on the books – The shy girl – Hundreds of nurses – A misguided publicity scheme.

In the first few weeks we were beset with problems. For a long time we had on our books a large number of aristocratic girls and mostly working-class men. Then we had an influx of widows for whom we had to find middle-aged husbands, preferably widowers, because they did not want to marry what they called 'a set bachelor.'

We gathered a 'set bachelor' was somebody who had already made a home for himself to his own liking and intended to move his wife into it like an extra piece of furniture – either that, or he was so accustomed to going his own sweet way that he would probably never be at home anyway. Our clients imagined him womanish and fussy about the house, or else surrounded by collections that must never be dusted. At all events they thought he would be concreted into some way of living that would not appeal to them.

Quite early on we found that young men of about twenty-one to twenty-three were difficult to marry off – that is to say, those with a public school education followed by Oxford or Cambridge, who perhaps were articled to some profession or were just beginning a job. This is because most of the girls of twenty and twenty-one in that class want to marry men of twenty-eight or thirty. In the normal way, a girl might meet one of the younger ones and fall in love with him. Having fallen in love she decides to marry him and hopes that he will make a success of what he does. But if she is a client of the Marriage Bureau she naturally chooses to meet somebody whose success is more assured.

Working-class men of twenty-one to twenty-three are much easier because they probably started in their job at sixteen and have already held it down for several years. By this time they are earning quite a good salary, and as they have no traditional high standard of living to keep up, they have saved well.

Some of our earliest clients were missionaries (the first one came from the Gold Coast), and rather to our surprise and confusion we soon found we had half a dozen of them on the books. We thought they really were going to be a problem, until we discovered we could generally marry them to school-teachers, most of whom seemed to have a combined craze for religion and travel.

Ever since we opened we have nearly always had a steady half-dozen missionaries on our list, and they get snapped up quite quickly. They are generally in some remote part of Africa, from which they never seem to get leave, and the courtship usually takes place by post with an exchange of photographs. I suppose we are really a great service to them. It must be very exciting, when you are cut off somewhere quite lonely and uncivilised, perhaps for a lifetime, to be courting somebody by letter – and then persuading her into making the journey of her life to share a rather hard pillow at the farthest ends of the Christian earth.

We try to persuade every client who is near enough to come to the office for an interview, but sometimes the distance or their jobs prevent them from coming to see us until they have been corresponding with us for quite a while. Fortunately, we find that you can get to know a person quite well from letters because they are less shy over writing their innermost thoughts than they would be talking about them. Perhaps this is why the postal courtships often turn out so well.

Now and again we do get a shock when we finally meet someone. There was a young woman dispenser from the Midlands who wrote us wonderful letters, but when she eventually came to see us she turned out to be a grotesquely plain young woman who had tried to get herself up as a novelette vamp. She wore a long dress before lunch, a fur cape, a turban, and quantities of different-coloured necklaces. When she was talking she drooped in an affected languor before the fireplace, while a pair of bony little hands fluttered nervously among the beads.

It was the hands that reminded us that she was not a pantomime character but really a forlorn human being in search of happiness. Had we asked her for a photograph we should have been saved the shock.

We did begin by having photographs sent to the office, but we soon got so flooded with them (people would send *all* their photographs, beginning with a fat infant sprawling on a bearskin rug) that we had to ask clients only to send them to each other.

A surprising number of our clients are mothers and daughters, both of whom are on our books, but in many cases the mothers are most anxious that we should conceal this fact from their daughters.

Mrs Smart, for instance, arrived like a breezy shopper.

"I've come about my daughter," she announced brightly, and we felt she was going to be business-like and easy to deal with.

She was good-looking, graceful and knew how to dress. And we hoped fervently that the daughter had inherited her attributes, for we sometimes find that very smart mothers have unattractive daughters.

"Can you tell us how old your daughter is, what she is like, and something about the kind of person you think she would like to marry?" I asked, when we had settled her in a chair.

"I want her to marry somebody with plenty of money, a good social background, and a great many friends."

It was exactly like a visit to the milliner, and she had probably chosen all the girl's clothes for her the same way.

"Then she's fond of entertaining?" I said politely. I was wondering whether the puppet daughter was even going to be allowed to fill in her own form.

But the mother was bent on her shopping expedition. "Who have you got?" she asked briskly.

Somehow I would have to explain to her that we were not the poulterer's, where she could have all the goods laid on the counter and pick out the plumpest bird ready to carry it away.

"Well, I expect there are some young men on the books that your daughter might like to meet. But first of all I need to have all sorts of details as to the type of person she would be happy with. We want to get a very good idea of what she is like herself and the kind of person she wants to marry. Then we can choose some likely young man for her. I think, as you live in London, it would really be best if I could meet her."

"Oh, but she's not to know I've come to you. Not at all."

I suggested that perhaps I should go to tea with them as an ordinary guest, and we could talk about young men quite incidentally. So it was settled – I was to go that Sunday. I had no idea what form the conversation would take, but I was afraid it might still only be between the mother and myself.

It was.

For half the afternoon Mrs Smart extolled her Rosalind, while the daughter twisted a handkerchief round and round her wrist and stared at my hat. I saw a slim, attractive, dove-like girl of twenty-one with pretty hair and enormous grey eyes. All the time I was wondering how I could get her alone, and whether she would confide in me when I did.

I thought it polite and more diplomatic to wait until the maternal extravaganza came to an end, so I nodded and smiled automatically, waiting for a chance to pick up the conversation and take it over myself; but having finished her sales talk about Rosalind, the mother made a clumsy dive into the subject of matrimony.

"I've always said that directly a girl grows up she ought to think seriously about getting married and having a lovely home of her own. Isn't that so, Miss Oliver?" she said, holding the teapot in mid-air.

Fortunately I was not expected to reply.

"It's stupid to waste time over silly things like a career, when there are such wonderful things as darling babies waiting to be born. Could *you* understand *anybody* wanting to put off thinking seriously about something so wonderful, Miss Oliver?"

"Yes, I could, easily." I was startled at my own courage. "I think a girl might feel she needed to have a chance of meeting a good many people first and getting to understand them. And she could do this while she had the interest of her career. It would all help to make a better wife and one probably much happier, and easier to live with."

Out of the corner of my eye I saw the handkerchief stop twisting.

Mrs Smart's eyebrows had gone up quite a distance and she looked most disapproving. "Yes, but think of all the simply delicious things she is missing while she muddles round with that career."

I ventured to suggest that the career might be successful.

This time the eyebrows descended in a frown of annoyance.

"I'm surprised at that coming from you, Miss Oliver." She turned to Rosalind, "Miss Oliver is an expert on marriage," and she then proceeded to give a completely inaccurate description of the Marriage Bureau, which I bore patiently.

Suddenly, in the middle of it she was called away to the telephone, and directly she left the room the girl became entirely self-possessed.

"Ma's a nuisance," she said laconically. "She always tries so hard to get me married, but the fact is she's broken off three engagements for me."

"Intentionally?"

"Oh, no. She just scares everybody away, she's so embarrassing. Either that or I feel so ashamed of her anxiety about marriage that I have to break off the engagement myself. I think it's really because she's terrified I'll be a secretary all my life, and that would be too boring for her."

"A lot of mothers are like that," I assured her. Then I arranged that I should introduce Rosalind to several young men whom she should meet *away* from her home and leave the mother out of the whole business.

We spent three months preventing Mrs Smart from plunging into Rosalind's affairs, which took a good deal of tactful manoeuvring. But eventually she was very happily married to a successful young solicitor.

One day we opened a letter from a daughter in Liverpool who asked if we would try to find a husband for her mother:

> "She wants someone with a love of gaiety and enough money to live in comfort. She is the small feminine type and would probably prefer the kind of man who would fuss over her. I am enclosing a snap of her with my baby. I do hope you can do something about it. It seems such a pity for her to live alone when she could be happy making a home for someone."

I supposed she was very fond of her mother and had been miserable about leaving her alone ever since she married.

One way and another we have a busy time with parents. There was a retired bank manager in Bath who wrote to us about his two daughters:

> 'My wife died 18 months ago. If anything happened to me, my daughters would be left very lonely, as they have made very few friends here and I consider that marriage to a proper man would be desirable in the event of my decease. They are too shy to make a move, and if I do not do so on their behalf now, I feel it would be too late.'

He then went on to describe the girls, and give full particulars of what their exact financial position would be when he died, adding—

> 'It is not proposed to make application to you till after my decease, and then only if they wish to do so. In the meantime I wish to put the position fully before you so as to simplify matters later on.'

He was over eighty and the daughters were a long way under thirty. The dear old man must have felt he could not live much longer (he said he could only walk a few yards) and he was doing all he could to ensure their future.

Security had been his motto and he wanted it for them. He had guaranteed their financial security, but he could not guarantee them against loneliness. Perhaps he would like to have seen them married before he died so that his mind would be at rest on this point. And yet, if that was so, why did he ask us not to set our machinery going till after his death? Maybe he would miss the daughters as chauffeuses, because he mentioned they could both drive a car.

Anyway the meticulous financial brain had left all his affairs in exemplary order, and some day when the perfect will is disclosed, it will contain one surprise hidden in the pedantic phraseology.

So far this is the only time we have heard of the Marriage Bureau being featured in a will.

One mother asked us to have her son on the books so that we could introduce him to some of our loveliest clients and distract him from marrying a girl she thought was 'flighty.' He was quite eligible, so we gave him heaps of introductions and he took everybody out that we put him in touch with, so we imagined the plan must have succeeded. But he still married the 'flighty' one. He brought her in to see us one day when he announced they had fixed their wedding, and we liked her, and hope they are happy.

Then there was a great furore over a young Italian nobleman, whose family were really trying to sell his title to the highest bidder they could find.

First of all a friend of theirs came in to see us and find out all about us. Then we had a letter from Italy from the young man's father, whose English was a little extraordinary.

He wrote that his son had 'absolved all his studies in England,' and that he himself possessed an 'antic' palace in Rome and another in Naples, both of which, he said, were national monuments and full of valuable pictures.

'He does not care if his bride is Catholic or Protestant, but the fortune of the young girl must be adequate to keep up to his title and the high rank she will occupy.'

The 'antic' palace had an appeal for several of our wealthier clients, so on the optimism of our reply the young man's mother came over.

She asked to see some of the girls, and we were to arrange for them to go over to Paris and meet him there, and either Heather or I were going to be chaperones. We were looking forward to it and were already trying to settle which of us went over (we both wanted to go and do some shopping) when the war drew nearer and the matter was dropped. I suppose they decided an English chatelaine to the palace might be rather inopportune, for they suddenly cancelled everything without any explanation and we never heard of them again.

We often come across match-making fathers as well as mothers, but the strangest one was the father who had three sons aged twenty-one, twenty-three and twenty-six.

He wanted us to send the girls down to their home in the country, so that he could decide which girl each son should take out. How he thought he was going to keep the matter under control at all we simply could not imagine. We did suggest there might be some sort of confusion, but he seemed to have a very definite idea as to how it would work out.

From his point of view it was quite a sensible plan. He had spent a great deal on his sons' educations and had taken a lot of trouble to set them up in their careers; he was naturally anxious that after all this they shouldn't have the drawback of an unfortunate marriage, so he proposed to take that question in hand as well.

Some of our girl clients lived in his district, and the father went round calling on them before they were allowed to meet his sons, who meanwhile came up to London to see us. They were extremely unspoilt and very charming.

Apparently the scheme was successful, as they were devoted to the father (we liked him, too) and quite welcomed his help in choosing their wives. I think they all got on very well together, and the girls used to say they loved going there.

Since then the middle son has married one of our clients and the eldest one is courting another.

Many of the difficulties we anticipated at the beginning did not seem to occur. We were afraid some of the clients might be given to romancing about themselves and we should never get at the truth, or that they would fill in their forms inaccurately. We find, however, that people are extraordinarily honest about themselves, and we often get a woman filling in the description of her figure as 'well upholstered' instead of concealing it, like some of them do, behind the vague term 'average' (which we discovered may mean anything up to fifteen stone).

We usually have no trouble in getting people to talk about themselves, and probably in no other circumstances would they talk or write so freely. It seems almost as though it is a relief for them to turn out all the cupboards of their mind and put the contents on a table to be dusted and rearranged.

One very taking little Yorkshire stenographer came and told us all about her shyness. I think the mere fact of having braved coming to us had given her a new sort of confidence when she arrived for her interview.

"I was sitting in the dentist's waiting-room when I read your advertisement," she said, "and then I thought of the old saying: 'If you don't help yourself no-one else will.'

"You see," she hesitated, "it's very difficult to explain, but if I'm with anybody I like or admire, either men or women, I always appear at my worst. I get embarrassed and self-conscious, and so tongue-tied they must think I'm awfully dumb. I think it's why I never get taken out more than once by any young man, because I'm such a terrible flop directly they get to know me."

I saw her sad little procession of friendships that tailed off so needlessly. Each time she began a fresh one she would anticipate its fall, and the same fit of nerves would take control.

If she could have one success she would probably be cured for life, so somehow or other we needed to nurse her beyond the danger-point with anyone she met.

"I expect it's only because directly you like a person, you're over-anxious to please them, and that unconsciously puts you out and makes you unnatural. If you could only make up your mind you didn't care a scrap whether they liked you or not, you would get on grandly. Because you see, you have an ample amount of simple natural charm."

Her eyes opened widely and a look of relief came over her face.

"It's partly that," I went on, "and partly that you mayn't have met many people. If you had a much wider circle of friends, so that it didn't matter much if you lost one now and then, you'd probably never get those fits of shyness again."

Her story ended happily, because I used to tell the young men I introduced her to that she was liable to get a sudden fit of uncontrollable shyness and they all managed to get her past it. Quite soon afterwards she married one of them and settled down in her native Yorkshire.

About a hundred of the women on our books at any one time are nurses. There are more nurses than anything else and all are very keen to get married – so much so that we often wonder why they ever bothered to take up nursing at all.

A few of them suddenly think of getting married only because their best friend has married and then, having realised that no young man is taking enough interest in them, they come to us. We had a young midwife like that who was only twenty-nine—

"My best friend, whom I work with, married last week, and we were always together so I shall miss her terribly. This is an awful blow and I feel once she goes I shall get into a groove from which there's no escape," she explained.

It often strikes us how strange it is the way people will settle in a groove and sit in it for years without realising. Then suddenly some stray thing (like hearing of the Marriage Bureau) will stir them and they come hurrying to us to pull them out of it.

Our midwife had another reason for wanting to get married – she had developed into a type which was far removed from her romantic conception of what she would like to be.

"I'm kind Auntie Brown, whom dozens of worried mothers ring up for advice," she said, "and I feel I shall be kind Auntie Brown till the day I die if I don't give myself a jerk."

We were ready to try and help her change her type and set her up again in her own estimation. But in the end she was so much in demand for her work that she did not get much time to come and see us, and I think she decided to remain in the role of 'kind auntie' in which, after all, she had made such a success.

Nurses, we find, are easy to marry off if they come to us young. But nurses over thirty are very difficult and we have to work hard over them. I think the men don't like them much because they are apt to get bossy and to develop a domineering strain.

News of the Marriage Bureau spread very quickly, but in a rather misguided moment we thought we would try a little original publicity as well.

Instead of ordinary circulars, we had silver printed cards made out like wedding invitations:

MARY OLIVER AND HEATHER JENNER
REQUEST THE PLEASURE OF FINDING
MR JAMES BROWN
A PARTNER IN MARRIAGE.
THEY ARE IN THEIR OFFICE FROM 10 A.M. TILL 5 P.M.
AND EVERYTHING IS PRIVATE AND CONFIDENTIAL.
R.S.V.P.
THE MARRIAGE BUREAU

These we sent out in hundreds to people whose addresses we got from the telephone directory, and we thought everybody would be enchanted with them and that we would be overwhelmed with delighted replies.

Next morning I took my first telephone call of the day—

"What are you doing to Mr Brown?" an angry feminine voice pierced my ear.

"Mr Brown?" I murmured foggily, rather taken aback.

"Don't tell me you don't know. I want to know what you're trying to lead him into." Her tone lashed me again.

"But I don't understand."

"Oh, yes you do. I want an explanation, and anyway, I'm going to call the police. Sending that disgraceful thing to a respectable married man."

Then I remembered our lovely silver-printed invitations.

"Oh, you've had one of our new circulars," I said benignly, though I felt very flustered at the unexpected nature of the response to our cherished campaign.

"Circulars! It's criminal, and I'm taking it straight to the police station."

"I'm very sorry it should have been sent in error to a married man," I apologised, "but I don't think it's a crime. If you got a circular asking you to drink Bovril and you didn't like Bovril, you wouldn't take it to Scotland Yard."

That minute she cut me off, leaving me with a sinking heart, wondering if all our circulars had had the same effect.

I did not have to wait long – all day we were interrupted by angry men and women accusing us of trying to break up their homes. We had a very disturbing time for weeks afterwards, especially as the secretary had amused herself by picking out all kinds of celebrities and public men who were resentful enough to call up Scotland Yard and complain.

We did, however, have plenty of the right kind of responses as well, and about fifty per cent of the people to whom we sent the invitations answered enthusiastically and came on the books.

A few of the married ones to whom we unwittingly sent the 'wedding invitations' were evidently most amused, and took it all in very good part. We had one very nice refusal from a Norfolk bachelor:

'Mr— begs to inform Mesdames Oliver and Jenner that the receipt of their kind offer to find him a partner in marriage has given him a great shock, to recover from which he will be obliged to degustate a good bottle of burgundy.

Having by the Grace of God and a good deal of luck arrived at a mature age without succumbing *en permanence* to feminine charms, the sight of his name surrounded by silver print struck home like a blitzkrieg.

These ladies, his correspondents, will gather from the above that Mr— has every intention of dying, as he has lived, in single blessedness.'

We also liked the reply we had from a man who wrote and told us that he had been happily married for years, and gave us the names and addresses of some of his friends and relations who were still single.

Chapter IV

Discussions in the waiting-room – A mother and child – Rush hour – Some of the many diplomatic tasks involved – Odd visitors – The fortune tellers – Couple who got engaged by post – How the Marriage Bureau checks on whether people are genuine – Guiding courtships – Introducing the Bureau wallflower.

Our receptionist has an interesting time and a good deal of responsibility. Merely by her presence she must make people feel that they are not doing anything out of the ordinary in calling at the Marriage Bureau – it might be the photographer's, the hairdresser or anywhere else they go to in the normal way. Her manner reassures them – she welcomes them, notes their appointment, and if there is a rush she asks them to wait.

In those few seconds she has carried them past the phase of longing to turn round and run down the stairs again. She has also transmitted the idea that we ourselves are equally business-like, and that the whole thing will not be a bit embarrassing after all.

Her desk is in the waiting room, and after a very busy afternoon I asked her what it had been like out there. I imagined it must be very similar to a dentist's waiting-room, where everybody looks at everyone else to see if they have false teeth, and tries to mesmerise their neighbour into giving up the newest magazine.

On this particular afternoon nobody read the magazines at all. One man, who was a civil servant from Glasgow, sat leaning forward on the edge of the sofa with his head well down in his collar and studied the floor. He looked like an ostrich that had buried its head in the sand. Perhaps after travelling down on the night train he felt that way, but I am inclined to think he does it all the time, so unless I can find a female ostrich for him he may be difficult to marry off.

Beside him a bright-eyed young woman in a bonnet hat with mink on it looked as if she was waiting to see an exciting mannequin parade. Every time anyone new came into the room she watched them with quick, bird-

34

like turns of her head. Then she glanced at her small child with a reproachful 'don't-stare-at-strangers' expression, as though it would make everybody forget she had stared at them herself.

The child weathered these reproaches by avoiding her eye. She was quite a pretty little girl of five, and she wore a bonnet hat exactly like the mother's – even to the mink trimming.

The ostrich man interested her intensely. She leant against her mother's knee and studied the top of his head. Then she swung one foot about till she kicked him gently on the shin.

Whether he felt the impact of the small kid shoe one couldn't tell, but he did not look up. So she tried sliding her foot to and fro along the floor under his face, till he must have felt that if he did not respond soon she would be making a fool of him. The mother was probably afraid to stop her in case the child disobeyed and made her look a fool too. Anyway, the sliding went on until the next client made her forget it.

This time it was a Naval officer. The receptionist knew he had been corresponding with some of our clients till he came home from China, and he had come to ask us whether the girl who wrote him the most entertaining letters was also the most attractive one for him to meet first. While he waited he dragged a bunch of letters out of his pocket and began reading them.

The mother looked round the room more brightly than ever. She was not interested in the ostrich man and she didn't mind if he never raised his head, but here was somebody more promising. She smiled encouragingly at the child, who was watching the bunch of letters as though the Naval officer was going to do a trick with them.

But a child is never a good ally under such subtle circumstances – her interest in the Naval officer was only transitory and her attention soon returned to the ostrich man.

She tried a fresh kick, less casual than the first one, and perhaps it was the pain inflicted on an old wound that made him move his foot a couple of inches. That, of course, delighted her; she was like a cat playing with a mouse, waiting for it to move again. The mother opened her mouth to remonstrate, but decided it would only start a scene and draw quite the wrong sort of attention to herself.

Suddenly there was a loud babble of voices and two women burst into the silent waiting-room. One was middle-aged and very smart, looking her best in expensive tweeds, while the other was younger and less metallic; she wore myriads of little frills and bows on the bosom of her frock.

"Now, darling, you go in first. I'll sit here and read the papers." The older woman took up *Vogue* and began rustling through its pages.

"No, Loo, darling, it's your turn."

"Well, I'm only going to pop in and out."

"So am I."

"Nonsense, darling – after having lunch and tea *and* dinner with the same man you'll have a lot to tell Miss Oliver."

"I really don't know whether I shall see him again."

"But how absurd; didn't you ask him to call you up?"

"No, I just hoped he would."

"Supposing he doesn't?"

"I only saw him yesterday."

"You sound very lukewarm about him, darling. I believe you're going to let him slip through your fingers. If I'd met him he would have telephoned me first thing this morning and told me what *hours* it seemed since he saw me last night."

"Who *did* you meet, darling?" asked the younger one, suddenly growing defensive.

"Oh, he had lots of money and a Rolls Royce, but the Rolls was a very old model and he was so dull he might have been stuffed."

"Did he like you very much?"

"Fascinated, darling."

Just as the people in the waiting-room felt they were going to hear the complete private diary of these two women, the secretary warned me they were there, and we decided to get them out of the way first.

They always come in together, and the elder one, Miss Mannering, manoeuvres her friend, Miss Knox, into having her interview first. Then, having previously drawn all the information she can out of her about the men she has met, she comes and tells us that she does not think Mr-- is quite the type for Miss Knox, and how much better it would be if *she* were introduced to him.

According to her, every man she meets is 'fascinated' with her. Actually they usually invite her out to lunch and she takes them back to tea at her flat, which is full of taffeta cushions and smells faintly of Harris tweed scent (she always wears expensive tweeds and diamonds). After that she rings them up incessantly for days and frightens them away. Meanwhile she becomes more and more determined to pin one down, chiefly because she wants to be relieved of the worries of a dwindling alimony.

Miss Knox, on the other hand, is far from pushy, and gets on quite well with the men she meets – until Miss Mannering arrives on the scene and tries to annex them, which promptly frightens them away.

One would think that sooner or later the friendship might be broken up on this count, as Miss Knox would very much like to get married. She seems very complaisant over it, however, and watches Miss Mannering's skirmishes quite blandly before she comes to us for another introduction.

As usual, that morning we gave her a new introduction and put fresh heart into her, then she joined her friend, who was waiting outside ready to ask whom she was going to meet next.

Then the mink bonnet came in with the small child. It was her first appearance, and when they walked in dressed alike I wondered whether she always took the girl about as part of her outfit.

I found it a little embarrassing to be discussing her future stepfather while the child stared penetratingly at me. Especially as the mother went into all kinds of domestic details of how the girl's father had fallen short and could be improved upon by number two.

Heather tried hard to come to the rescue and divert the child's attention, but she preferred to stay and drink in the conversation, keeping her eyes fixed on me while stealthily helping herself to the paper-clips on my desk and hiding them in her hand warmer.

As a proposition for the Marriage Bureau the mother was promising, as she was really quite attractive, and we introduced her to all the men who might suit her and who did not mind an encumbrance. Unfortunately, she used to drag her little girl along on the dates and tell them that the child was 'provided for until she was fifteen'. When the men thought that in ten years' time they would be landed with an obstreperous school-girl for whom they would have to provide limitless pocket-money, they used to take fright.

In fact, she made it look as though her main objective was to get the child fixed up with a new father, which I think was partly a form of feminine pride and partly a way of not appearing too over-anxious. Eventually we had to suggest tactfully that she kept the child more in the background.

The waiting-room had been full all morning, and we found that by now we often had to interview as many as thirty clients in one day. But having a rush in this new office was nothing compared to the complications in the attic where we began.

There we had no waiting-room, so we made people climb the ladder and go through the trap-door onto the roof to relieve the congestion on the stairs. They must have thought we possessed the most delectable roof-garden (perhaps it was the way we invited them up), but in truth there was nothing beyond a grimy square of concrete surrounded by chimney-pots.

While we were interviewing in the office, we heard people tramping up and down above our heads, and we used to get terribly nervous lest they were growing angry. Fortunately it was late spring and nobody seemed to mind. I do not think we were ever overcrowded on a rainy day, chiefly because so many of the clients come to see us in their best clothes.

Although it was consoling to think they were not on the roof these days, I still found a rush of clients a strain, merely because you simply cannot be too hurried and business-like over people's matrimonial problems. They all want to tell their life-story in such detail, and I like to hear it, both in order to get to know them and also to make them feel they can put their confidence in me.

We have to learn their character off by heart as well as their looks, and be able to carry it in our heads when we are looking out a possible mate for them. Details like their income, hobbies, and what kind of partner they want, can all be written down and filed. But their character and disposition cannot be docketed so easily and we have to remember these as clearly as their faces.

This often has to be done while there are endless interruptions on the telephone. Somebody has lost the address of a girl we put them in touch with – could they have it again? Another person wants to register – do we really have *nice* people on our books? Then a young man rings up to find out what headway he is making with the girl he is taking out. I am non-committal except to say she told me how much she had enjoyed her last outing. (We never try to push on the courtship or make use of our clients' confidences.)

Next a young woman rings through and talks about the weather. I discuss it patiently, until the casual little sentence comes along, flung with such studied carelessness into the rain: "I went out with Mr-- and I haven't heard from him since. Is he away or something?"

Mr— is now going out with another client because he complained this one was too old and he thought she might run to fat.

"Oh, I think he's working very hard just now," I tell her, struggling to remember whether he has any profession at all. "How about your meeting someone else in the meantime? I'll send you another introduction."

And I make a mental note that it must be done at once. If I think she's the type who might try and run him to earth again I say: "Oh, yes, he told me he thought you were a very nice girl, and he admired your looks, but he thought you a little too *young* for him." And I quickly pull another partner out of the bag.

Often I get incomprehensible calls from some client who has a friend in the next room listening to the conversation, but it's someone from whom they want to keep Marriage Bureau a secret. It's rather like doing a verbal acrostic, and as I cannot suddenly appear very stupid in front of the client I'm interviewing, it tends to be awkward.

That day, as usual, I had all this sort of thing to contend with, as well as the morning's mail of nearly three hundred letters, of which we had only answered a quarter before the clients began arriving.

In the middle of this whirl a very striking young woman was shown in to see me.

"I've got the perfect bust bodice," she announced with a flashing smile.

I struggled to get over my astonishment at this extraordinary opening to the conversation.

"It's just what all your brides will want to have," she continued.

It dawned on me she was not a client, but was trying to sell me something, and a dreadful apprehension came over me that she was going to smother my desk with corsets just before a male visitor arrived.

"Have you got a floppy bust, Miss Oliver?"

I was speechless.

"Because if you have, you probably hide its alluring beauty in a cumbersome bust bodice. Now I've got a bust bodice that holds you firm *without* hiding the beauty of the feminine line. It makes you look just as attractive as if you were naked, and you have no shoulder straps and nothing to show that you have any garment on at all. Would you like to see it?"

Before I could answer she flung open her coat – she had no blouse and no underclothes above her waist. All she was wearing were two pieces of pale pink adhesive plaster with holes in the middle. She certainly had a lovely figure and really did not need to wear a bust bodice at all. I was curious to know how the same contraption would look on someone less gracefully moulded, and was trying to picture it on several of our clients who immediately sprang to my mind.

"It's very good of you to bring them along," I began, "but we really shouldn't have time—"

39

"Never mind," she pursued, "I just want you to wear one *yourself*, so that you can't *help* telling your clients about it."

And she took a couple of the 'bust bodices' out of her handbag and flung them on my desk. I just had time to push them under the blotting paper before a very pompous elderly stockbroker was shown in to discuss his marriage.

That night, out of curiosity, I thought I would try them on. I regretted it for three weeks, because that was the time it took before I could get them *off*. I lay in over-heated baths and then tried to peel them away, but they clung villainously to the soft skin on such a tender part of my anatomy, that at each attempt I winced and gave up. Until at last they became so grubby I was forced to be more brave, and in an excruciating struggle I got them off.

We had all kinds of startling visitors soon after the Marriage Bureau was into its stride. Prams, maternity gowns, nursery furniture, and all had very insistent representatives who came to the office at awkward times. They used to get in to see us by saying: "Yes," when the secretary asked if they were registered with us.

Fortune-tellers were the greatest invasion we had. I should think nearly all the fortune-tellers in the country turned up on our doorstep. Their great idea was to start a kind of racket with us: when Mr X was walking out with Miss Y we were to send him along to her, and she would tell him he was going to marry a slim, fair girl (making him believe this must be the girl he was taking out), and so hurrying up the marriage.

We had a busy time putting off the fortune-tellers. But one of them could not be discouraged so easily, as she wanted to register with us. She kept a seaside boarding-house and fortune-telling was her side-line, which she found quite profitable on rainy days.

According to her circular, she could divine your future from tea-leaves, cards, bumps, and everything imaginable. On the same circular her boarding-house was said to be 'only a stone's-throw from the sea,' and one was assured that every room had a sea view.

She asked me to go down and see her (I think she hoped I would send honeymoon couples there) so I decided to go for the day.

When I got there I found it was a long way from the shore, and if you wanted to look at the sea you had to open the windows and put your head right out and nearly twist your neck trying to see round the corner. Inside, the house was crammed with the antimacassar type of furniture, while the rooms smelt of damp plush and stale cooking.

I had lunch with all the lodgers, while the fortune-teller landlady sat at the head of the table and told me how psychic she was.

She informed me she could see something passing over her left shoulder. I couldn't gather what this phantom shape was, except that it had some great significance with how I was going to affect her future. Actually I think her psychic illusions were closely connected with a bottle of gin, so I carefully evaded putting her on the books.

The next visit I made was very different. It was to a very charming middle-aged peeress who had divorced her husband. She felt she would be happier if she married again, and that it would be better for her two daughters to have a man to look after them.

"I don't wish my girls to know about this," she said. "If I do meet anyone I must pretend he is an old friend – at least to start with."

When she invited me to go down and see her, she asked me to say I was in the Voluntary Aid Detachment with her in the last war. So I had to write and explain that as I was in baby clothes in the last war, I didn't think that particular introduction would be very convincing.

I believe she thoroughly enjoyed putting her name down with us.

"I feel I'm doing an awful thing really," she said with a delighted giggle when we met. "What *would* my relations say!"

And she looked as if she had just ordered six dizzy new hats after wearing a dull one for years.

We are quite accustomed to people being shy about letting anyone know they have joined the Marriage Bureau, and we frequently have situations where clients ask us not to give them away in front of their families or friends. In any case, we write to them in plain envelopes, and we never leave telephone messages from 'The Marriage Bureau' to be put on the hall table.

We particularly liked the couple we had who got engaged by post and did not want either of their parents to know they had met through us, much less that they had never even *seen* each other.

They made me say they had met on his last leave at a party at my house. She was a Colonel's daughter in Cheltenham and he was a successful young business man in Delhi. They wrote to each other for over a year and then she sailed out to Delhi and married him.

When they got engaged she went down to stay with his people at a large country house in Devon, where she was a great success and they all liked her very much.

41

Last December they sent us a Christmas card with a photograph taken on their wedding day, and inside they had written a little note:

'Dear Mary Oliver,

Just a line from two very happy people to wish you all the very best and thanks for what you did for us. It's all really marvellous and we hope to come home one day and tell you all about it.'

And their respective parents do not know to this day that they met by post through the Marriage Bureau.

We are so often asked how we know whether clients genuinely want to get married. To begin with we can usually tell by talking to them when we get all their particulars.

Very few men who are not serious would come to us, pay five guineas and fill in our long form, when they could meet any number of 'easy' girls at dance halls without their meeting being recorded on paper.

If an application should get through from a man or woman whose intentions are dishonourable, it is very easy for us to find them out as we always ask *both* sides to tell us what they think of each other. And if there are any complaints, we then send the offending party out with someone we know and whose judgment we can rely on. They will come back and tell us their honest opinion, and if there is anything wrong, we say to the offender, "Look here. I'm very sorry, but we've had two reports about you which we don't like. We are obliged to give you back your fee and take you off the books."

We also tell our clients that we give no references and we take no references. But we do ask them, before they get engaged or married, to meet the opposite party's friends and relations, as they would do in the normal course of events had they not met through the Marriage Bureau.

Many men spoil their chances at once by being mean when they take a girl out. No girl likes to feel that each extra sixpence he spends on her is searing him to the soul in spite of her attractive company. Without vaunting in a vulgar fashion that money is no object, he can at least let it be of no concern when he is taking her out. She likes to be made to feel that it doesn't matter a scrap if he spends the earth on a single evening, even though she probably knows it is going to matter considerably for the rest of the quarter.

If she is a quite ordinary, thoughtful girl, she will want to remain in the first restaurant they go to for the rest of the evening, rather than drag him to a string of night clubs to be fleeced in each of them. She may even suggest a simple evening, and out of pure consideration say she has a craze to go to a sandwich bar, just because she knows he has taken her out a good deal and his resources must be badly strained. But she likes that to come from her, and would think it a slight to her charm if he suggested it himself.

It is better to take a girl to the cinema once in the week and buy the best seats, than to make her queue for the cheaper ones two or three times. Not that it would be agony for her to sit in the cheaper seats, but just because she would rather have the compliment of being given the best. This is one of the rules that apply after marriage as well, for the reason that a man must never stop courting his wife.

We had a middle-aged commercial traveller on our books who fell down at once through being a trifle calculating over an afternoon's outing. He told us the story himself, I think because he was afraid her version of it would be worse.

"She wrote a letter to say I was twice her age and she didn't like me talking about expenses," he complained. "My only mention about expenses was over the afternoon tea dance. If we had tea in the ballroom itself it was 2/9, but if we had tea just at the door entrance it was only 1/6. You see sometimes the ballroom is packed, and then you have to have tea on the landing entrance anyway. It makes no difference to the dancing."

"Yes, but I take it the ballroom wasn't packed," I explained, "and therefore you weren't exactly flattering her when you could bother so much about one shilling and threepence while you were in her company."

There are many things young men forget, and of which they might well be reminded. Like that fact that a woman is a more fragile being than themselves and must always be treated like fine china. He must assume that even stepping over a kerb is a dangerous exploit, and watch her progress over it with a hand under her elbow.

If he is in a hurry not to miss the first act of the play, he must forget it and not go racing ahead, leaving her to try and keep up like a faithful spaniel. Her comfort should matter more to him than the empty seats in the stalls, even if she did keep him waiting when he called for her.

In spite of what the French say about it, the English language does lend itself to pretty compliments. Everything he notices and likes about her he should mention, because if she is smart and attractive she will have taken trouble with herself, and the more she is appreciated the more beautiful she will look.

Nowadays we do not take on men clients who are not able to support a wife in at least a certain amount of comfort. A widower, for instance, who only had £3 6s. a week, and already had a child to support as well, was discouraged by us from adding a wife to the burdens of the weekly budget. Not that we deny there may be plenty of people managing to find a degree of happiness on the same budget or less. But we should not like to bear the responsibility of letting two people risk a marriage that had a ready-made reason for going on the rocks.

Mr Dewlap's budget was not very promising, but we were sorry for him. Also he was really very nice, so we thought somebody would perhaps pity him and like him enough to marry him.

I had just finished interviewing a mother with a debutante daughter when Mr Dewlap was announced. He was an oldish man with grizzled hair and a lined face, he wore an old mackintosh that hung open, and he carried his hat. But there were stains on the mackintosh and his hat looked as though he had dropped it in the river when he was fishing. His expression was rather hopeless, and as I hate to see anyone feeling hopeless about life, I prepared to be very sympathetic and see if I could not make him feel the world was a pretty good place after all.

During the interview I discovered that he was 57 and lived in Cumberland, and his income was £250 a year, on which he had to support a little girl. He had been a widower for about nine years and the little girl was living with relations.

His only assets were a small wayside garage with no electric light and no sanitation. He also had twenty acres of land, a pony and somebody else's cows.

He told us with pride that when he first took the garage it was very 'old-fashioned,' but now he had a petrol tank and a pump. Evidently he had enjoyed installing that pump, and now the excitement of it was over he was feeling lonely. Not that he confessed to being lonely. The reason he gave for wishing to marry was that he liked singing, and he wanted someone to play his accompaniments.

He informed us he had no car but he held a driving licence, and he said he was 'batching it' by himself. We gathered that meant doing all his own cooking, washing and housework, and I think he hoped for a wife who had a car and could do the cooking while he installed another pump.

"I don't suppose anybody will want to marry me," he said pathetically. "It's very lonely there. I don't mind it, but I think most women would object."

"Some women wouldn't mind if they loved the countryside enough," I replied encouragingly, for I felt terrible sorry for him, "but I do think they might object to there being no sanitation. Couldn't you have that put in while we're looking out some introductions for you?"

But he only shook his head sadly and said he did not think he could.

"It's very pretty," he murmured, as though that would cover a multitude of discomforts all the year round.

In my pity for this lonely figure I put him on the books, hoping that heaven would send us someone without any sanitary ambition, and a mania for housework and gardening.

Then he gathered up his crumpled hat and walked out of the room with his mackintosh swinging forlornly from his shoulders.

Chapter V

What it is like to meet somebody through the Marriage Bureau.

What is it like to meet someone through the Marriage Bureau? Since we cannot describe it ourselves, we have asked a girl on our books to write the next chapter for us.

When I rang her up about the man we had chosen for her to meet, I said, "He's thirty-six, Church of England, 5'9 in height – slim – and he's got an income of about £1,000 a year – in the army, stationed in London. He's travelled, fond of riding but not horsey, likes entertaining and people, and he's good-looking. I'm sure you'll like him."

Then I rang up the man, and said, "She's twenty-eight, slim and fair – has £300 a year of her own – dresses well – attractive, intelligent and travelled. Fond of entertaining, keen on horses, but looks fragile, not tough – doesn't like winters in England and wouldn't mind living abroad. I think she's just the type of girl you're looking for and you must meet her as soon as possible."

Well here she is and we leave her to continue...

First of all he wrote me a letter:

Dear —

Mary Oliver gave me your address and has asked me to drop you a line.

If you can come up to London, please give me a ring and we can arrange a meeting. I think that it is essential that we should like each other when first we meet and then greater affection may develop.

I do not know whether Mary gave you any particulars about me. I give you some here, but I am afraid that they do not form an attractive array. I am nearly thirty-six, dark and slightly grey hair, blue eyes, athletic figure, ruined by 'child-bearing hips.' I am in the Regular Army and have a good future. I have lived most of my life abroad in India and Egypt and would like to go abroad again.

I am keen on shooting, games, gardens and dancing (but I can't waltz). I am not one of the real 'old school tie' and never could be.

My office phone number is ——

My home number before 9am and after 6pm is in the telephone book (see —— Hotel).

I shall be very pleased to hear from you if the above details do not deter you!"

Yours sincerely, ——

This was my first introduction as I had only just joined the Marriage Bureau, and I was very shy about meeting him.

I used to pick up the letter and take it to the telephone, then lose my nerve and put it back in my handbag.

When he met me he might think I was like a bad drawing of the undiscovered girl he'd imagined, and be very disappointed. Or I might be terribly disappointed in him. All the week I wondered what he was like.

I had lots of fun with that letter, and I must have read it a dozen times. After I switched the light out at night I used to get up again and fetch it and try to shape this man from the sentences.

"I think it is essential that we should like each other when we first meet and then greater affection may develop."

That meant I would be crossed off at once if I wasn't in the running. It also reminded me of the reason we were being introduced, and I wanted to delay meeting him more than ever.

All the same I kept kicking myself over putting it off. It's all nonsense, I told myself. Supposing Mary Oliver didn't run a Marriage Bureau, and she gave a dinner-party and invited us both because she thought we would like each other. I shouldn't feel he was inspecting me in case he wanted to marry me. It just wouldn't enter my head. Why should it bother me now?

All the same I did wish he *had* met me at a large party and picked me out of a room full of people to ask me out, then I shouldn't feel he might be hating every moment of our date.

The bit about not being old school tie puzzled me. I know Mary wouldn't have chosen somebody who ate his peas off a knife. But it made me a little alarmed as I thought he must be excusing himself for some odd trait in his behaviour.

Of course, the more I tried to imagine him, the more freakish he became in the pictures I conjured up, and that made me put off the meeting longer.

Then I saw Mary Oliver and she asked me if I had rung him up yet, so I promised I would.

I collected a lot of courage and picked up the telephone. He was out of his office. I didn't leave a message, and phoned again. I missed him, and I missed him in the evening at his hotel. After that I got cold feet and didn't ring up any more and felt quite relieved about it.

Of course, as I didn't leave a name he couldn't tell if I had telephoned, but he wrote another letter saying he wondered if it was I who had rung him up, and explaining how I had missed him. "Please ring again!" he finished.

I liked his second letter better than the first. I was glad he had written it and felt encouraged.

This time I rang him up at his hotel, and while he was being paged I nearly took fright and rang off. I almost prayed he wouldn't be in. But he was.

"Thank you for your nice letters," I said politely.

He said something about being sorry he had missed my calls. Then there was a gap, and I felt as if I were drowning. It was no good, I couldn't act this part at all – playing at an ordinary insignificant social telephone call.

"I'm terrified," I said.

I was just going to ring off on this explanation when he laughed. And because I liked his laugh I felt less frightened.

"I thought you were travelled."

"I am, but I'm still terrified."

And he laughed some more.

"How can we allay your fears?" he asked.

Then he invited me to lunch and asked me where I wanted to go. I didn't like to say 'The Ritz' to a stranger, who might hate the sight of me when he saw me, so I left it to him.

We fixed a day and a place and I was to have a blue hat. But when the day came I was ill in bed with influenza, and with the greatest relief imaginable I rang up and put off the meeting indefinitely.

Of course, I thought about him when I was ill. Now that I had his voice, and the laugh, I had two more pieces to fit into the puzzle of what he was like. Sometimes I looked forward to getting better and ringing him up, and sometimes he became such an ogre to me that I rejoiced in not doing anything at all.

But eventually Mary Oliver discovered I was better and encouraged me to ring him up again. This time perhaps he thought I was becoming rather a myth, or maybe he was busy at his office, but he didn't sound so much as though he wanted to see me. Being timid I probably imagined it. So I accepted his invitation to meet him for a drink at six o'clock, and I made it several days ahead so that I could think up an excuse not to go at all.

But when the day came it seemed pretty silly to put it off, though I was still feeling far from well and I didn't want to go looking my worst.

On my way in the taxi I tried to bolster up my courage. Really it was just the same as when friends in England had introduced me to young men abroad and I had to meet them without having seen them before. So why should I be frightened? Still I did wish we'd met at a party and he'd asked me out, instead of this alarming business of the Marriage Bureau being mixed up in it. And I got out of the taxi convinced he was going to be frightful.

I put my weight rather tremulously against the darkened swing doors of the West End restaurant, and they whirled me into the red-carpeted entrance hall. I had been there many times before, but this time I felt as if I had been flung up on the beach in an unknown island.

There was only one figure in army uniform, and he was standing squarely in the middle of the hall, reading an evening newspaper.

He looked up rather covertly over the top of it and then went on reading. It was probably the Major, but I didn't want to recognise him first, so I went over to the fireplace and passed the time by trying to warm myself, until I realised it was a synthetic one and had no heat.

I couldn't go on warming myself by a false fire indefinitely, so I peeped out of the shadows at the uniformed figure, still reading his newspaper. Then I suddenly remembered I had the wrong coloured hat, so the next time he looked up I started to walk towards him and he hurried forward and greeted me. I explained I hadn't liked to disturb his work just to tell him I had changed my hat.

The moment I met him I forgot all my fears and was as much at ease with him as if we had often met before. I even forgot to wonder whether he was disappointed in me.

We hadn't any friends in common, so we couldn't talk about them. The only thing we had in common was the Marriage Bureau. I told him it was the first time I had met anybody through it, and he told me about the others he'd met. There was one who had too much money, and another who grumbled all evening and had no other form of conversation.

I found he had a very nice smile and an equally nice expression. He was good company and light-hearted, but serious about fundamentals. His marriage and his home he would take very seriously, and his home would be his citadel. One saw he had set himself definite high standards, and he would expect his wife to have values like his own. He wasn't in the least self-important, although he must have achieved a great deal. I had a feeling he would have lots of interesting things to tell if he chose but he didn't try and build himself up.

He said one reason he had joined the Marriage Bureau was because he was finding London lonely. It seemed absurd to me that anyone so likeable and friendly should have had to spend Christmas Day alone. But he'd been abroad for six years and then he'd come home to war-time London, full of people who were too busy worrying about themselves to make new friends. The people he used to know in London were scattered, and he found himself in the middle of an anxious, inhospitable blacked-out town where neighbours meant nothing even in peace-time. And he found it lonely after India where everyone knew everyone else. At the same time his career had reached a point which allowed him to marry.

He told me how he'd been going to make a will, like everyone else who was living in the air raids, and then he realised he had no one to leave his money to except a brother he didn't like. He wanted to feel that the money he had saved and worked so hard for would go to someone he was fond of.

We talked about the hypocrisy there was among relations, pretending to like each other just because they were related. I liked hearing him say he didn't like his brother because I never have anything to do with people I don't like either, even if they are a relation.

I felt all his friendships would be very genuine, and when he married, he and his wife would have a very happy circle of friends.

He said he'd only told one person that he was going to write to the Marriage Bureau, and that was an old aunt. I saw he was devoted to her and respected her advice, and that he often went to her to get her approval on things. There were also old ladies in the hotel where he lived, and I think he was very good to them. He would be just as nice to old ladies as he would to somebody pretty and young and I liked him for it.

There were scraps of things he told me that came up in our conversation, from which I learned more nice things about him. Like the story of his tin box with all his treasures that got mixed up and sent to Malta by mistake when he was on his way home. That made me think that he would cherish his home and notice the flowers and appreciate all his wife did to make it attractive. It was just the way he spoke of the tin box.

I discovered what it was about the 'old school tie' business, for he brought it up himself. It was because he hadn't been to a public school, and I think he had a complex about it. Anyway, he told me all about the school he went to abroad, what they learned and all the sport they had, which was much more varied than usual. I didn't know him well enough to say so, but my reaction, especially after seeing him, was to want to write and congratulate the headmaster. As it was, I didn't quite know how to reassure him.

It seemed strange that the first day I met someone he should discuss his financial position and his future with me, but then I suppose we were several moves ahead of an ordinary meeting. I think he has planned his life very much to a set pattern, and he doesn't want his financial pattern to be upset. He put it very nicely that he was anxious for his wife to have a little money of her own, because it made just that much difference, and for her sake it would be happier for her not to have to ask him for everything.

The only thing that worried me was whether he would be very upset and reproachful if one *did* ask for anything. I wasn't sure.

He was just as keen the girl shouldn't have too much money.

"I'd hate to think she felt she had so much money she could get married with the idea of walking off as soon as she wanted."

I saw from this he wanted to be top dog, and I liked him for that too, because nobody wants to marry a man who isn't. That is unless they are a bossy type of young woman. But I felt his would be a very kind, considerate authority that would rest lightly on his wife's head and not make her rebellious.

He disliked people who were bad-tempered in the early morning. I thought it would look rather odd if I immediately assured him I wasn't, so I laughed and said I didn't see any point in being disagreeable then either.

Sometimes in our conversation I would think, 'Isn't this extraordinary, we're talking about all the things we wouldn't otherwise talk about unless we'd known each other for months.' Yet it didn't seem in the least unnatural that we should be doing it.

After we'd chatted for a little he asked me to have dinner with him, which meant he was happy to put up with me for another two hours, so I had passed grade one or something.

Once he apologized for talking about himself – not that he had been doing it in anything but a very nice, unassuming way – and asked me about myself. But I avoided this because it would have interrupted, and I was enjoying listening to him. Anyway I'm rather reserved as I don't like women talking about themselves.

My mother used to have a great gift for getting her guests to talk about themselves, and it was something I wanted to be able to do when I had a chance of becoming a hostess. I couldn't imagine any good hostess sitting at the head of the table talking volubly about herself. And as I suppose every man, when he is thinking of marrying, unconsciously tries to picture a girl sitting at the head of his dinner-table.

I was still recovering from the surprise of being asked out to dinner, when he told me he liked me best of any of the people he'd met. I thought he was only being polite, but he sounded so convincing I wanted to think it was true. (Mary said afterwards it was because he was a very genuine sort of person, and two days later he rang her up and said the same thing to her. I was glad, because the fact was I liked him very much too.)

When he said he liked me best I didn't immediately think, 'Oh, dear, now I'm in the running as a possible bride. I must try and make a good impression' – as I might have done since we met through the Marriage Bureau. I merely felt very pleased and intensely relieved that now I could settle down and enjoy myself, knowing that he wasn't putting up with somebody he never would have chosen to take out himself.

We went to a restaurant that was gay without being too crowded and noisy, and he was a perfect host. We talked more generally then, like any couple who are dining out after an ordinary meeting.

One of the things I had been afraid of was that he would ask me a lot of questions – or worse still, try and find out why I hadn't been married already, expecting me to divulge my former romances in self-defence, which is an annoying thing I've suffered before.

He told me he didn't want to marry anyone younger than I was because he thought they probably wouldn't know their own mind. And that made me wonder whether years ago he had got engaged to a nineteen-year-old girl out in India, one of the many who are sent out every year by parents who want them to get married quickly. And then, either by a designing parent or her own changeable mind, she had broken it off and married someone else. I thought this might have happened as Mary Oliver said he didn't want to marry any of the type of girls he met out in India.

Lots of my friends used to think they would be 'on the shelf' at twenty-six, and in a wild rush had married the wrong man. I thought of them then and wished they could have heard this man talk about the age of his future wife.

We left the restaurant quite early, partly because I was still tired after being ill, but mostly because I was afraid of outstaying my welcome. When he asked me to dinner he said, "You don't want to be very late, do you?" which I had translated as a tactful way of saying, "I'm working very hard just now, so I don't like keeping very late hours." Though he might have meant it because I had only just got up from influenza.

I was glad he asked to telephone me again on a definite day – because if he'd just said, "May I ring you up some time?" I should have considered myself cancelled. And I was really rather glad I wasn't cancelled because I liked him.

When I was going to sleep that night I suddenly realised that the fact we met through the Marriage Bureau hadn't spoilt the evening after all. And I knew I should never get in a panic again over seeing anyone else Mary Oliver or Heather Jenner arranged for me to meet.

Chapter VI

Hints for would-be brides – Mannequins and why they come to the Marriage Bureau – Pretty girl who could never get set up – People from remote parts of the Empire – Grandee who was too fond of animals.

I chose that girl to meet the major primarily because they had the same tastes. Although she had put her name down with us, she was very detached – she was not a husband hunter, which would have frightened him, and she had the take-me-or-leave-me attitude towards men which I wish all our clients had. She wouldn't try and create an impression; she was sympathetic, and would say just enough to make him enjoy talking to her; and I thought she would have the same values and much the same outlook as the Major, who was one of our nicest clients.

She was an easy 'subject' for the Marriage Bureau, but we have so many very difficult ones, and some of the prettiest girls are the most difficult of them all.

People often wonder why this or that young woman with apparently everything in her favour – good looks, fortune and luck – remains unmarried, but this overlooks the fact that, welcome as such possessions are, they are not the *vital* spark for attracting a husband.

If I had a daughter I would give her a long list of 'Don'ts' before I allowed her to marry.

Man is a nervous animal, rather like a horse. Frighten him with a lot of noise and fuss and you may not be able to control him. Don't frighten him by gushing, I would warn her. Have no traffic with a sugar-coated tongue; everyone knows that it is not sincere, and sincerity is one of the magnetic qualities – not to be confused with intensity, however. Never get intense about things. When you find yourself getting hot all over with enthusiasm it is time to stop, as you will only alarm people.

Don't wear ultra-smart clothes, I would warn her. Anything flamboyant frightens the marrying man to death. And don't give him the impression that you are a snob about your family, clothes or surroundings. Snobbishness is very distasteful to a man – except, of course, the man who is a snob himself, and then he may just as easily take exception to it in other people.

Never try to make an impression by being affected. Giving yourself airs, exaggerating your job, position or family background will only alienate the man. He will either be intimidated by you or will laugh at you.

Show an appreciative interest in other people. Don't let this be artificial – it's as easy to see through as an empty glass, but really feel it. People will be drawn to you in exact proportion to the interest you show in them.

When you don't understand what is being said, don't sit about with a dentifrice smile, trying to indicate that everything is too, too fascinating. He will either think you know more about the subject than he does, which will madden him, or that if it's so easy to understand it can't be very interesting. Worse still, he may think that you are just not listening.

Be honest. Say (with interest), "I don't quite understand. Tell me more about it please." He will be delighted.

And, of course, don't be more than five minutes late for an appointment.

There are many more don'ts I could mention. For instance, one very pretty girl who came to me seemed, on casual acquaintance, to present no difficulties. But I was wrong.

She is the kind of girl who tries with all her might to impress a man the moment she meets him. Instead of making him talk, finding out his interests, and making friends gradually by finding things in common, she instantly tries to dazzle the unfortunate man with splendid accounts of herself, her friends, her family, her income and her expensive tastes.

She once told a man who was interested in her that nothing in the world would induce her to go into a sixpenny store. It was so *vulgar* in her opinion!

From the man's point of view, it was so vulgar that he never wanted to see her again.

The worst drawback of all, however, is the inferiority complex. I find that a woman who suffers from this has very little sex appeal. And this applies to men also. To be modest is one thing, and quite attractive, but to persist in thinking of yourself as unattractive and stupid is repellent.

If you really want to be liked, give interest, appreciation, understanding and tolerance. Anticipate friendliness for that is the way to make people friendly towards you. And do not assume that if someone is a little quieter than usual or more brusque, it is because he dislikes you. It is much more likely to be a reflection of some private concern or worry.

One of our difficult clients was a really lovely model girl who posed for photographs. She had a pretty face, a perfect figure, and the most beautiful skin I have ever come across. Heather and I were always swept away by that complexion, and it interrupted our work because we simply had to stop and talk about it every time she had been in. It was real 'peaches and cream,' and she knew she could be very sparing with make-up.

Of course, the men were in raptures directly they saw her, and used to take her out at once to the smartest place they could think of. But there was always trouble, because in spite of her beauty she hadn't enough poise – at least not enough to last a whole evening. I think out of sheer nervousness, she used to say the most frightful things.

One poor man who had the most honourable intentions towards her, stopped to talk to the taxi-driver to carefully tell him the way because he didn't think it would be easy to find in the black-out.

The girl was already seated inside, and heard only the low voices in conversation. Suddenly, to the intense embarrassment of both the young man and the taxi-driver, she sprang out like an angry virago and accused the man of instructing the taxi-driver *not* to take her straight home.

We heard about it from both the man and the girl; of course, she was written off at once by the young man in question.

Yet she was a charming girl to meet, and at heart a very nice one, and we were certain these maladroit things she did and said were only forms of shyness.

Even when we tried to teach her tact, she still had a way of being awkwardly frank at quite the wrong moment. We could not help being amused over the time a young man said to her, "What a pity your teeth aren't quite even." (She had a little chip in one of her front teeth.) And she looked him straight in the eye and replied, "Yours need scraping."

This sort of frankness, coming from an otherwise apparently gentle but exotic creature, used to bewilder the men she met. Probably they were afraid she would suddenly say the wrong thing to her mother-in-law or their boss at the office, and thereby embroil them in some awkward situation.

We almost had to give her up, but in the end she married a young planter from Assam, who took her out there after the wedding.

Quite a high percentage of our prettiest girls are mannequins or model girls, and we have had hundreds going through our hands since we started. You might imagine it would be only too easy for these glamorous creatures to find a husband, but they come pouring into the office saying they never meet any eligible men.

It seems the men they meet are generally married already and only want a little distraction, and there is no question even of friendship or any real admiration for the girl.

So in reality these glittering, sophisticated girls who seem to sweep all before them are immeasurably lonely and have an almost childlike ignorance of their fellow human beings. There is a degree of pathos in them that is all the more poignant because it is in such strange contrast to the picture they present to the world.

But whenever I visit them at home, I see the back of the picture. Instead of an exotic salon and a roomful of admiring faces, the girl is in a bed-sitting room where her chief companions are a teapot and an ironing board. She either has to sit up late washing and ironing her underclothes and manicuring her nails, or else she has to get up early to prepare herself for wearing fifty-guinea haute couture outfits.

There is no time for reading or having any leisured interest, because there is always tomorrow when she must still look the same. And in any case, she is tired out because she has been standing all day, and she has dressed and undressed countless times, and sat patiently beneath stifling incandescent lights while a photographer takes those cool *soignée* pictures that make hundreds of women with a dozen other interests say: "I simply *must* get some new clothes."

Although she may make four times the amount which many a good stenographer is paid, often she is no better off, for she must buy so many expensive underclothes, shoes and gloves; if she is posing for cigarettes or outdoor shoes she is expected to have the rest of the outfit ready to hand.

She has no real circle of friends. There are only these men she does not really like. And her girlfriends are limited to the others in the salon who may want to borrow her hats. So in these narrow confines she has little opportunity of learning to understand human beings, and we find we are taking on someone who has to be taught a great deal before she can be a success.

This lonely Cinderella is the supposedly 'hard-boiled' girl who is thought to know so much about men. Actually she knows less about them than anyone, for she has usually only met one type of man.

When they first come to us they seem to think that a husband is just a means of being relieved of a considerable amount of financial anxiety. They want to marry somebody who will have a great deal of money left over after paying the rent so that life will be all the easier for them. At this stage they have not given any particular thought to their side of the bargain and all the million things they will have to do to make their husband a happier man.

We try to show them the true perspective, and in the end they usually marry some nice young man with a comfortable income, and learn all about real affection.

Mannequins and show girls nearly always want to marry men from far-off parts of the Empire, and luckily for us the men from these places are all attracted by them and want them as brides. You might think they would look for stout Scottish lassies or someone more able to stand up against the buffeting of climatic extremes, but they don't. They come home and sweep these girls off their feet, and so far these marriages have been very successful.

Many of our men come from all parts of India and Africa, including Nigeria, Morocco and the Gold Coast, besides Canada, New Zealand, Australia, Ceylon, Palestine, China, the Straits Settlements, Lisbon, Gibraltar and Singapore.

In a way Heather and I get the biggest thrill of all meeting people from these distant places. To begin with they are lonely, so what we can do for them means far more than it does to a man who is living in England and has plenty of friends. And the girl who goes out to them has perhaps found her own life narrow and colourless. She is someone who has longed to travel, and yet never dreamed she would ever have the opportunity. She is lonely too in a way, and sometimes she is overworked as well. What she needs most of all is a really violent change and something terribly exciting and new in her life. In other words, she needs romance in its broader sense.

So when we bring off one of these matches and get, as we so often do, a letter saying how happy they are, we feel we have done something rather important and worthwhile – even though the arranging of it has been a big responsibility.

It may be several times in one week that we open the post to find something like this:

I am now Assistant Manager in the —— Oil Company, and am responsible to the General Manager for all operations. I live at the Oil Field, and have a large, delightful bungalow, beautiful garden and enjoy entertaining the many visitors, including Governors, Commissioners, etc., who visit this Field.

I motor a lot, having a car given to me by the Company, and in the summer one gets up to the hill station, a very cheery place in the season. From my house it is only two and half hours' journey and one gets up to 7,000 feet. In the winter we ski there.

There are quite a number of Europeans and Americans on my staff and they have wives ... I am very easy to get along with, and am very light-hearted, enjoying life and am not set in my ways. Financially, I am well off and hope to retire in comfort, say ten years hence.

Well, there is Opportunity for some deserving girl, just waiting on our desk in Bond Street. We have put him in touch with several girls and at the moment he is writing to them. As there is no chance of his coming to England while the war is on, he is probably going to choose his bride by her letters and photograph. So far we have no indication of whom it will be, and we are still sending fresh entries. When he feels hopeful about anyone, we are to arrange for her to meet his mother in England first.

Next a policeman from Southern Rhodesia pops out of the post-bag, telling us 'when reaching my age, twenty-six, a fellow thinks of settling down. I am permitted to marry in another year's time according to Police Regulations.'

Then there is a shipping man in China, and a young man in Singapore, who was counting on his next leave to come to England and look for a wife, but now the war has prevented him getting over. He has an income of £975 a year and his recreations are tennis, golf, dancing, bridge and racing.

A twenty-nine-year-old engineer in India also has a good income and says his pastimes are *big-game hunting* (underlined), oil painting, photography and motor cycling. And he says he likes to be jovial and enjoys talking politics. I think he, too, is awfully disappointed about his leave being cancelled, and all those English girls he was going to come and meet over here. Anyway, he asks us to hurry up and find him someone.

One of our remote clients is a young man who lives on the Seychelles Islands, where he has his own boat and crew and spends all his time catching whales. He told us he makes about £1,500 a year, as every part of a whale can be sold.

He didn't try and gild his island life, and when he asked us to find him a wife he said she must be 'one who likes heat, whales, flies and natives.' But adds that he has a very nice little bungalow and the island is lovely.

Heather and I have taken rather a fancy to him, and think from his letters he must be very nice.

When war broke out he had just become so interested in one of our nicest girl clients (she has the loveliest eyelashes we have ever come across) that he was coming home to meet her, but so far the war has held up his return. Meanwhile (for the interest is mutual) she has gone into one of the services, and says she does not want to meet anyone else till he comes home.

Of course, all our distant applications are not so promising as the ones I have just mentioned.

We had a vast correspondence from an old man in the backwoods of Australia whose name we never put on the books. Letters, some of them in verse, came pouring in, together with a quantity of snapshots. Quite incidentally he did want to find a wife, but only because he thought she might be induced to buy him a caravan, in which he planned to roam the world looking for buried treasure, with a lion cub as a pet. He also proposed to take frequent sun-baths in the nude en route.

As far as we were concerned he was lonely, and we were glad he applied to us, but we did wish (for we have a very busy office) that he didn't have to give us his views on everything from criminology to pedestrians' bad manners.

We were initially alarmed when we had a letter in Hungarian (which is not on our language list), but then were relieved to find a translation was sent with it.

It was from a doctor who said he wanted to 'sail into the happy haven of marriage', preferably with a Hungarian, but he did not really mind what nationality she was.

Having begun his letter with such poetic romanticism, he then became extremely calculating. Evidently the patients were not queueing up in sufficient numbers, and he wanted his wife to be 'a very cheery, domesticated lady, into whose business, shop, factory or agricultural estate I would enter as her collaborating partner in addition to my professional work.'

After this starkly practical statement, the gentleman of the Blue Danube kissed our hands in farewell and asked us to let him know if we agreed to attend to his case.

Sometimes young men on leave from the East write to us from the boat on the way home. Like this one...

> I am coming back from India for a short holiday, and if you can introduce me to a good-looking and well-to-do young lady or Society lady, I shall be glad if you will let me know.

He did not trouble to tell us much about himself, except to assure us airily that he belonged to 'all the important clubs.'

One letter that came from Tunis made us very interested in the man who wrote it, simply because he was so candid:

> I am not young (61), not rich (income rarely up to £200), not good-tempered. I live out here partly because I like the sun, partly because it is the cheapest place I know of to live in, partly because I don't like going to afternoon teas and being polite.

If would-be clients are living in other countries their letters to us are, of course, extremely important as we need to get as clear a picture of them as possible before we choose people for them to write to. So many times we either get scrappy letters which tell us next to nothing, or else numerous pages which also tell us nothing except about matters quite beside the point, which we find exasperating to read.

The most helpful, practical business-like letters of all seem to come from Americans. Here are extracts from a letter that came from New Jersey a year before the war:

> I am an engineer, mechanical, having worked both in the domestic field and in Canada and Europe as well, and am divorced, without children. Married in 1929, lived together a year and wife skipped. I divorced her upon my return from Europe ... Am of English ancestors, 46 years old, 5ft 11ins tall, 220lbs, fine health, blue eyes, grey hair, comfortably fixed as to money and property.
>
> I work a five-day week, and have 26 days' vacation with pay a year, and 15 days' sick leave, ditto a year – a real decent job. Am an alumnus of Yale University, class of 19—. Own car, of course.
>
> I have been too busy tending to business since I came home from Europe to look around much for a wife. It is hard to find one interested in anybody over forty years old to boot – at any rate here.
>
> Have thought seriously of travelling to England next summer to look for a wife, say 22 to 32 years old, non-Catholic, and not a widow, one who is a homebody. Would like a fairly attractive personality, at least 'easy to look at.' Also one who really wants to have one or two children, as I love kids. Ditto a good dog. Like music deeply, also art.
>
> I suppose there is one chance in a hundred that you will get this, or if so, even consider it a moment, me being a 'foreigner', so if the Dead Letter Office reads this far, I hope they will not bother to return this to me – I would get a laugh from the small-town busybodies at the Post Office here if they saw the returned letter.
>
> Nevertheless, I want a good wife, and like English girls, what I have seen of them in Canada ... I could come over to meet them if we proved congenial by mail to start with. Would be glad to contribute to any cost for the service you might care to ask.

This is just the type of letter we like to have, informative, brief and to the point and easy to read. This American was engaged – by post – quite soon after he came on the books, to a very attractive young English games mistress.

Before the war we always had at least thirty American men on our books at a time, and they were very much in demand. Most of them were business men, aged about forty or a little over. They were generally over on a short business trip on which they might not have time or opportunity to meet many people. And as they wanted to take back an English wife, they asked us to help them find one.

Americans carry out their courtship very well, and with much more verve and acumen than the average Englishman. After all, it is the time when a girl does like the man to make a really big effort to please her – not, like so many Englishmen, by telling her what a little god he is in some place she has never even seen – but by doing things that have given him some amount of trouble and thought. Americans make an art of this when, in their own term, they are trying to 'rush' a girl.

Flowers, letters, long-distance telephone calls – he does something every day and really goes to it with energy. He does not leave her, apparently forgotten, for two or three weeks because he has been too busy to call her up.

And when he is married he still makes a big fuss of her. It may not be quite so hectic a fuss, but at least he doesn't regard her quite like the old mare put safely in her stable. Anyway, if he started to feel that way about her there would probably be a divorce, because in America tolerance isn't allowed to reach the state of hypocrisy. They say, "This doesn't work, let's wash it up," and perhaps it is often better that way than dragging on in a state of apathy or even dislike.

We also found there was a great demand for the American girls who came on our books. Most of them were about twenty-four to thirty-two, very slick and smart and easy to talk to. They usually had an adequate amount of money of their own, and were all anxious to marry Englishmen. And they wanted to live in the country in an old English country house. We cannot help wondering how they are liking some of those old country houses in the winter.

When war broke out we still had some American girls on our list, so we put them in touch with Englishmen in other parts of the Empire. They were very pleased with that idea, and several of them took trips to India and got married to the young men we introduced to them.

The American men especially used to love their first meeting through the Marriage Bureau. They usually appeared with a red carnation in their buttonhole to identify themselves, and regarded the whole procedure as a pretty cute idea.

As clients we found the American girls charming and likeable. They were always frank and interesting about the men they met, and were very intelligent in discussing anybody's character. In many ways we found them a great help to us.

We also have several foreign clients who have lived in this country for many years. We have reason to remember the South American who had a large, very richly appointed mansion in Scotland...

He was about fifty, fair, and good-looking except for his nose, which was so big he looked rather like Mr Punch. He was well turned out, although his shoes and his finger nails shone just a little too much.

His wife had died some years ago, and he wanted to marry somebody very smart, who would entertain his guests well. One of the chief things he stipulated was that she should be fond of animals. That was easy to find, since so many of our clients put on their forms that they are 'fond of animals' as one of their assets.

We picked out a Mrs Dale for him, who was extremely smart, a little over forty and quite convinced she would enjoy his pets.

It looked like an easy match, and when he invited her for the weekend we pictured her making a very decorative appearance at the mansion, walking through the trees in the garden with a couple of handsome Borzoi hounds. The South American would be grinning with delight from one ear to the other, and very soon she would be installed as the Marquise.

A few mornings later she was announced at the office, and Heather and I nodded gaily at each other. We both looked up, expecting to see a radiant face, and prepared for a flow of enthusiastic chatter.

But Mrs Dale was not radiant. She was incalculably annoyed.

"*Apes!*" she said fiercely, throwing her handbag on my desk and sitting down in the chair without waiting to be asked. "He keeps 'Apes.' There were five of them, great big ones, curled up in baskets in front of the drawing-room fire. What's more, one of them was ill. Have you ever seen a sick ape?" she asked with a genuine shudder, as she recalled the spectacle.

We blinked at her in some confusion, and I murmured apologetically that we had no idea he had such unexpected pets.

Heather rose to the occasion: "Oh, he's probably only keeping them there till he presents them to the Zoo."

"No," said Mrs Dale dramatically, "they *live* there. And you won't get them out. He adores them."

"Well, how did you like him?" I asked as brightly as I could after the shock of the apes,

"Oh, I hated him at first sight. Couldn't stand him the moment I saw him."

Even as she said this, Heather was already doing some quick thinking and looking out another introduction for her.

Shortly afterwards the South American himself came in to see us, also looking highly aggravated over something. We presumed Mrs Dale had said something very rude about his apes, but as we thought it best to look as though we suspected nothing at all, we asked him how he liked her.

"I took an instant dislike to her," he waved his polished finger-nails as though to eradicate her name from an invisible wall. "The very moment I saw her, I said, 'Not for me.' She is dreadful."

"Here's quite a young widow whom I am sure you would like," announced Heather with remarkable poise, while she plucked out a file. "She did a good deal of entertaining when she was married before, and she's got a really lovely figure. We've seen a photograph of her in a bathing dress."

Eventually he bowed his way out of the office.

"Perhaps Mrs Dale was making it up about them," I suggested hopefully. "And anyway we may find somebody who thinks it's rather interesting to keep apes in the drawing room."

We decided not to warn anybody first, as they might refuse to go down and meet our South American client. Instead we would hope they might be so entranced with the mansion that the little item of the pets would not matter.

But they all came back shuddering, and said they could *not* marry anybody who expected them to share the domestic hearth with apes.

Chapter VII

Girl who wanted to meet the attractive young man who lived up the road – Some statistics about clients – Wealthy man who was mean – The only marriage that nearly foundered – Couple who always quarrelled and yet got married – Popular attributes – Women who think every man has fallen for them.

She was young and pretty, and she came in smiling. A slim, brown-haired girl with large grey eyes and quietly expensive clothes. After some of the depressing figures who had drifted through our office that morning, it was like spring sunshine to see her, and we liked her before she even spoke.

I offered her a chair and watched her take off her gloves, thinking how every time she took them off somebody must have fallen in love with her. She had very small, transparent hands with fingers like spun glass, so fragile and beautiful one wondered how she even did up her dress.

"I've just heard about you, and I thought perhaps you could help me," she said hesitatingly. "You see, I want to meet somebody just in case they might happen to like me."

We told her in all sincerity that we could introduce her to a number of young men who we felt pretty certain would like her.

"Oh, no," she said quickly. "I don't want you to do that."

We looked at her in perplexity and wondered why she had come to see us.

Then she unfolded the story of a young man who lived only three doors away in the same road in London. Good-looking, successful, owning his own house where he lived alone, and above all he seemed to have the most attractive personality.

For three years she had passed him in the road, watched him play polo, and seen him at race meetings in the country. Before she went to bed she had gazed at the trees showing over the top of his garden wall and said, "One day perhaps I shall meet him." And in the morning she had looked round her curtain at the same trees and thought, 'It might easily happen today.'

But it never did, because she never met anyone who knew him.

It was one of the vagaries of chance that they should belong to much the same set of people and live almost next door and yet never meet – it happens so often in London; and one of the rules of convention in those circles is that they should wait for an introduction.

No matter with whom she was going out in the evening, she would still hope he might pass when she was crossing the pavement – because that would be much more interesting than the dinner, the theatre or the dancing with the young man who was taking her out.

"Perhaps he's just as anxious to meet you," I suggested, being the most sympathetic comment I could make.

"I don't know really," she said distantly. "Anyway, I always look away, just because, you see, I want to get to know him so terrible badly."

That I appreciated, and nodded understandingly.

"I know one couple," I said, suddenly remembering, "who were neighbours for a long time, just like you are. And they both wanted to meet each other very badly and didn't know it. They lived right next door to each other, then one day a tree fell down from her garden into his and he had to go and see her parents to complain about it. So they finally met, and soon after they got engaged and were married. It was all very romantic."

The grey eyes were wide with interest while she drank in the story.

"I'm afraid our trees are terribly firm," she said a little sadly. "The point is, can you possibly – I know it's asking a lot – but could you – somehow, I mean could you arrange for us to meet – I don't know how? But it would be very nice of you."

She smiled and settled more happily in her chair, as though she had unloaded herself of a vast burden and was prepared to be swept along in any current of consequences.

"What's his name?" I asked.

She told me.

"Well, to start with, he's not on our books, so I don't really see what we *can* do."

But she only smiled trustfully. Then I had a sudden impulse to try out some mad scheme and see how it would work.

"I'll give it a go," I promised. "It's quite outside our province, but we'll do what we can. Only don't count on anything because I may not get very far."

And she drew on her gloves over those lovely little hands and thanked us warmly before she went out.

"Mary, you're crazy," said Heather laughing. "What *are* you going to do?"

"I'll have to think of something," I said. "Wasn't she sweet?"

That evening I went home to my flat and looked up his name in the telephone book. I stared at it for a considerable time while trying to work up my confidence. Then I cleared my throat and started talking out loud to myself to see how my voice sounded, (which is a trick I used when I was seventeen and very shy and had to make an important telephone call).

Mary prepares to hit the phone on behalf of her client

Then I called. He was in, so I had to go through with it—

"Is that Sir—?"

A voice said he was speaking.

"Oh, this is Mary Oliver here. I run the Marriage Bureau. I'm so sorry I was out when you telephoned this morning to invite me to lunch with you tomorrow. And I just rang up to say I shall be so pleased to come. Only could you make it half-past one at the Berkeley instead of one o'clock?"

"Marriage Bureau – I think there must be some mistake."

Luckily he sounded mildly amused rather than annoyed.

"A mistake," I murmured in a mystified voice, "but that was the message I got. Heavens!" I added, as though suddenly seeing daylight. "One of our friends, either yours or mine, must have been playing a joke on us. I'm so sorry. How dreadfully embarrassing."

He laughed, really very engagingly, and said, "We'll have to get to the bottom of this. Let's have our lunch anyway, even if they *have* played a trick on us."

I accepted, and rang off in the most jubilant mood imaginable. But as I wandered back to the fireplace I reminded myself that this was only the beginning of the story – we still had to persuade him to register with us.

When we met I could quite understand why this girl was so stirred by him. He was a delightful, easy, attractive personality, and in spite of the delicate mission it entailed, I did enjoy my lunch.

I do not quite know how I did it, but when we were having coffee (I know it was getting perilously near the end of our meeting) I persuaded him to join the Marriage Bureau – chiefly, I think, because he simply did not believe it was true that Heather and I were running it, and that we had so many clients. He was very interested in the whole business.

When he joined, the first person I introduced him to was the girl three doors away.

The end of that story was a happy marriage, and since then we have had several other clients who have come into the office and said there is someone they have been longing to meet, asking if we could do something about it. I often wish secretly that someone could do it for me.

Another case of this kind did not end so romantically. She was a woman of about forty-five, who wanted to meet a man who lived in the same block of flats in Brighton. In her case we were not particularly astonished that he passed her by because she was not very attractive and had a forbiddingly square jaw.

Frankly we were surprised she had not spoken to him first, for she looked the type who would. We gathered she went up and down in the lift with him a good deal, and suspected she took multiple lift rides just in the hope of seeing him. She seemed to know a tremendous lot about him, so whether she tipped the porter to give her tit-bits, or secretly went through his mail, we do not know, but she took up hours of our time telling us all about him.

We got him to join the Marriage Bureau by sending him a circular, but just as we had arranged the first meeting she came in and said she did *not* want to know him after all, because she had discovered he drank. In the end we refunded their money and told both of them we had no-one to suit.

The Baronet and the girl who lived three doors away were married quite quickly, about three months from the day they met. Often the engagements last from one to six months, but the most whirlwind of all the romances was a young Austrian girl who came to us soon after we opened the office. Her father was a big shoe manufacturer in Austria, and she was at a convent in England learning music.

"I am so simple," she kept on saying when she arrived for her interview, but she got engaged the very first week and came in looking radiant. Three weeks later she was married.

Our advice to clients when they ask us should they marry so-and-so is: "Don't do it quickly – no sensible man will mind your wanting to think it over." This is partly because we feel that if they have to come and ask somebody else about it, they cannot be very certain of their own mind.

Outside people, when they first hear of the Marriage Bureau, are apt to imagine it as the last resort of hopelessly shelved individuals who have left their youth a long way behind them. But the majority of our clients, both men and women, are under forty.

We find most men want children, and most of the younger girls want them, but the girls over thirty would rather be without them.

A lot of widows about forty want to meet widowers with small children, and as we always have a number of widowers looking round for somebody 'settled' to mother their family, this fits in very well.

Last year we had many retired widowers on our hands but even *more* independent widows; fortunately the more attractive of the younger widows were much in demand with our bachelors, so things evened out fairly well.

Nobody seems to want to marry a dentist (luckily we only had a few to deal with last year), but doctors are popular, and we have at least sixty on the books at once. Women usually refuse even to meet the dentists. If they did they might like them, as we've had some very nice ones who were also very good-looking. But directly they hear the word 'dentist' they say: "Oh no – no, I shouldn't like to marry one. Can't you introduce me to somebody else?"

If they don't mind doctors, why mind dentists? We can think of no explanation.

Bank clerks are also a little difficult because they have so little money, though it is at least steady and certain work. So we have to send them girls who are prepared for a long courtship, preferably ones who are working in an office themselves. We took on about sixty bank clerks last year, and half as many accountants. The latter were a much better proposition, as some of them were young accountants with a partnership in the offing.

Unless he is rich and can travel and supply a good deal of active diversion, a retired bachelor is not a popular idea with the average girl or young woman. They nearly all say, "I'd hate a man knocking about the house all day."

The point being, of course, that they are unhappy about him seeing the house with its hair down in the throes of the morning cleaning – it is too much like having a stranger in the bathroom. Also, even if a man has got a pretty mundane job there is always some chance of promotion and a magical future on which to build a wonderful castle of dreams.

We have a continuous supply of retired bachelors on the books, and we should like to advise most of them to take jobs.

Civil servants seem to flock into our office, but we get few artists or musicians.

A good many men say they want a wife who is musical and can play or sing to them, but the only man who specified that he wanted to marry a professional musician (she had to be a violinist) was nearly stone deaf. He was also very keen on dancing and had a wooden leg.

We had thirty-five lawyers last year, and four MPs. And out of the many men and women who wrote to us from abroad, fifty of the men were tea-planters.

Business men are generally aged from forty-five to fifty-five, and we have a number from the North who are self-made men and want somebody decorative to sit at the end of their table.

What might surprise some people is that out of the fifty odd business *women* who were with us at the same time, a large number were big business directors with their own firms.

They were not very easy to find husbands for, as they had left the question of marriage till too late. There was one, for instance, who was head of a big wholesale clothing manufacturer in Lancashire. She was only forty-five, extremely nice, very broad and heavy, neat and quite nice-looking. The only way to describe her, if one can do it without defacing her bountiful charm, was that she was the sort of persona any jealous wife would want her husband to have as his secretary. I think she was outstandingly capable, and she must have been popular with her work-people or she would not have been able to build up a successful business as she had. But there had been no other side to her – for the best years of her life she had been solely in love with her business, steeped in it, giving it her all and not wanting anything else.

Now the brother she lived with had died suddenly and she found she was lonely. Mentally she began to look out of the window and see what she had missed. She herself had a business with a remarkable six-figure turnover, of which she was in complete control. Her income was huge for a working woman, and her savings established her for life. She could retire in clover, but what then? It was like being given a brand new motor car and not knowing where to go.

"I've been lonely since my brother died," was the only explanation she gave for coming to us, but we saw the whole story when she told us about the clothing firm.

For a moment I thought of not letting her register. Then I reflected that if we did not take her on she would probably fall into the hands of a fortune hunter, or somebody who wanted an easy berth in her business. And so in the hope of averting that tragedy we decided to take a chance.

Another idea outside people have when they first hear about Marriage Bureau is that we are only patronised by working-class people. I do not know why they immediately jump to this conclusion. In actual fact, out of our register only approximately fifteen percent are working-class men and women.

This is because the working class have more facilities for meeting each other: there is less convention, there are the Saturday 'hops' when a man can dance with a girl and make friends with her without waiting to be introduced; and it is not odd to speak to somebody who travels on the same bus every day.

Several workmen have tipped me after I have arranged their marriage. I found it a little embarrassing the first time one put two shillings on my desk, but then I realised he meant it in just the same way as the grander clients who send me bouquets of flowers. "Please buy something for yourself," he said, as he put the coin on my blotting pad. I thanked him warmly and said I would get a new supply of cigarettes.

We try as far as possible to keep the numbers almost even, and this means we have a long waiting list of women. Directly an extra batch of men come along we add some more women from the waiting list.

The average income of our men clients is £600 to £700 a year. A third of the men have an income of four figures, and the highest income for a man so far is £15,000 a year.

You might think some women would put up with an awful lot for an income as high as that, but one man who fell into this category was refused a great many times.

He was an industrial widower who had seven children and lived in the North in a large gloomy mansion with red plush sofas; pictures of his first wife in embossed silver frames hung all-round the house.

The trouble was he used to take our women clients to dine somewhere garish and cheap, and then drag them out into the cold and say, "Now let's get on a bus" – which from somebody with £15,000 a year struck rather harshly on feminine ears.

We used to warn the women we introduced him to that he had seven children, but directly they heard about his income they hastened to assure us they *adored* them and that it would be such fun to have a large ready-made family.

Few of them got as far as seeing the children or the red plush sofas, because the bus ride shook them so badly they never wanted to see him again.

Some men ask us not to tell the girl what their income is until they know her pretty well, so when she asks us about it we have to say vaguely that it is 'adequate.'

We did have one, an Australian sheep heiress, and nobody, not even ourselves, knew anything about her income until a month after her wedding.

I remember her coming into the office. She was a quiet, mouse-like little thing about twenty-six, with a flat expression and not at all smart, and she wore cotton gloves that were all bitten at the fingers.

"I've got a little allowance of my own," she said. "And I want to marry a man who lives quietly in the country. I'd like him to have about £400 or £500 a year, not more."

We found an educated young farmer for her in Somerset and they got married. Like most English farms his was barely holding its own, but he said she did not seem to worry when he told her they easily might become poverty-stricken later on.

So they settled down very happily, until a month afterwards when we received a bombshell in the form of a furiously angry letter from the young man.

Heather and I read it in turns several times over, for we could hardly believe our eyes. Apparently her 'little allowance' was £8,000 a year, while any day in the future she would inherit over a million. And she had never said anything about it until she told him casually one day after the wedding.

But the worst shock to us was the way the husband had taken the news of her wealth. We gathered there was a pretty big row going on, and one of our happiest marriages was in danger of breaking up.

Of course, we wrote at once and explained that this was the first we knew about it ourselves, and that we did not see why it should make any difference to their happiness since her tastes were obviously just as simple as his.

I believe the storm lasted for weeks, and we were very glad when she wrote one day and told us they had made it up.

That, so far, is the only occasion we have heard of when one of our marriages seemed in danger of going on the rocks.

The marriage we have always expected to founder seems to be surviving quite harmoniously. This was a couple who always quarrelled every time they went out together, but yet got married in the end.

The man was a very intelligent, amusing, but very self-opinionated doctor, who adored arguing. A friendly argument was no good to him. He simply had to take his gloves off over it, and the only person who bothered to stand up to him was this girl whom he eventually married.

She was not a particularly spirited girl, but she used to offer a stodgy resistance to his arguments that at least kept them well kindled, which was what he liked – until she would get fed up with it and hurl at him any retort that came into her head, so that it always developed into a real row.

Then he used to come into the office and say he was never taking her out again. Altogether he had thirty-six introductions (the record number for a man), but nobody else could be bothered to oppose him, and each time he went back to her, which meant, of course, a fresh quarrel.

For two pins he could have started an argument with Heather and me, but we were very careful not to let him begin.

Our highest income for a girl so far is £10,000 a year, while the average is £200 or £300. A great many have a dress allowance of £150. Nearly all the men say they want their wife to have a little money of her own, but most of them are anxious it should be very much smaller than their own income. Working men do not seem to mind if their wife has no money at all as long as she is domesticated.

Each client has a number, and we keep a large Black Book in the office containing the names of all our clients. Beside their names are the 'numbers' of the people they have met. Then by simply looking up their names we can see whom they have already been introduced to, and make sure we do not give them the same introduction twice over. We happen to have a divorced husband and wife who are *both* on the books, and neither of them know the other has registered with us. Our Black Book helps us not to make the awful mistake of arranging to send them out together.

At the moment a schoolmistress holds the record for women in the number of introductions – she's had thirty five. But in her case very few of the introductions have led to a meeting, I think mainly because she writes to the men on school exercise paper and that frightens them.

If anyone asked me what attributes most men want in a woman I should say three of the chief things they state are that she should be healthy, adaptable and have a sense of humour. Nearly all of them want her to have a slim figure and lovely legs. They put the figure before a pretty face and it has to be a very beautiful face indeed that can carry off a pair of bulky legs. There are occasional variations like 'plump but not fat' and one man specially stated he wanted his wife to have 'a plump bosom and lovely legs.

Most men want to marry girls with a fair skin. They do not mind so much about the colour of her hair as long as she has a fair complexion. Voices matter to them enormously, and so do pretty, well-kept hands.

'Intelligent, vivacious and well-read,' is a phrase that often appears in the forms. Many of the men lay great stress on sincerity and ask for her to be fond of a home and children.

'A good conversationalist' is another qualification that appears pretty often, but they nearly all add that this does not mean somebody who never stops talking.

Men dislike loud voices. I had several complaints about a girl who seemed to think the whole restaurant wanted to hear all she had to say. When I sent her out with a very nice Naval officer, he reported back: "She would talk about the wrong things in the wrong place. You know – talking loudly about workmen and criticising their families while we were in the tube, and then discussing all sorts of things in the restaurant so that people looked round at us. I wished I could just disappear!"

After this Heather and I had two alternatives: we either had to send her out with a series of rather deaf clients, or else we should have to tell her, and see if we could get her out of it.

We often take on the task of telling people their faults, which, of course, has to be done very tactfully and well wrapped up in praise for their virtues. But half the time we do not have to bother because the clients do not hesitate to tell each other their failings. There seems to be a good deal of plain speaking between them.

The women usually want a husband with a sense of humour. They don't seem to mind whether he is fair or dark, though a good many take exception to red hair. And most of them want him to be athletic more than good-looking. They want him to be sincere, unselfish, generous and sympathetic. On the whole they have a much less clear picture in their mind of the type of person they want to marry than the men have.

We often get asked by our women clients what men like them to wear, even though what the men generally write down as to their taste in feminine clothes is 'smart but not ostentatious.'

I remember a girl asking me what she should wear when she was going to meet a man for the second time and he was taking her out to a big cocktail party. So I wrote back to her:

> I really think a plain black woollen like the one you were wearing the other day, is quite suitable for the cocktail party; as not many men care for loud colours, you are quite safe in black. It does mean a lot if a man approves of your clothes when he takes you out, and I only wish that all our clients were as wise as you are.

Now and then we try and smarten up our men clients, and we made a very earnest endeavour with Bert, an East End van-driver, aged about thirty-four.

We began by advising him to put on his best suit instead of calling on the girls in his uniform, (we forbore to point out the oil-stains that rendered it so unattractive). This turned out to be a bad suggestion, however, because his best suit must have been put away somewhere damp for a great length of time and it had not occurred to him to have it pressed. Still, at least we got the idea out of his head that it was effeminate to have clean finger-nails.

He was keen to marry somebody 'intellectual,' though we never quite knew what he meant by this, as after he met anybody he would always come into the office and tell us they were 'too stupid.' I think he felt a little awed by his own intellect ever since the day he had a letter printed in the popular press.

His chief hobby was going to first-nights, which he said he only did to study the people. And one time he came to the office he treated us to a loud socialistic tirade on the price of a society woman's frock being enough to feed a family for a week.

Nobody would believe the things we have to listen to in the course of a day's interviewing. Diseases are a pet topic, and we often have to endure the demise of somebody's late lamented husband in all its lingering stages. We must listen politely because we can hardly dismiss the subject in a breezy way and say, "Well, anyway, he's dead now. Let's hear what sort of a man you want to marry next."

I even had an afternoon session with one woman hearing all about the laying out of a corpse, which I did not find quite the best form of entertainment after a delectable lunch.

But that was a cheerful interview compared with a woman who arrived in such floods of tears I thought someone must have died that morning.

"Come in and sit down," I said kindly, when she appeared round the door, hoping fervently that the tears had nothing to do with one of our clients.

Then I waited patiently while she dabbed her eyes with a soaking handkerchief.

"I can't marry him," she said in a voice cracked with sobs.

As she spoke more tears welled up in the swollen eyelids.

"Who?" I said, wondering if I ought to part with my clean handkerchief.

She told me; it was a Government official in Somerset who we'd put her in touch with. Frankly I hadn't expected alarming developments of any kind from him, and thought he would be slow over his courtship as he seemed so staid. All I could imagine from her tears was that he had proposed to her and then she had unearthed some unknown vice.

When she had dealt with the fresh tears and prevented them running down her cheek she explained: "You see, he can't leave Somerset because of his job, and my little girl is at school near London, and I should never see her unless I put her in a new school in Somerset – and then she mightn't be happy."

This seemed such an anti-climax to what I had expected that I couldn't find anything to say.

"It wouldn't work, would it?" she added dramatically, as though he had invited her to settle down in a harem.

Meanwhile I was thinking how quickly he must have made his proposal, for as far as I could recollect she had only just met him.

"When did he ask you to marry him?" I asked, trying hard not to sound too curious.

"He hasn't yet," she said.

And then it seemed as if my voice was a distant person answering, for I was so dumbfounded.

"I really shouldn't worry just yet," I replied.

It always astonishes Heather and me how many women think that men are *sure* to propose to them. They seem to have a glorious time pretending that every man they meet has fallen madly in love with them.

Sometimes we find it necessary to explain that just because they meet through the Marriage Bureau, it doesn't mean they are half-way up the aisle the first time he takes them out. And that if they do have this illusion, the man will probably sense it and disappear in considerable trepidation.

Chapter VIII

The wallflower has proposed – Too well-known to marry – Wife by instalments – Lucy was blind for ten years – The clergymen – Debutantes and Society mothers – Arranging wedding receptions – Furnishing homes.

It was a lovely warm sunny evening towards the end of our first summer, and Heather and I were working hard at the office, trying not to think how nice it would be to tip all the unanswered mail into the desk drawers and sally out into Bond Street before the shops closed.

"Can you see Mr Dewlap?" asked the secretary, closing the door behind her. "He says he's only got a few minutes before he catches his train, but he's got some news for you."

When clients say they have 'news' it usually means they are engaged, but in his case we were afraid it only meant he had installed another petrol pump. However, when he came in he was looking like a changed man.

He still wore his mackintosh in spite of the day, but several of the lines had vanished from his face and he seemed a few inches taller because he wasn't stooping so much.

"I've done it," he announced proudly, and there was almost a sparkle in his eyes when he said it.

For a startling moment we thought he must have gone to a registry office and got married by special licence that afternoon.

"It's Miss Jordan. She's thinking it over," he added, without a trace of anxiety.

Then we realised – he had made his first proposal, and in the thrill of this achievement he had forgotten that her answer might easily be in the negative. Of course, we hadn't the heart to suggest such an eventuality, so we invited him to tell us all about it.

He told us quite boyishly, and was even prepared to laugh at the picture he must have cut when he was doing it.

"You know Miss Jordan's very kind and sensible. Well I did it in Regent's Park. We were sitting on a bench having a rest, because we'd spent half the afternoon looking for my hat which I'd dropped a long way back when I was thinking how I should say it. And then I made an awful fool of myself and forgot my wonderful speech, and just said, 'Will you marry me? I'm rather lonely.' So now she's thinking it over," he repeated proudly, as though he had definitely been accepted.

We were afraid his luck would be out. She was a plain, cheerful, middle-aged district nurse, who had only been out with him twice before and said she didn't find him very interesting. We put them in touch because originally he asked us only to introduce him to people who were within cycling distance of his garage. This woman lived fifty miles away, but she had a motor bicycle.

So far she hadn't gone to see him as he had become shrewder and only invited her to meet him in London. Perhaps he was beginning to guess that he would have to get a plumber before he could take a bride home.

We used to hear about the garage from the clients who did go and see it. Apparently he only lived in the kitchen, and nobody seemed terribly impressed with the idea of taking on the garage after he had been 'batching it' there for years, though most of them were sorry for him and said he was a nice man.

When he left the office that afternoon we had to stop our work to talk over how we were going to cheer him up, because we felt he was going to be so terribly crestfallen if Miss Jordan turned him down, which we had every presentiment she was going to do.

She rang us up next morning to tell us about the proposal, and how she hadn't the heart to refuse him on the spot, so she told him she would think it over. As we ourselves hadn't the heart even to suggest she might turn him down when he came into the office, we felt we couldn't blame her.

Every day the Marriage Bureau seems to have its strange event. That afternoon it took the shape of a very eminent retired foreign diplomat living in London, who came in to discuss his matrimonial future after a heavy lunch and promptly fell fast asleep, full length, on the settee in our decorative interview room.

Somehow we did not feel it would go down very well with our women clients if they arrived and found a figure lying asleep with a florid face, and a cigar hanging out of the corner of his bushy beard. So we tried delicately to wake him up, first by jangling the telephone, and then by dropping books, but he never stirred. We didn't like to risk annoying him by prodding him, for he was a man of means as well as eminence, and we hoped to arrange his marriage quite easily. And so, after making a lot of noise all for nothing, we decided we could only trust that no visitors would arrive before he woke up naturally.

I said we hoped to arrange his marriage easily, especially as he is so well known, but he has proved a heavy burden to us. We thought so many women would like his money and the limelight of marrying him, and there was no doubt he would be a very impressive figure to accompany to public dinners because he would be wearing so many orders.

But the type of London society woman he wants to marry all say they know of him and would hate to meet him. We gather all their friends would think it a huge joke if they married him.

Another complication is that he will only meet people who are within a reasonable taxi-ride from the West End, so we don't like to introduce him to anybody farther away than South Kensington.

The only women who are anxious to meet him are the ones who have led very ordinary London lives and would like a little excitement (this is before they have listened to his boring stories). Then he goes off to have a look at them 'in their own background', as he puts it, which really means he polishes off their whiskey. Meanwhile he tells them some interminable story they cannot follow at all, until the whiskey is finished. After which he departs, to eat a large dinner by himself.

In a way he is an interesting case because in spite of his material success he has never been married, and in his own eyes he has always been a hero to all the prettiest girls in Europe. I don't know what he was like when he was young, but you would think he must at least have tried to get married at an earlier age.

When he first appeared he looked such a light-hearted and cheerful old dog we half feared we should find ourselves having to tell him that only people who seriously want to get married are allowed on the books (a task which on rare occasions we have to perform). But he asked for someone nearly his own age and was evidently quite serious about his intentions.

He has had plenty of introductions since then, but there are still no signs of a successful result. I suspect what he really enjoys is getting letters from unknown women and then seeing what they look like, so he doesn't mind a bit when they cannot face his anecdotes a second time.

While he was still prostrate on our settee, another visitor was ushered in. Fortunately it was not a woman client, but a grey-haired little man with a pale face and very thick spectacles, who glanced hazily at the recumbent figure as though it were nothing more extraordinary than a dog lying asleep on the mat.

"I've just come from Liverpool," he said, and we remembered his writing to us for an interview.

Before he shook hands he had to take his hand out of his overcoat pocket, and then he found his umbrella was still hanging on his wrist. He looked as though he must have hung it there when he left Liverpool and forgotten all about it till he got to our office.

"I'm so glad you could come up and have a talk; it makes things so much easier," I replied encouragingly, for he seemed quite perplexed.

Then he came out of the clouds and told us his story. "I've had two terrible losses which were almost too much for me to bear," he said, looking down at his boots. "They happened in the same week."

We maintained a sympathetic silence.

"You see, all my life I've had one great hobby. I was building a big boat in a special shed I had made for it. And just as the boat was almost finished the shed collapsed in a severe gale and my boat was destroyed. The same week my wife died," he finished, with his eyes still on his boots.

The way he told it we did not know which had been the worst disaster, the boat collapsing or his wife's death. However, we commiserated in an even manner with both his bereavements, and gradually he came to the point.

"You see, my wife always fought the battle of life for me," he explained, "and now that I haven't got her, or any occupation, there's no incentive to begin life again unless I could meet somebody so charming she would compel me to make an effort for her sake.

"The trouble is I shall never meet anybody on my own because I've always shrunk from society. You know for years I've been working in a room by myself, making up prescriptions for a chemist all day and then building my boat in the evening. I think that's really why I've got some sort of inferiority complex. I've got hardly any money and really nothing to recommend me, so I shouldn't be a social asset," he added forlornly.

"Well, I think the right wife, if we can find her, would take away your inferiority complex and give you all the incentive you need to start a new life," I said, for he made me feel anxious to cheer him up.

"I don't want to inflict sorrow on any woman," he said, "but I do wish I could see in life what others are able to see."

"Well, you're naturally feeling a bit hopeless at the moment. And I'm very glad you came to us to try and get you out of it."

There was something very touching and tremendously likeable about the little boat builder. It made us want to do all we could to help him. We could picture him working lovingly on his ship, living happily in his dream of when it was finished, and being an absent-minded but devoted husband to a wife who rather indulged him. Now his whole world was swept from under him and he was feeling lost and thoroughly lonely, but he only wanted a little affection and encouragement to set him on his feet again.

We talked to him till he had to catch his train back to Liverpool, and when he left our office we were glad to see he was already beginning to take a much better view of life.

I do not think he even noticed the eminent gentleman on the sofa when he left. We ourselves had been so wrapped in the boat builder's story we had quite forgotten him, but just as we decided something should now be done about him, the secretary took the matter into her own hands.

"Would you like some tea?" she called loudly in his ear.

"Tea! Good gracious!" he said, sitting up with a jolt. "I beg your pardon, I must have dropped off," he added, without apparently feeling any embarrassment.

"We didn't like to disturb you," Heather said politely, but he just shrugged and hurried off without waiting for his tea. I think he must have missed an important meeting in the City.

After he went we had a woman who came in and complained she couldn't *think* of marrying some man because he drank his soup from the point of the spoon instead of the side. And she demonstrated his deportment at the dinner-table with one of the pencils on my desk.

The nurse who eventually married the boat builder had a way of finding something wrong with every man she met. This we had tried to correct by the time we introduced her to him.

When they were in the courting stage she did have something to say about the ship building making a mess, because he brought pieces for it into the house and laid them about everywhere. But we were able to point out how little it mattered when he was such a nice character.

What was so gratifying to us was that, since knowing her, he has started rebuilding, for surely it is evidence that he has started life afresh. She must have given him the "charming feminine influence" he said he needed to make him do it, so we felt very glad to have found her.

Before they were married she used to go down and spend the day with him. She found the garden covered in weeds and the house looking sadly as though it had been without a woman in it for some time; so in a quiet, capable way she began to set it in order, preparing surprise meals for him while he was working. Having begun the task and seeing him thrive on it, she was encouraged to continue.

I think as a nurse she was accustomed to going into households that had crumpled up from lack of attention, and setting them running again to please and soothe the person who was ill. And at first the boat builder was just another invalid, because in a sense anybody who is very unhappy is ill. To begin with it was like doing her job and she fell into it automatically, and while she was doing it she discovered that this sad, distraught figure of a man was unfolding into a happy, loveable character. Then they grew fond of each other, and the practical friendship turned into real devotion and romance.

There is a type of woman, especially when she is not so very young, to whom a reliant man has a tremendous appeal, and she was one of them. Judging by his letters she was exactly what he needed. As far as we can gather she has taken up 'the battle of life' for him with great success. And until the boat was finished he was paying us for his wife in instalments of half a crown a week.

While we were trying to settle the boat builder's future we had a visit from somebody who will always be one of our favourite clients...

Lucy is the gayest thing on earth. I remember the first time she came to see us – a tiny creature only five feet high, with the most sparkling personality I have ever met, came cheerfully round the door and won our hearts at once. She wore a round hat and a bright-coloured frock and although her curls were grey, she carried with her such an abundance of youth it must have infected everyone she met.

Her freshness, and the way she seemed poised on the edge of a world she had just discovered to be wonderful, were difficult to reconcile with the homely type of woman who stood before us.

"I was totally blind for ten years," she explained, "and then I had an operation on my eyes, and now I can see perfectly. Oh, it's just the most wonderful thing that ever happened! I still can't believe it. And now I can see, I thought perhaps I might be able to get married?" She glanced inquiringly at us both.

No wonder she seemed on the threshold of an exciting new world – all the time she was blind she never thought there was a hope of ever getting her sight back. We could see her taking it bravely and philosophically, but it needed little imagination to know how she must have suffered in mind over it. She had worked energetically at handicrafts with other blind people, and done gardening in a garden where she could no longer see the flowers, and I should think as far as it was humanly possible, she was very independent.

Now Lucy was revelling in an orgy of sightseeing over even the most ordinary things in life, going about with all the excitement of a tourist on her first holiday abroad. Among all the new possibilities that she felt had returned with her sight, she thought somebody might now want to marry her, which had felt quite out of reach while she was blind.

Her bright-coloured frock was an expression of pleasure at being able to see colours again, and she wanted to marry somebody good-looking – probably she would enjoy his good looks all the more because she would be perpetually delighted that she could see his face.

"Did you find you liked people better when you saw their faces for the first time?" I asked her.

"No, mostly I was disappointed," she said candidly. "Chiefly because I found I'd imagined them looking quite different, and I was rather cross they didn't look like I expected."

It was not an immediate cure with Lucy's blindness.

"I could only see in a haze at first," she said, "and that went on for two or three years. I shall never forget the day I was going to post a letter and thought I saw a pillar-box, but I was a bit puzzled to find it was moving about – just as though I might have had one over the eight or something. Anyway, when we got close up to it I said to my friend, 'Here's a pillar-box. I can post my letter.' And my friend said, 'That's not a pillar box. It's a Chelsea pensioner!' We had some funny times, but I can see better than that now," she added gaily.

All the time Lucy was either smiling at us, or looking at everything in the room with rather penetrating interested eyes, like a child with a heap of new toys in front of her.

"I must marry somebody with a sense of humour whom I can have fun with," she said, and we agreed it was very important. We were wondering whether we could find someone with the same joy of living, or whether she would have enough for two.

One of these days, when she gets married, we are going to miss her visits to the office. She comes in very often and always livens up our day. She nearly married a clergyman, but then decided he was not amusing enough, and she didn't think she would be good in the parish.

Chelsea Pensioner versus pillar box!

We have many clergymen on the books from all over the British Isles, most of them middle-aged. Usually they have very little money, and some are widowers with a family to support. As far as the Marriage Bureau is concerned, we find they come in very handy for the not-so-young spinsters who have a secret passion for the vicar in their own parish. If we can persuade them to transfer their passion it works out very well, as they are already accustomed to helping with Church work.

Heather had one interview with an elderly clergyman who couldn't make up his mind whether he should marry somebody middle-aged, or whether the parish would be scandalised if he married an attractive young girl, which was what he really fancied. So Heather suggested it might cheer the parish up a lot if he married the young girl, (though his teeth were so far apart she felt a certain trepidation that any young girl would be carried away by his smile).

There is a country clergyman of about sixty who has settled down in the rectory with one of our clients as his housekeeper. She is about the same age and helps him with the parish as well as the housekeeping. Periodically we write them as tactful a letter as we can, saying we hope they are happy and will they let us know when they are going to be married, as it's only then that we can invoice for the remainder of our fee. But there is still no response and we are beginning to feel a trifle embittered, especially as these letters are not easy to compose.

Soon after we opened the Bureau a great many debutantes were brought along in a very business-like way by their mothers, who wanted to put them on our books either because they had already been launched unsuccessfully in the London marriage market, or because the parents were cutting out entertaining in the difficult times before the war.

The trouble with pre-war 'deb-dances' was that most of the young men who went to them were not eligible, so except from the shop-window aspect, these dances meant a lot of wasted outlay. Several of the mothers said openly they thought it more practical to bring the daughters to us.

Many of these Society mothers had been too ambitious, and had prevented their daughters marrying before in case later they met someone more impressive. We had one very contrite letter from a mother who had twice broken off her daughter's engagement.

> The great sorrow I am suffering from now, is that I refused to sanction my daughter's marriage when she was nineteen, and again when she was twenty and had a most devoted fiancé, but I thought she was too young to go abroad.
>
> Unfortunately she listened to me, although it was a most desirable match, and since then she has had several offers, but never now takes much interest in men.
>
> Night after night I go through the most terrible retribution and feel I have broken into her dear life. Of all my children she is the finest and noblest, and so kind to me.

I am glad to say we were able to answer this poignant letter by introducing the girl to several of our nicest and most eligible young men. She is very attractive and well worth the mother's regard for her, and we expect to see her married to one or other of them before very long.

While we were getting the first debutantes married off, we decided to strike out on a side-line and organise wedding receptions as an additional Marriage Bureau service. Heather took this in hand very competently, and we were rather proud of the way she was able to prepare a reception for three hundred guests at considerably lower cost than usual.

But it meant a great deal of extra work, and we were quite relieved when people gave up having big receptions because of the war.

It was not only the work of seeing the caterers, florists and everyone else, and planning all the details; there were many other duties that descended on us unexpectedly, such as:

...dealing with a bride who discovered immediately after the wedding that she was in love with the best man and attempted to run away with him after the reception.

...finding a fresh bridesmaid, the same size, to deputise for one who was taken ill.

...concealing somebody's elderly aunt who wasn't used to champagne, from the disgrace of being intoxicated in public, by piling her into a taxi at a side door.

...staying behind to watch the last dregs of the guests, who were frequently intoxicated; seeing the caterers left the house tidy, and finally being buttonholed by the bride's mother for a belated "Do you think they'll be happy?" conversation after it was all over.

Heather's capable hands

Another side-line we started was furnishing our clients' houses, and we are still doing it and find it much more interesting and satisfactory.

Heather does all the designing and furnishing, and she nearly always has several houses or flats on her hands at once. Often nowadays the couple have a short engagement because the man is going away on active service; they want to see as much of each other as they can and not be bothered with furnishing, so they tell Heather what they want and she does it for them.

There are many dramas here, too, and she remembers painfully the task she had trying to furnish a home for a couple who had taken a small semi-detached house in the suburbs.

The bridegroom had no ideas at all beyond huge creaking wardrobes and the sort of heavy tables you see under a red plush tablecloth with a fringe. And all his fiancée kept saying was, "I want it done in the Oriental style."

As Heather didn't see how she could make either of their ideas look in sympathy with the little building estate house, she suggested a scheme of her own. But the young man merely regarded her sketches with bovine indifference, while the girl kept on reiterating, "I like the Oriental style."

So Heather took them both to a big furniture store, hoping that when she showed them the kind of furniture she had in mind, they might see something they liked and begin to see her point of view.

She led them to a section which had the light, plain, modern furniture she knew would go with the house, and waited while the salesman opened drawers, swung mirrors, turned things round back to front and did everything he could to prove they were good value.

The young man watched the process gloomily and registered no interest at all, and the girl looked scathingly at the salesman as though he were merely making a fool of himself.

"I want something rich," she said icily.

Heather spent an exhausting morning trying to find what the girl meant by 'rich' furniture, which was difficult, as she didn't seem to know herself.

Eventually she persuaded them to let her go ahead with the original scheme. But when she went to have tea with them after they were married she found the 'Oriental style' had won, and the house was filled with brass trays and elaborate bric-a-brac which smothered her simple decoration.

Sometimes Heather has designed homes on paper for people living abroad. This is generally in the case of young men who are living in the East and want their bride to go out there and find an attractive home waiting for them.

But I think what she enjoyed most of all was furnishing a small motor-yacht for a man who wanted to live on it the whole summer when he got married.

He managed house property in London, and he got engaged to a girl who was manageress of a block of service flats in the West End. They both thought it would be very romantic to live on the yacht for the summer, but when he wrote to Heather it was clear he was very anxious—

> As you know, Isobel is greatly attached to any kind of boat, dinghy or even a barge, and the thought of living on the *Mermaid* simply thrills her. But I feel I would like it to be absolutely super when she comes aboard for the first time.
>
> Being rather a weather-beaten bachelor for so long, I have never really taken any interest in the interior decoration, hence the dilapidations and the enormous amount of lumber, which has gradually accumulated in every possible space of the *Mermaid*.
>
> At the moment there are faded cretonne curtains somehow attached to the windows, and a well-worn orange-patterned carpet.
>
> I think I had better tell you, although I am ashamed to admit it, that the curtains where I sleep are mauve, with orange and green daubs and zigzags. Funnily enough I have never paid attention to them, but on seeing them now I believe they are bound to make anyone feel sick before the boat even moves.
>
> I suppose by now you are feeling utterly ill, and am sorry on behalf of the *Mermaid*. However, if you will come down one weekend I will book you a room at a nearby hotel, and will gladly pay any medical advice you may require.
>
> I have not told Isobel anything about this as I want it to be a surprise for her, and you know her happiness means everything to me.

So Heather went down to Hamble and set to work on the *Mermaid* at once. He did not want to spend a lot of money, so she found a local boy to do the painting, while she went back to Town and chose the new curtains and furnishings.

Before she went she persuaded him to throw away many of his bachelor possessions. Much of the 'lumber' consisted of easels and paint, and those she stored away saying he would not want to paint on his honeymoon. There were also a rare quantity of saucepans and frying-pans in various stages of neglect, for the cleaning of them defeated him and he always bought new ones when they got too dirty. But with true masculine sentiment, which is often so oddly misplaced, he had not thrown the old ones away.

When she finished, Heather had transformed the *Mermaid* into a vision of new white paint (with a thin blue piping here and there because he wanted something blue), attractive curtains and fittings, and even two hidden bunks so they could have friends for the weekend.

And when the man wrote and thank her, he said he could not believe it was the same boat, while apparently his Isobel was enchanted with it.

Chapter IX

An old-fashioned spinster unfolds her wings – Who will buy my title? – How the Marriage Bureau deals with a fortune hunter – Dealing with divorcees – Widowers at a premium – A lesson in love letters – Some of the photographs – More hints on marriage – A disastrous meeting – Loneliness, the reason why most people come to the Marriage Bureau.

We don't always encourage clients to get engaged to each other; if we think it best we sometimes do exactly the reverse. For instance, we had a client whose best years had gone in looking after an invalid mother (who in the end became very difficult) and in running a large old house in Wales where she had no existence of her own. The mother was well grafted into this Victorian monstrosity because it had been the family mansion for generations. She had the sort of matriarchal power that I thought only existed in fiction, and the daughter was completely enslaved.

I saw it myself because the daughter, who was called Fanny, got in touch with us before the old lady died, and I was invited down under a promise that I said nothing about the Marriage Bureau.

Directly the mother died, Fanny stepped out into the world like a new-born butterfly unfolding its wings. She found herself with £2,000 a year and no ties of any kind, so she plunged gaily into her belated youth with all the spirit of seventeen.

First she sold the Victorian mansion and its entire contents with all possible speed and without letting it hang about by putting a reserve on it. Then she took a bright, comfortable little modern flat in London, and furnished it in complete contrast to everything she had left behind. And when she came on the books of the Marriage Bureau she bought herself an expensive fur coat, though she still clung to some dangling necklaces and lumps of amber on black ribbons that belonged to her former life.

She launched ardently into a timetable of Turkish baths and slimming exercises and showed us the result proudly. Everybody likes Fanny because she is so kind-hearted and full of fun. We are able to tease her and she always enjoys the joke – such as the time somebody took her (I believe in all innocence as he had lived abroad for much of his life) to a West End rendezvous which, in Edwardian days, acquired a racy reputation that now clings to it like disreputable hangings.

"Such a fascinating place, with wonderful antiques," she told us, "and such an *interesting* old woman in charge of it."

When we told her she had been to tea in a high-class brothel she was very amused.

We never charge for interviews, but when Fanny comes to see us she insists on paying us a guinea each time, which she lays firmly on my desk, saying, "There you are, my dears, business is business, you know."

It is certainly to her credit, in view of her former dull life that she didn't lose her head and marry the first person who came along, but she is very sensible, and I think when she does marry she will have made her choice wisely.

She wants to marry a widower for preference, with one or more children, but not children over ten years old as she is afraid they might be too big to grow fond of her. She would make a wonderful stepmother.

"I'm too old to have any myself, you know," she tells us, and we have to be polite and look faintly incredulous.

One proposal she discussed with us came from a very brilliant man who was covered with intellectual honours, but he had quantities of relations, and as Fanny was scared of relations after the powerful possessiveness of her mother, we dissuaded her from marrying him.

The other man we advised her not to marry was a retired Major who wanted her to put some money into a business. We are always on the watch to protect our clients from fortune hunters.

So far the most arrant fortune-hunter we've come across was a Spanish marquis who wanted to sell his title for £50,000. Fortunately we discovered this before he came on the books and refused to let him register.

He approached us by introducing himself in a very flattering and grand form on the telephone, which we felt was in very poor taste, and inviting me to lunch with him at the Hyde Park Hotel. According to his own account he was tall, with a good figure and plenty of hair – "Quite good-looking, you know, and I wear a monocle."

But when I met him in the cocktail lounge I saw a small fat man with bleary eyes, a white face, and rather a bald head.

"Splendid, perfectly splendid of you to turn up," he said in a throaty voice, while I, having taken an immediate dislike to him, was thinking it would be perfectly splendid of me if I stayed.

"What will you drink?"

I asked for a dry martini.

"Dry martini, nonsense! I never drink anything but champagne in the morning," he said loudly, and ordered two champagne cocktails, which we drank while he complimented me noisily on the Marriage Bureau, till I became aware of the enthralled silence of the eavesdroppers at the other tables and wished I could get up and fly through the swing doors.

All through lunch he told me about his divorced wife who was French, and how he now wanted to marry for money.

"Very good family, you know," he repeated emphatically for about the ninth time, while I wondered how I could sit through the remaining courses with the entire dining-room hearing our conversation.

I asked him whether he would prefer somebody dark or fair.

"I don't care a bit what she looks like as long as she has money," he shouted blatantly. "Push her around in a bath-chair, you know, if necessary."

Of course, I had long since made up my mind that he should never come on the books. Nevertheless, I put through a few inquiries about him, and found his title was genuine but he had enjoyed a rather chequered career, which included selling racehorses for his friends and keeping the money. He had also sold aeroplanes to Spain in the Civil War which had involved him in various international difficulties.

His married life began with a poor wife whom he divorced because she had no money (of course, the official reason was rather different). He then married a rich French woman, but soon went back to live with his divorced wife whom he kept in style on the second wife's money. The French woman having become wise to this then divorced him, and now he was evidently looking for a *third* wife who could afford to support himself and his first wife for the rest of their days.

Another man who in a sense was a fortune-hunter, we did put on the books, but he was in a very different category. One of his sisters came in and registered him with us; she would have the girls we suggested to tea first, and if she liked them she passed them on to meet him.

When we finally met him we liked him. He was working for his living in London, but he had on his hands a big estate in Scotland which he had to try and maintain on woefully insufficient means. I think his sister thought it

93

would be tragic if he had to sell it, and that was what made her come to us to find him a reasonably rich wife.

In the end, he married a fairly young widow who had been left quite well off by her last husband. I remember she was very nice and very overdressed, for she used to wear a pale pink frock and a long coat made of silver foxes, with another silver fox on her head. Beyond hoping she would not wear these clothes in Scotland, we had no misgivings about her, and I believe the marriage was a great success, especially as she rallied to the support of the home.

We have a good many divorced people on our books, and whenever possible we like to know *why* they got divorced as it helps us find them a fresh partner. But unless they volunteer to tell us, we cannot very well ask as it's really none of our business. Some of them are so eager to meet someone else that they come to us before the divorce has reached its final stage, so actually we must be careful not to let them have any introductions until they are quite free to marry again.

I think the most extraordinary divorce case we heard of was the couple (it was the woman who came to the Marriage Bureau) who had lived in the same little suburban villa for a whole year never speaking, and merely writing notes to each other. The quarrel only started because he said something she didn't like and then wouldn't apologize, so she refused to speak to him. How they managed to endure life in such a small house for a whole year of note-writing was quite beyond our comprehension, and we had to be careful to see that her next husband wasn't as stubborn as herself.

For a few months, widowers were at a premium as we had so many widows between forty and fifty who wanted to marry. The situation was so urgent we almost had to go out canvassing, and Heather and I even wrote to our bachelor uncles asking them to marry.

In this hasty whip round we collected my father's tailor, who I discovered was a widower, and married him off to a widow in Richmond with about four or five hundred a year.

Even when there was such a demand, Mr Dewlap was one widower whose marriage still seemed an unlikely event. When Miss Jordan turned him down he wrote us an abusive letter, but repented of it about a month later when he came in for advice.

He wanted to know why so many women he wrote to never wanted to meet him, and I spent an afternoon coaching him on how to write his letters. I suggested that instead of writing pages on all the things he was going to do to his garage, which might bore them (I did not add they might look unfavourably on the fact that it needed so many improvements), he should tell them about himself. And instead of drawing a depressing picture of a lonely man 'batching it' on twenty acres, he should tell them how travelled he was, that he was fond of music and gardening, and generally write himself up in a more encouraging way.

Sometimes we have to tell clients to stop sending their photograph with their letters, because while they themselves have at least a certain amount of charm, the photograph is so unflattering that it brings the correspondence to an abrupt end.

One girl who was really quite attractive sent round a photograph of herself wearing glasses, and some men used to send it back saying they did not want to meet her because she wore spectacles. Yet all the ones who did meet her found the spectacles didn't detract from her charm in the least.

The most memorable photograph of the many sent to the Marriage Bureau, was of a family group in old-fashioned bathing dresses, taken very obviously in a studio and not on the sea-shore, with a row of shells and an oar. The small child on the extreme right of this bizarre little gathering was now a man of sixty who wanted to be put on the books. We wanted to frame the picture and hang it on the office wall.

Ninety per cent of the snapshots show the client taken either with a dog or a chair, which proves how self-conscious the average person is when being photographed. And a trick some of the widowers have is to send women a photograph of their first wife, which never goes down very well. I suppose they do it to say, "Look, this attractive woman married me, so I must be a pretty decent sort of chap." The clients' reaction is that he probably never stops talking about her.

Our advice ranges over all kinds of serious and intimate matters. One young man told us in confidence that a girl we introduced him to had felt she must unload a confession about an affair the very first time he took her out. Of course it embarrassed him and put him off, and we wondered how we could stop her doing it to anyone else without letting her know he had told us.

Confessions to anyone – parents, fiancé or husband – should be avoided. In most cases, it is indulged in as a form of selfishness or exhibitionism, intended to draw sympathy or attention; as such it tends to confuse rather than clarify the emotional atmosphere. One of the important things a man asks for in his future bride is that her moral values should be as high (if not higher) than his own, and that she should be a good and affectionate wife. Confessions on either side are only distasteful and don't help anybody.

We find the best marriages are founded more on liking than on romantic love. There is something deeper and more reliable in marriage than the bubble of romance that we all know can break at one wrong word, because romance by itself is one of the things that cannot be invisibly mended.

Most people look for a real companion to share their life, and true companionship is a blend of the right mentality and the right temperament. If two people have the same values they will have similar aims, and therefore are unlikely to quarrel. As a great many people find to their cost, physical attraction, which so delighted them at first, eventually turns to revulsion if they are totally unsuited mentally.

Much of our time is taken up with women who, like the church mouse who arrived soon after we started, have to be mentally and physically refurbished before we feel we can suit them with the right husband.

There are many things a shy, lonely and sexually unattractive girl can do to make herself into a happier and more popular person. The graces of the drawing-room and ballroom can be learned, just as they have to be learned by an actress, who may have to practise for hours merely walking across the stage. And if a geisha girl can be trained in all the arts of pleasing and entertaining a cultured man, why should not the average girl who wants to marry take trouble to learn how to attract?

For her, a few dancing lessons are an infinitely better investment than packets of cigarettes or even new clothes; not only for the mere asset of being a good dancer, but because they will teach her command of her body and grace of movement, and help her to 'wear' her clothes. In fact they will take her a long way towards charm.

Then there are the women who say to us, "Yes, but look at these teeth of mine," or "How can I get round my nose and fat ankles?" Some of the most attractive married women I know have had some physical defect to overcome. Yet they have charmed men into overlooking the flaws. In fact these defects often force them to take extra trouble over their appearance.

Unfortunately some of the women who come to us try too hard to please when they meet a client, and become unnatural. There is all the difference in the world between making the best of yourself and then not caring whether, to use a vulgar term, you 'click' or not (which is the right way) or behaving as if you are sitting for a stiff examination on which your whole future depends.

There was a woman who had lived a very local life but had now broken out of this small circle which held no romance for her, and come to the Marriage Bureau. I remember the day she was to meet a man at the office. To begin with she arrived much too early, which was a mistake. Her manner was rather prim and precise, and she was spruced up to such a degree one could almost feel her praying a hair would not slip out of place. Every detail about her clothes had mattered beyond all else, and she had put them on far too early and done nothing in them for fear of spoiling them. When she sat down she never relaxed, but sat as though she were wired inside.

Presently the man arrived and was introduced. He was on time but gallant enough to apologise for being late, and, feeling her tenseness, he assumed an unnaturally cheerful manner. I wondered whether this foolish woman had queered things from the start by putting him in the embarrassing position of finding her there first. However he took her across the road for coffee and made another appointment to meet her, but then he dropped her because her eagerness was so apparent.

Most of the meetings take place in a hotel or restaurant, and I believe both men and women thoroughly enjoy the excitement of meeting a complete stranger who has been introduced to them by the Marriage Bureau.

Sometimes couples do miss each other, either by accident or casualness, and we have to calm the injured party and find out what happened. Anybody careless about these things in the beginning naturally has to be rebuked, but usually there has been some mistake and everything is put right.

We shall never forget the day a young city typist arranged to meet a bank clerk from the provinces under the clock at Waterloo station. They met successfully, and then they went to a cafeteria for tea where they had to stand in a queue and pile things on a tray.

He left her standing in the queue saying he was going to secure a table and would come back to carry the tray for her. Having laden it with delicacies for two, rather indiscriminately because she thought he might be hungry, she looked round and couldn't see him anywhere. She waited and waited,

The Great Clock at Waterloo Station, still a well-known meeting point

growing more dismal all the time, with the tray planted at the end of the counter and the waitress eyeing her because she was expecting the young man to appear and pay for all the things on it.

But he never came, and after hanging about for three-quarters of an hour, she gave him up. She appeared at our office next day looking distinctly ruffled.

Of course, we thought the young man had been very naughty and run away after seeing her (though we were surprised because she was attractive), so we tried to get in touch with him to tell him it was not the way to treat our clients.

Three weeks later, just when we thought he had vanished inexcusably from our horizon as well, we got a letter from him saying that just as he was going to find the table he saw a friend in the army, whom he hadn't seen for months, and thought he might never meet again. He dashed out into the street and across the road to try and catch him, and in doing so got knocked down by a car and quite badly injured. And while the girl was waiting in the tea queue, he was taken off to hospital where he couldn't remember her address.

So we apologised for having misjudged him and sent her off to the hospital to see him, and a few months later they got engaged.

When people are particularly coy about approaching us, they often write and say they are making inquiries 'for a friend'. Then as they get more confident they usually say 'the friend' is not interested after all but *they* are thinking of coming on the books themselves.

We had one letter signed 'M. & O. Two friends,' written about some girl they were particularly anxious should marry a New Zealander, and we were inclined to suspect it originated from a young man who wanted a clinging girlfriend out of the way so that he could concentrate on another.

We did have a man who came in and said quite openly he wanted us to get his girlfriend married off. He paid five guineas and talked it over with us, and next time he brought her along with him. She took it all quite calmly and didn't seem to mind in the least, although of course, it must have been a little like pensioning her off because he was interested in someone else. He was about twice her age, while she was thirty-five and very good-looking.

Another day we had a letter from two girls who were great friends, saying they wanted to marry 'two brothers who are good friends as we are.' It can be imagined this was quite a difficult thing for us to arrange, and in the end they married two clients who were not brothers, but lived in the same town, so that did nearly as well.

Before this there had been quite a patch of trouble because one girl fell in love with a man in the North and the other fancied one in the South, and they had a long quarrel over who should give up her young man. Finally we managed to settle it by finding another man in the same town in the North.

It was an extraordinary friendship that even made one of them give up her young man, but they had not only been to school together, but had always worked together behind the haberdashery counter in the same shop.

Immediately after this we sailed into another storm, over two daughters who wrote to us trying to get their mother married again. The mother agreed with alacrity to meet some of our clients, and we found a retired widower who had all the attributes she wanted, and sent him down to the country to call on her.

Unfortunately the eldest daughter came into the room and he fell for her straight away and ended by marrying the daughter instead. After this, mother and daughter were not on speaking terms. We did our best to get the mother interested in someone else, but after several angry long distance calls she faded out of our existence.

People who really exasperate us are women who follow the stars and bring in their horoscopes, which they expect us to study before looking out any introductions for them.

"Oh, Mr—, what month were you born in? Really! That comes under Jupiter. I'm afraid Ms— can't meet you as you weren't born under Cancer. I'm so sorry to have troubled you."

Somehow I don't fancy our clients would be very impressed with our methods if we carried on like that.

One woman even refused to deal with me and insisted on dealing with Heather instead, because my birth month was unpropitious.

We didn't take her on although she was very attractive, because she had a persecution mania. The first day she came to the office she looked fixedly at the closed door behind her before pouring out her confidences.

"I must be very careful," she said mysteriously, "in case any of the gang are following me."

At first we were a little startled by this remark, but suggested calmly that it might be quite a good idea if 'the gang' did come along as then we could put them on the books.

She had a fantastic plan about what should happen when Heather went to see her at her flat in Margate. How she must knock twice and then go to the other side of the road, while she hid behind the curtain in an upper window. Then directly she dropped a white handkerchief onto the pavement Heather would know the coast was clear and that the door was going to be unlocked.

Waiting in a coastal town in war-time for signals to be dropped from windows did not appeal to Heather, so she never went to see her.

It was sad really, because in every other way she was quite a rational person and very attractive, and I am pretty certain 'the gang' would never have originated if she hadn't been lonely.

Loneliness is the chief factor that brings people to the Marriage Bureau, and we find it in every walk of life. In any typical bunch of our letters the word 'lonely' appears time and again. I am looking through a little pile now in which I have come across a band of lonely men and women, some of them with every sort of blessing except enough human companionship.

There is a retired Army man, between forty and fifty, with a lovely country house and riding, fishing, shooting and sailing on his doorstep. He describes the full social country life and how he breeds racehorses as well; he describes the wife he wants, who has to be good at all these outdoor sports. It is quite an ordinary letter from a man who is well off and has a good many interests. But the postscript is the real headline:

P.S. – All this perhaps sounds very commercial, but believe me I am not really so, as I am lonely and desire someone to love and to be loved in return. And someone to look after and care for and to interest.

Then comes a letter from a rich widower in Scotland, whose name heads a long column in *Who's Who*. He says he is lonely too.

'I did not dream that it could be so lonesome in a city like London,' writes a Canadian in the next letter. And an Australian Naval commander says, 'I am a total stranger in England. I do not know a soul and I feel very lonely and depressed.'

In the same little group is another widower, whose children have all grown up and left home, and he finds himself marooned in a big empty house in the North with only the servants round him, feeling very lonely indeed. Then a girl in Glasgow who says, 'Although I have many friends I am very lonely. You see I was going with a young man for quite a number of years, but he became infatuated with another girl and married her.'

Next comes a young man who, between concentrating on his job to earn promotion and sticking to a widowed mother, has no time to make friends let alone meet a girl who might become his wife. 'Being just another lonely male I can't resist writing to you,' is how he begins his story.

There is another girl of twenty-two who works in a shop where the long hours tire her so much she has had to give up going to dances, so she no longer meets any young men, and spends lonely evenings in lodgings by herself.

Saddest of all is the letter in copy-book handwriting from a private who was then in hospital in France with the British Expeditionary Force. 'I receive letters from home just like the rest of my mates, but when they open letters from their sweethearts it causes a pang within me and makes me terribly envious.'

We did not know how badly he was wounded, whether he would ever get well, or how his future would develop. But we got some of our clients to write to him, and we wrote to him a good deal ourselves, just in case it helped him round the corner.

Before the war we used to find there were many more lonely *young* people than older ones. Young men and girls living in rooms by themselves in London, without much money to spend and no opportunities to go out and meet other young people, feeling their youth was going while there was so much to miss. They were far more lonely than the middle-aged retired people living in hotels, who had money for bridge, and the pastime of minding other people's business in the same hotel.

Now the war has reversed all this, and it is the *older* ones who seem lonely, as they have evacuated to the country and are missing the few friends in the old rut where they had dug themselves in. But the young people now have more chance of making new friends and less time to be lonely, because several of their evenings are filled up with war duties where they meet others of their own age.

Our experience proves that lonely people are not necessarily friendless because they are unattractive, penniless or stupid. We find the most attractive people are often bitterly lonely, just because they have lived abroad a long time, or merely that their luck is out over meeting any friends.

In fact, if any outside person could see our files they would be astonished at the number of lovely young women and eligible men whom we could point out as having come to us mainly because they were prompted by loneliness.

It is making these people happy that gives Heather and I the best satisfaction from our job. Anybody who has ever been lonely at some time or other in their life (and who has not?) can easily appreciate how great that satisfaction is.

Chapter X

Another move for the office – The 'mating'.

A t the end of the first year our filing system alone was beginning to call for more space than we had available, so we decided to move into a bigger suite in Bond Street. This time we had four rooms instead of three, a waiting-room, the secretary's office and two front rooms. The secretary's office was separate from the waiting-room and had space for several large filing cabinets. We made one front room the interviewing room, while the other is where Heather and I do the work of the day including, of course, the match-making.

The mating, as we call it, is the most important part of our work, as this is when we decide whom each of the clients should meet. And as we devote most of our time to it, and certainly our most painstaking efforts, perhaps I should describe how it is done.

If you came into the waiting-room during a lull, you would find a large attractive room, with an off-white carpet, red satin curtains and a long settee. There are love-birds twittering in a cage hung above the writing-desk, and the only ornament is one of those Victorian bunches of highly coloured everlasting flowers mounted on velvet in a glass case. It's the sort of ornament that looks appalling in company with a lot of antimacassars and a horsehair sofa where it belongs, but surprisingly effective in a modern setting.

Now push open the door of the front room where we work...

Picture us sitting one each side of a desk piled with card index boxes and correspondence. Letters have overflowed the edges of the desk and floated on to the floor. And on the only clear space of carpet a white Pekinese is rolling in delicious comfort before the gas fire, gnawing a rubber bone.

We use the floor a great deal, because no desk was ever made large enough to sort our correspondence into groups which will help us answer them more promptly.

If you could see us at work in that room you might wonder that we ever come out of it sane. There are two telephones that seem to ring incessantly, while the mail that arrives in legionary quantities twice a day has to be opened and dealt with at once.

Of course, we are young and we try to be smart, so dress boxes and new hats arrive as well. And we are often so busy that lunch gets forgotten until all the offices in Bond Street are closing their doors for the night. But neither of us notices the whirl we live in, or how the room gets lamentably untidy, because we are doing the 'mating' and it takes so much concentration. All the time we are looking up names and details, we are remembering the faces of our clients, their characters, their dispositions.

As we sit there we are painfully aware that the destiny of twenty-five to thirty couples a day may hang on how accurately we can pick out the epitome of their dreams. And so we are never tempted to grow slack and shuffle them carelessly together, in the hope that a few chance happy marriages might appear from the melee.

We have kept to the same system of filing and indexing for 'mating' purposes that we had when we started, for it worked out very well.

People still on the books waiting to get married are entered in 'The Black Book.' This volume tells us their name, religion, age, income, and where they live; they are also entered under alphabetical headings of towns, as well as the people they have met.

When they have paid their registration fee and become an official member, each client is put into the Black Book and given a number. They also have a card in the card index box, which has on it full details, both of themselves and the type of person they want to marry. And the card has a record of the 'numbers' of the various people they have met, so there is no fear of our sending them the same introduction twice over.

Anybody who overheard the odd scraps of conversation in our 'mating' office, without being able to read the serious detail of our thoughts, might think we had gone out of our minds. Here is a reproduction of the actual dialogue between Heather and me (only, of course, the clients' names are fictitious) during part of an afternoon's 'mating'...

Mary: Heather, who can marry a policeman in Singapore?
Heather: How about Mary Minter in Glasgow? She's also a Roman Catholic and she wants to live abroad.
Mary: Let's look her up. Can I have the 'M' women?
Heather: Ah, here she is. Oh, yes – she's an orphan. Her mother's left her a confectioner's shop.

Mary: What's she going to do with the shop if she marries? Oh, anyhow, as she wants to go abroad I suppose she's prepared to sell it.

Heather: If she makes sweets it's obvious she can cook. Will it be lost on the policeman?

Mary: It will in Singapore. I should think he'll have a certain amount of servants there. She'll be quite useful for all the local police bazaars, though, making sweets for them all. Anyhow, they seem to have a lot in common. Look, Heather, she's the right age and she's attractive, and she wants children, which he does.

Heather: Yes, and the great thing is I should think she's very adaptable, and he seems a good-hearted, easy person to get on with. One *must* have a good-tempered husband in that climate. Who's next?

Mary: Mrs Bootle.

Heather: What does she want?

Mary: She wants somebody 'well proportioned, cleanliness essential, fond of country life.'

Heather: What about Wilkinson?

Mary: Yes, hold on, I'm looking him up. I think Wilkinson's her man. He's three years older. Oh no, Heather, they're not a match after all. Mrs Bootle's 5ft 9ins, and the man's a shrimp, only 5ft 4ins. Perhaps she won't mind. We'll call him 'medium'. He's got the sort of figure she wants, income, same religion and everything.

Heather: In fact he's got more income than she's asked for. Maybe that'll cancel the height. Does he live in the country?

Mary: Yes, that's right. He's retired and stuck there for life with the sort of house he'll never sell. By the way, she's a bit bossy, Heather. What will she be like with a small man? She'll probably kill him in two days. I'm sure she ought to have a tall one towering above her with a very loud voice to keep her down.

Heather: Oh, now, Mary, you know it's always worked when we've put the bossy ones with the quiet ones. Let's introduce them.

Mary: I shall cry if I don't find my grey hat. Anyway, Mrs Bootle's got her first man. We're doing her well starting her off with £2,000.

Heather: Now for the next one. Mrs Lime – my dear, she's not awfully gay. I suppose she's still feeling her widowhood.

Mary: What a pity – because I thought Carter would do for her, but he says he wants somebody to cheer him up. They do seem to have a lot in common – he's sixty-eight and she wants someone about

	sixty-five. They both love music, travelling, motoring and home life. And, my dear, he even likes photography, which she does.
Heather:	And they live near each other, which is half the battle before they meet. I don't think she's so bad, and once she got married again it might make a new woman of her.
Mary:	Yes – she's sympathetic, and I don't think she'd be too difficult to live with. Anyway, they'll soon tell us if they don't like each other. Heather, do you know anything about Eileen Scales?
Heather:	Hasn't she been on rather a long time? Very attractive looking?
Mary:	No, I think she's new. Yes – she is new. No objection to widower with children, especially young ones. You know, I think secretly she's madly keen on children, and she'd rather like the widower because she would be so disappointed if she couldn't have any herself.
Heather:	Couldn't she have Mr Brown?
Mary:	Yes, good old Mr Brown. He's so sweet and he's quite lost with those children of five and six. They both live in Suffolk and they're both fond of dogs. They must be soul-mates. He has £800 a year and she wants £800. He's forty-five and she's thirty-two. He wants someone with a pleasant face and hers is quite cheerful and sweet. That's another match – we hope.
Heather:	Certain ones get stuck for no reason at all.
Mary:	Can I have the Black Book, Heather?
Heather:	Who are you looking for?
Mary:	I'm looking for someone who lives in the same hunting county as Miss Barrington-Smythe. Heather, what are we to do? She's had five men already this week.
Heather:	Well, you know why she scares them away.
Mary:	Why – what's her line?
Heather:	Thought-reading. She's very bad at it.
Mary:	Well, she'd better have Mr Vincent. Good lord, no, he's only a half-gent and she *must* have a gent.
Heather:	Violet Grey, a lady's maid. She's lady's maid to Lady—. She says, 'Don't worry, I quite realise it's no easy task for you, so please take your time.'
Mary:	There's Page the butler. And ladies' maids and butlers do get on well.

Heather: Yes, let's try him. She's terribly nice, isn't she, Mary? She's a sweet woman.

Mary: Well, he's nice too. But wait a moment, how far is Nottingham from Coventry?

Heather: I'll look on the map. There it is. It's about forty-five miles.

Mary: Oh, good. They can easily nip over and see each other. That's Violet, off with her butler.

Heather: Mary – this baker with £500 a year who wants someone 'nicely curved.' There's Mary Martin, who calls herself 'medium,' which is bound to be plump.

Mary: I'm looking her up. Oh dear, he's only half an inch taller than she is, but I suppose that'll be all right if she wears low heels the first time she goes out with him, because he's got an inferiority complex. You remember her, she's an awfully enthusiastic sort of person and I do believe she would help him to get rid of that complex.

Heather: I think she might.

Mary: Can I have the Black Book, please – Heather, we've got to find someone for Joan Spinks whose father's a retired greengrocer – you remember, that nurse of twenty-eight – quite pretty.

Heather: Oh, send her Mr Halesham, He's screaming for someone of twenty-eight.

Mary: No, he won't do. He isn't dapper enough and her idol must be dapper. Where's the box of C. Men? Let's look up Cullen. I think he's the man for her. Yes – she might like him. Now in the Air Force, and was something to do with bananas.

Heather: Yes, my dear. Bananas has just the right money she wants.

Mary: And she wants 'a refined home lover.' Let me see, he says he's fond of boxing. Would that help about the house? Also debating – rather dangerous. But he's fond of music and children, which she is, and they both want somebody with a sense of humour.

Heather: Bananas is nice. I thought he was gentle and kind when I saw him, and he certainly had a sense of humour. I think they might click, don't you?

Mary: Now for Mrs Rocksmith, who's swathed in mink from top to bottom – jewels sparkling when she walks into the office. We've just married her daughter to a baronet's son. Now Ma is trying her luck.

Heather: Shall we try her with Major Toptown?

Mary: Yes, she's just the girl for him. She wants to live in the country and he's a landowner. And keep her flat on in town.

Heather: Would he like the flat? Did you see it?

Mary: Not bad – a bit ornate. He *can* afford it on top of the land. He's Master of the Foxhounds, and she likes that sort of thing. She'd be a good hostess and she wouldn't worry him too much. I think we might have a wedding there soon. He says here he's got a stately figure, which means portly, but she doesn't seem to mind about figure.

Heather: Mary, *what* are we to do with Elizabeth Green?

Mary: She's had about twenty-four people now.

Heather: Yes, she never takes the trouble to answer their letters or remember their names.

Mary: She writes about a month later, by which time we've given them someone else. Why she ever joined I can't think.

Heather: Waste of stamps on all sides.

At this point the secretary announced a visitor for me – we can never carry on long uninterrupted – so I laid down the last letter and went over to the mirror on the wall to tidy my rumpled hair, before I left Heather to go on 'mating' alone.

I came into the interviewing room to find a middle-aged Army officer studying the Victorian flowers with a great deal of intensity. He was a new client and he looked surprised when I appeared.

People so often look astonished when they see us that we always long to ask them what sort of person they expected. Perhaps they think we will both be old and rather eccentric-looking. Fortunately it doesn't seem to put them off when they find two perfectly normal-looking young girls, though I sometimes wonder if we should do better wearing white wigs, as we have to receive the confidences of people sometimes twice our age.

The Army man had already written for particulars, and now he wanted to talk over his marriage and register. I do not know why people make such heavy weather over filling in forms, but they all do. "What shall I put for so-and-so?" they ask us, as though we know more about them than they do themselves.

We often long to adopt the crude technique of a harassed civil servant in a labour exchange and tell them curtly to "go over there and fill it out." But of course, we have to be very patient and sympathetic however pressed we are for time, as our clients' matrimonial affairs are none the less personal for being put on a business footing.

This man must have filled in plenty of forms to join the Army alone, but he seemed to want assistance over nearly all the questions.

"What shall I put for 'Colour of Hair'?" he asked gravely, raising a very bald head.

As almost all our women say they must marry a man with a sense of humour, and I was rather pleased because I thought this must be an attempt at a joke. I was just going to laugh uproariously when I realised the gravity was genuine and that he could not have a spark of humour.

"Put fair," I said solemnly, looking hard at his bushy eyebrows.

And I realised that the dice were loaded against him.

Chapter XI

Extracts from letters.

Here are extracts from some of the letters received by the Marriage Bureau which we reproduce without comment:

Above all things my correspondent must be a GENUINE animal lover. This is most important, for without it there would be no peace. I am a Catholic (not a nun).

From a dentist:
I have no particular ideas as to how my future wife should be, but I do make this one stipulation. She must have false teeth – I am forced to give enough benefit to my family.

The other day I was watching a facial demonstration, so thought perhaps this would help improve my looks. After having my face pulled about for twenty minutes I got up to go. The girl who had performed the operation went away to get my change, and another attendant came up to me, and to the amusement of all who had been watching, said: "Can we give you one of our facials, madam?"

This, Miss Oliver, will give you an idea of my looks.

From a prominent Member of Parliament:
My future wife must be intelligent but uninformed.

I do not want a husband who will be attached to an odoriferous pipe, and who finds the mantelpiece more comfortable than either a footstool or slippers.

The most popular phrase:
I am considered good-looking.

I want to marry a man with melting violet eyes.

I am what people call 'a gay young widow.' I have been happily married three times, and all my husbands have passed peacefully away. My first husband was a grocer, my second an egg merchant and my third a butcher. As I am now thoroughly used to these three occupations, I would like my next husband to earn his living in one of these lines.

I am attractive with plenty of sex-appeal ... everyone believes I am about twenty-four, but really I am forty-three ... it should not be difficult to find me another partner ... of course, he must be good-looking and not fat, but tall and strong (like my late butcher husband) ... as all my husbands were fond of a merry and carefree life I want to go on living that kind of life because I know this would be their wishes. Besides, I am too young to settle down to a quiet home with children.

I think that is all I can say about myself, except that I have a good figure and was Miss Margate in 19—. I was chosen from 400 girls and some of them were beautiful, but I am modest and do not believe in having a good opinion of oneself.

From one client to another:
Dear Mr—
... I liked you but I feel I must be frank and tell you I could never marry you. First, you have so little hair; that puts me off a little ... I am also used to gentlemen who wear dark suits when they take a lady out. I had on my best hat and coat in honour of you.

PS – About your hair, don't worry about it; there are many things you can rub in to make it grow again.

From a boy of 19:
My mother says I should not contemplate marriage until I am twenty-two years old, but I should like to court two or three years before we marry.

I am unable to reply to quite a number of your clients because: their name is illegible; their address is illegible; their letters are signed with Christian name only; they give no address.

Dear Miss Jenner,
Thanks for the introduction which I feel I must return. Years ago I was engaged to a girl who was keen on dogs. In the end the dogs got her undivided attention, so the liaison was eventually broken off.

I find that women show a most delightful impartiality between fantasy and fact. Thus, a Botticelli in description becomes a plump Rubens in photo form.

Have kept a gin-soaked bawd for other men's diversion all my life, and am at last to be allowed my divorce. Am wondering what may now be possible.

From a man:
I stand 6ft 2ins and could pose for a sculptor. I swim a mile non-stop, skate fifteen, and drive 360 – petrol permitting. But these things do not defraud the clock.

The lady who would care to write to me with a view to matrimony in the near future must be willing to live on Public Assistance.

The following experiences will show that it is really a case of going on until the right one turns up:
Now Miss X of Epping, appointment made, kept me in an afternoon and did not turn up, not a word of explanation.

Miss Y, Kennington, an Australian girl. Big girl, large features, motherly and very plain. Spent lunch hour, had to be polite and gentlemanly and, note the joke, she did not like me. What a relief.

Miss Z of Harrow. Long correspondence, exchanged photos, made appointment, kept me standing on a cold corner 30 minutes, did not turn up. Two days later received post card saying could not come. Date on postcard same date as appointment (how honourable).

Mrs C of Palace Hotel, several conversations on telephone, appointment at the Trocadero, waited 30 minutes, page boy brings message lady finds it inconvenient to come.

Well, there you are, so now if you think it's worthwhile and you have some more promising material, we will go merrily on.

I have the patience of a fisherman and a photographer. Fussy unless I get plain food punctually.

I do rather deplore having to write to you as I had hoped to meet someone nice before, but have been strictly brought up.

I have had two boyfriends. The first one was when I was twenty-five years old and we had a small quarrel and somehow the friendship cooled off, and the second was when I was thirty-five and after we had been friendly for some months he told me that his wife was still alive.

Should there be any client upon your books willing to guarantee my mother's normal comfort for the residue of her days, I should be willing to marry the lady.

I have been engaged before. The last time was just before I went to Africa. But I was so keen about the job in the desert that I did not notice how the months were passing and finally came out of it to find that she had discovered someone else.

I am more concerned with what is under the hat than with the hat ... I can tolerate more easily a person who occasionally gets into a hell of a temper than I can a semi-animate doormat. I can swear like hell when necessary – and, so I am told, when unnecessary.

Chapter XII

The Branch in the country – A more successful country branch
– War-time boom in weddings – RAF weddings.

Heather and I were motoring along a country road in the direction of Aldershot one weekend at the beginning of September 1939. Like everyone else with a business of any kind we were very preoccupied with how we should run the Marriage Bureau in war-time.

"Anyway, Mary, if this week's a good omen the war is obviously going to make everyone want to get married."

"Yes, but supposing they bomb London and our office gets flattened with all our papers and records in it. Then where would we be?"

"We ought to have a second office in another street, with everything duplicated."

"That might get flattened too."

"Perhaps."

"Heather, I know, couldn't we have a country branch?"

"Is it worth it?"

"Yes, because to make it pay for itself, we could have it as a guest house and country branch combined. And we could offer rooms to our newly married couples who get married in war-time and don't want to set up house till the war's over."

"It's an idea, but where could we have it?"

"Round here. There must be heaps of wives who want to live near Aldershot now their husbands are in the Army."

"And lots of Army husbands who don't want to live in their quarters. Mary, it's *quite* an idea."

And while we were thinking it over we came across a house agent's board looking over the top of a high wall. Not a dusty old board that was bowing from its post, but a brand-new one suggesting the house had only just been left empty.

"Let's look at it," I said, so Heather stopped the car and reversed towards the gates. They were immense wrought-iron ones with a lodge each side of them. Even though the lodges were evidently occupied, nobody came out when we blew our horn, so we opened the gates ourselves.

It was a long drive, and when we got to the front door we found it was also made of regal patterned wrought-iron and nearly as large as the gateway. The house was a big grey stone building, with two turrets, rather like a Scottish laird's castle.

A pleasant-looking, plump housekeeper in a stiff white overall opened the door and showed us into a high marble hall with pillars, huge Spanish chests and lovely old high-backed velvet chairs. We noticed the doors bore impressive emblems, richly carved, and the windows in the ballroom had stained-glass emblems near the top.

From the housekeeper we learned that it belonged to an exiled foreign sovereign who had now decided to let it furnished for the duration.

We were so carried away by the sovereign's mansion that we forgot to ask how many bedrooms there were and how many servants it needed. I think the only thing we asked was the rent, and that, in our fever of delight, seemed reasonable. All we looked at was the ballroom, the library and the hall. And in the course of seeing those we came across a quantity of precious Persian rugs and three grand pianos, which helped to turn our heads a bit more.

The housekeeper probably thought we were making an easy escape when we waved aside all idea of seeing the rest of the house and asked her not to let it to anyone else, as we would be getting in touch with the agents at once. Anyway, she took it quite calmly and showed us out with a respectful little bow, and we drove home like mad things, full of excitement and in our imagination filling the house with visitors who would pay enormous sums to live in the romantic atmosphere of old Madrid.

We could hardly wait till the next day, when we went to see the agents. They presented us with a long printed description of the house, and with photographs that fanned our excitement. We learned that it had twenty-five bedrooms and nearly as many bathrooms, besides twenty-three acres of land. This was news to us, but if we thought anything at all we merely thought it was an even better bargain, and we asked to see the lease.

Perhaps everybody did something crazy at the outbreak of war. We certainly indulged in a strange piece of madness the day we took the sovereign's house for the duration, and having paid our rent for three months, went home to pack all our belongings.

We packed most of the night, including all our clothes and the office files, and in the morning we drove down to our country branch, taking two car-loads of luggage and two secretaries.

It was a strange cavalcade that sped down the Aldershot road, with boxes of stationery, dismembered filing cabinets and bundles of documents blotting out the entire back windows of both cars, and a few precious things from our flat crowning them unsteadily or pushed into odd corners.

When we arrived, the housekeeper looked as though she firmly believed she was dreaming.

"But where are the servants?" she asked with bulging eyes, when we each emerged gingerly from the two driving seats.

"We've brought two secretaries."

Heather said it as though they were better than a whole retinue of servants, while the secretaries looked rather glum.

Then we went to choose our bedrooms.

We walked for what seemed miles along corridors, and looked into palatial rooms with big four-poster beds and velvet hangings. They had accompanying marble bathrooms, formal groups of leather-bound books by each bed and elaborate writing-tables in every room.

The place had the kind of nameless smell that usually pervades houses of defunct celebrities that have been preserved as national monuments. I suppose it was really because they were afraid of opening the windows in case it faded the velvet.

In our tour we discovered that each turret had a small private suite inside it, so we decided to occupy these and leave the other rooms for the guests.

Then with sinking hearts we went into the servant question, and found there were only four installed in the house while it was empty, but it needed *fifteen* when it was fully occupied.

The housekeeper was quite capable, though we suspected she had hoped the house would never be taken, and the 'tweeny' who had stayed on was very good. But we hate to dwell on the memory of the mysterious 'sisters' who were also part of the sovereign's skeleton staff.

Neither of us could discover what their original duties were. But in our time they occupied a room in the servants' wing from which they never once emerged to do a stroke of work. If we sent a message saying we wanted to see them to tell them their duties, we always received word that the eldest had 'rheumatics' (which we suspected had their source in a bottle), or else her sister's inside had 'turned right over' (which seemed to happen *whenever* we suggested she should do any work). Unfortunately, the sisters were let with the house, so there was not much we could do.

Anyway, nothing chilled our enthusiasm that first day, for we thought both guests and servants would flock to the house. But when we tried to amplify our staff the only result from a thorough combing of the neighbourhood was a cook who, it transpired, could hardly cook at all.

Then we turned out attention to the more enthralling task of finding the guests. We made the secretaries spend several days typing out circulars about the house and polishing the bathroom floor. Meanwhile we tried to help with the housework ourselves, and Heather and I would dictate letters to clients while we dusted the carved furniture.

We rode round Aldershot on bicycles, distributing the circulars; we expected a deluge of requests for rooms, and felt very worried about our meagre staff.

After a long, discouraging silence the only response came from an elderly Colonel, who rang up and asked what we charged for a single room.

"Six guineas," I replied cheerfully.

"Too much. I'll pay four – move in tomorrow."

And he rang off without waiting to hear if we agreed, so we decided to put him in the attic. He sounded so testy we thought he must have quarrelled with his wife that morning and was leaving home in a rage. Either that or else he had a pretty bad liver.

There was no bed in the attic room we chose for him, so we got a collapsible iron bedstead that we found in a box-room and fitted it together as best we could, trapping our fingers painfully in the process. It did not look right somehow, but we made up the bed and hoped for the best.

That night, when the Colonel had gone to rest after a very indigestible dinner prepared by our inferior cook, we heard a loud bang and clatter, followed by some angry barrack-room oaths.

He left before breakfast without paying for his night's lodging, and leaving a collapsed iron bedstead lying in pieces on the floor in silent evidence of his complaint.

A whole fortnight passed before we had another inquiry for rooms, and that came from a woman who rang up to know what we would charge for herself and her maid.

"Too much," she said when we told her, and vanished from the line before we could lower our fees.

Meanwhile the September sunshine was waning and we felt cold in the turrets at night, so we made a few tentative inquiries from the housekeeper and found the house burned a ton of coal a week, besides an equally alarming quantity of coke for the central heating.

It appeared we should have to forgo the heating and shiver – at least until the house was filled with guests, which we were now beginning to suspect would never happen.

By October we had to go about the house in fur coats, and our zealous efforts with the carpet sweeper were purely to get warm. Then, as there were still no guests at all, we moved thankfully back to London, and tried to think how we could get rid of the sovereign's mansion as quickly as possible.

We thought no more about having a country branch until the first air-raids began on London. When one or two familiar landmarks in Bond Street had been levelled to a heap of rubble, we went down to Maidenhead and took two office rooms over a firm of insurance agents in the High Street.

Those two rooms are now our permanent country branch, and its main purpose is to house a complete duplicate of all our records and correspondence.

As we are so busy in London, we only open the Maidenhead office two days a week. But in spite of this we have had several marriages already, one of them being the wedding of a smart Bond Street dress designer who evacuated there and married a well-to-do local man with an attractive house on the river. She still keeps up her dress designing and it has turned out a very successful match.

The war brought a deluge of new clients from all over the country, and we soon discovered that many more people wanted to get married in war-time than in peace-time.

In the first few weeks we suddenly found the number of people on our books had increased by a quarter. But instead of being delighted at what might have been called a boom in marriages, we became extremely anxious on remembering all the stories we had heard about disastrous 'war weddings' in the last war. So we spent our time saying, "Don't be in too much of a hurry. Think it over first. Don't get married too hastily—" until all the couples must have thought we were dreadfully damping and tiresome.

We found the men wanted to get married so that when they went away to fight they had 'something to come back to.' And the women wanted to marry quickly because they were afraid of being left without a man at the end of the war. They did not say this in so many words, as naturally they did not wish to look like chickens running after grain. But from the little things they said it was plain they were thinking of all the old maids left after the last war when there were so many superfluous women.

More men seem to want to have children in war-time, but fewer women want them – which is not surprising when they have to look after them alone in as much, if not more danger than the husband who is in the Services. The men generally say they want them to perpetuate their name, which seems more important to them than the sort of life the child is going to have either in war-time or immediately after it.

We find very few of the couples want to set up a home of their own in war-time. Many of the girls get married and then go back and live with their parents. And we have had several RAF men who have specifically asked to meet a girl who could go on living with her parents. I suppose they feel happier knowing she is with somebody, in case they should get killed flying.

We have had applications from hundreds of Australian and Canadian soldiers who want to marry English girls while they are over here, and we found the Australians in particular went like hot cakes early in the war.

The girls were very keen to marry them because they said they found them sincere, and thought their bluntness was refreshing. Above all, they wanted to go and live in Australia after the war; we imagine because they felt it would not be reeling from the after-effects as much as this country.

The Australians invariably had the same system of approaching us. Usually the one who wanted to come on the books would bring a friend and make him do all the talking. The friend would tell us what a wonderful fellow he was and how lucky the girl would be who married him. Altogether a tremendous amount of back-slapping went on, and then we would get down to details in a very breezy manner (they always infected us with their breeziness) before we set things going for them. They were fun, those Australians, and we liked dealing with them.

When the girl client met her Australian she probably met him in the Overseas Club, and she very likely saw another Australian soldier sitting almost within earshot. But she probably thought nothing of it because there were bound to be plenty of Australian soldiers sitting about the Club.

That soldier was the friend again. This time he had been asked to hang around and take a look at the girl, and if he passed her she was definitely 'on,' for the time being at any rate.

A very touching romance we sponsored was the one between a young man in the Australian Navy and a girl who used to be his childhood love when he was ten years old. He was born in England, but went out to Australia to work when he left school; when war broke out he joined the Australian Navy and got sent back to this country.

Through us he met the girl who lived next door to him in England, and they were so delighted at meeting again they got engaged almost at once. Apparently when they were small they used to write notes to each other and push them underneath the garden fence, and then be very coy and pretend not to see them.

The Australians and Canadians all said they liked listening to English girls' voices.

In the first few months of war most of our Service clients were in the Army, next in number came the Navy and less than half were in the RAF. This was very harassing for us, as the RAF is far more in demand than either of the other services. In fact, ever since war began this has been our permanent headache, because every other letter nowadays seems to have the phrase, 'I want to meet someone in the RAF.'

This is generally sheer hero-worship on the part of the women, and we often wonder how the RAF marriages will work out after the war, when the heroes come down from the sky to a black suit and an office.

Meanwhile these young men make wonderful husbands, not because of their deeds of heroism, of which the average pilot's wife says she hears little or nothing, but because of their outlook.

Their emotions are fewer and finer, and they have the best sense of proportion in the world. You cannot fight 1941 air battles and have a mind for petty quarrels and disturbances.

Life and its purpose are like a clear-cut crystal which they are holding up to the light without anything fogging its surface. It is a beautiful thing, cut on very simple lines and inspiring them all the time.

One pilot told me that when he first started to fly he was unhappy and worried by human problems, which at once seemed infinitely small and stupid directly he was ten thousand feet above the world. When he was training to be a fighter pilot it took such a degree of concentration in those fast machines that it completely blotted out all his worries. And when he came down to earth again he found them not seeming anything like as formidable as before.

We are afraid of two things in the hero-worshipping wives. One is that they may expect every short leave to be a dazzling celebration – whereas relaxation to the average pilot probably means doing something ordinary and dull, like pulling a motor-car to pieces in the back yard.

The other is that they may nearly suffocate him with mothering, which is what hero-worship frequently turns into once they are married.

Men hate being followed round with scarves and overcoats. They only thing for a wife to do is to leave the extra pullover laid out with his clothes for him to take or not if he chooses. He is much more likely to put it on. And metaphorically this applies whenever she wants to get her own way.

Sometimes the war bride may have to do a little mothering, but she has to hide her maternal capacities very carefully, because a man hates to see the wheels going round. He cannot bear being fussed and bothered over little things, which is merely exhausting to him. Neither can he stand the complicated web of emotions over small matters that so many women weave round their unfortunate husbands. Women can usually take a lesson from men with their sensible, simple outlook and better sense of proportion.

And so to all future pilots' wives we would say try and have a sense of proportion like his, see life like the clear-cut crystal he sees it and let all his landings be happy ones.

Chapter XIII

More about war weddings – Millionaire wants a son-in-law
to inherit his business – Trying tricks of clients – Mary Oliver
goes to see the family of a client who is being difficult.

One of the things that both couples and parents seem scared about in a war marriage is that they can see so little of each other, even after they are married.

It always makes me think of a girl I know very well who is both happily married and working for her living. At one time she even had to stay at work several evenings a week, and when her employer called her up and said, "I do hope we're not breaking up your home," she simply replied, "I'd much rather my husband saw too little of me than too much."

Funnily enough, so few wives have the ability to imagine that perhaps the most devoted husbands may not want to see too much of them, and it is up to the wife to be the elusive one. Not, of course, to neglect his creature comforts and the smooth-working wheels of his home, but to arrange the home with changes and progress in it, and not so that she is sitting in his pocket day in, day out, for years and years. He will appreciate her much more if he has a few opportunities of missing her.

One sees so many married couples eating a meal in public, just like automatons, quite wordless and expressionless. You see the same couples everywhere in different forms – in smart restaurants, sitting side by side in the bus or going for walks – always the same, till one wonders why they bother to go about together at all.

War has done a great deal in bringing much-needed change into some of these homes – drastic tearing change in some cases, but it has stirred the dust of years and let people see things more clearly; monotony has vanished.

The result has been mercurial in some instances and I have noticed that many people take on a new lease of life.

So when anxious parents come to me and say, "But they've only met a few times, they can't possibly know each other well enough, and then he's going to sea and may not get leave for a long time," I would merely suggest, "Perhaps it's better than knowing each other too well."

The drawback to the necessarily confidential nature of our work means that we have to keep our heads through the most complicated intrigues created by clients who do not want their friends and relations to know they are having dealings with us.

War has increased these particular difficulties as Service people are often afraid of letters getting into the hands of their superior officers, again because they are terrified of being laughed at. There is one young officer who makes me sign my letters 'Auntie Gwen,' and put in a lot of family chatter. All the girls I suggest to him have to be referred to as though I have just met them at a party, and that as they live near where he is stationed I think he ought to meet them. And of course kind old Auntie gives their address.

We had one woman who lived with her two sisters and was convinced they held her letters over the kettle before she came down to breakfast. 'Please see your letter is *well stuck down*,' she used to repeat every time she wrote – until we put her mind at rest by using sealing wax.

Among our recent clients was a man with a big business who was trying to find a son-in-law qualified to inherit the family firm and look after it when he died. This way he felt his daughter's husband would have a safe job for life. He did not tell the daughter he was putting her on our books, and when I said I should have to meet her before I could do anything, he arranged for me to run into him 'by chance' at the Dorchester hotel. I was to walk past their lunch-table and suddenly recognise him (we were supposed to have met in Italy) when he would introduce me (not under my own name) and invite me to a cocktail party. When I came to the party I was to bring a young man (the suggested son-in-law) and then find I had to go early, leaving him behind.

I suppose the old man was frightened the daughter might fall in love with somebody who would not have enough brains for the particular family business. In any case, he was afraid she might get difficult if she guessed that he was choosing her husband for her.

At the moment we are still looking for the right young man, for there is the double problem of finding somebody capable of taking on the business as well as being an attractive husband.

This same old man annoyed us by giving himself another name when he applied to us. We found out his real name quite easily, for besides being a millionaire, he is well known and very influential. But we felt rather vexed at his deception for it stands to reason that we must know something about our clients, and it only adds to our work if they give us a false name.

Another mild deception on the part of some of our men clients is for them to pretend to the girls we introduce them to that Heather and I are personal friends of theirs. This is usually after they have taken one of us out to lunch to talk over their projected marriage.

Of course, the girls get angry and think we are trying to get them off with our friends. And then we have to ring up the men and ask them to stop doing it; our going out to lunch with them was purely a business meeting, and they must not try and make it into a personal friendship to impress the girls, because it has quite the wrong effect. All of which is very awkward to explain and a great nuisance.

When we are out in the evening or during the day, and clients walk into the same restaurant, Heather and I never recognise them unless they come over and speak to us – again because of this business of many people wanting to keep it a secret that they are on the books of the Marriage Bureau.

The ironic reflection of all this is that sometimes our own friends refuse to invite us to their weddings in case it should be thought we had fixed it up for them. Sometimes, when we are feeling mischievous, we threaten to avenge ourselves by appearing with bags of rice and confetti, and dropping pamphlets about the Marriage Bureau as we scramble into our pews.

The rather entangled process of trying to remember all the variations and plots for secrecy in the matrimonial affairs of several thousand clients can easily be imagined as one of the hardest parts of our role – whose parents are supposed to know, and whose are not; how they are supposed to have met; what we may say in a letter, and how we must deal with an inquisitive relation.

Now and again we have nearly made a mistake, but managed to retrieve ourselves by saying we had two clients with the same name and got confused.

One girl who came on the books and got engaged to a very suitable young man, forgot she had not told her parents, and suddenly let out by accident that she met her fiancé through the Marriage Bureau.

This happened long after we felt we had established our integrity, and thought there would be no more raised eyebrows and wild conclusions that the Marriage Bureau must be something quite sordid. Therefore it was all the more wearisome to us when the girl rang up and said her parents were very angry over her engagement since they heard how she met the young man, and would we do something about it to calm them down.

I promised her I would go down and see them, and next morning I put on my tweed suit and flat shoes and took a train to Gloucestershire.

If they had not lived so far away, and been so inconveniently placed sixteen miles from a station (where the only taxi-driver was away tending his vegetable garden when my train got in), I might not have minded so much. As it was I could only think of all the work I would have to make up in the office the following day.

I was still thinking of it when I walked through a conventional country hall with a large dinner-gong at the bottom of the stairs and one of those top-heavy coat stands that belong to families where there is a row if somebody hangs their things on the wrong hook. And in a rather oppressive library I waited for my interview.

Presently, after a good deal of creaking about on the floorboards upstairs, the girl's mother came in, looking as though she was going to deal with some very ugly situation with a striking display of competence.

I wondered what she expected me to be like, because when she saw me she seemed so nonplussed she hardly knew what to do next.

"*You* don't run this – this Marriage Bureau?" She spoke as if she were pulling the last two words off a garbage heap.

"Yes."

"Then what about this young man you introduced to my daughter?" she went on, determined to carry out her attack. "Do you know anything about him? Who is he? What is he doing going to a Marriage Bureau? And how did you get hold of my daughter?"

In her rapid torrent of questions I chose to lose the last one because I thought it would be worse for the daughter if I explained that she had approached us and applied to be put on the books.

I told her all I knew about the young man, and the mother nodded, less angrily.

"Still, the child can't get engaged to somebody she's met through a Marriage Bureau."

I asked why.

"It's unheard of."

I said nothing.

There was a long silence while I stared dreamily at the fire and wondered whether the taxi-driver had gone back to his vegetable garden.

"Anyway, I've stopped it," she said petulantly.

"I understood you originally gave your consent."

"Originally – yes." She made it seem a very long time ago.

"Then you must have liked him."

"I didn't know *then* about their meeting like *this*."

"You want her to make a good match?"

"Of course."

"Well she told me she never meets anyone out here."

There was no answer, so I pressed on.

"If you were going to put that right you would have to entertain a good deal and take her about somewhere where she would meet more people. Then, of course, you couldn't stop her falling in love with some particular young man. And you might find afterwards he wasn't a bit suitable, and there would be a lot of unhappiness all round."

"Yes, well, that isn't helping us out of this difficulty," she replied more calmly.

"Except that in this case, all the practical details weren't just left to chance. They were known before your daughter met the young man and fell in love with him."

Suddenly, before she realised what she was doing, the mother smiled. And then she laughed.

"Well, tell me more about this Marriage Bureau of yours," she said. "It's all very new and puzzling to people like us."

I stayed for lunch and tea, and altogether spent a lovely day with them. In the end the scandalous meeting of the young couple was forgotten.

It was the father, a dear old man in a fly-away collar, who drove me to the station. He was talking and chuckling amiably all the way, and I think he was enjoying a glorious reaction after the family storm which somehow, having been the cause of it, I had managed to dispel.

Chapter XIV

Honeymoon tours and the one that went wrong – On being turned down.

Honeymoons in war-time have ceased to mean the most extravagant holiday of your life.

The couples who are setting up a home tend to stay and enjoy it – just in case it's not there for them to enjoy next leave. And the others merely remain near where they were married, because travelling is not romantic in a smoky carriage with all the air and moonlight sealed out till daybreak.

We had a couple who thought they would spend a complete escapist honeymoon in a caravan. So they set off with all their saved-up petrol coupons, assuring each other they could cook. Actually neither of them could cook at all, and the petrol ran out when they were near some very noisy defences, so it was not altogether a success.

But before the war, when clients were spending real peace-time honeymoons, the Marriage Bureau often used to arrange their honeymoon tours for them. We whisked them off for anything from a month at St Moritz to a day at the Zoo, according to their means.

Sometimes Heather, our honeymoon organiser, had to suggest somewhere when they did not know where to go, but usually they had their own ideas.

Once she tried to persuade a young riveter who married a parlour-maid *not* to go abroad, but they were quite determined to go to the South of France. Neither of them could speak a word of French, and they spent the last part of their courting days struggling with gramophone records and a dictionary. After that they discovered the French understood them better when they spoke English. When they came back the young wife told Heather that although she would not hurt her husband's feelings she did not like France because there were not enough English people about. Next year, if they had a holiday, it was going to be Margate or Southend.

After Heather sent a Cockney couple touring in Scotland we had a shower of snapshots of them wearing the kilt and every other Scottish accessory, inscribed with 'from your two wee Scots pals.'

Unluckily, she suggested an elderly doctor and his wife should go to Bali just when the European situation led to their being turned back at Port Said. And a couple who were keen on climbing she sent to Llandudno to climb the Great Orme and Little Orme to their hearts' content, but they got lost after achieving the highest peak and spent the rest of the night cursing both Heather and the Welsh mountains.

The only honeymoon that went wrong through any fault of ours was when we sent a couple to a tiny sailing village in Cornwall and despatched their luggage somewhere else. They arrived, poor souls, in their brand new going-away clothes, from which stray grains of confetti still dropped embarrassingly out of odd corners, in a place where everybody was wearing slacks and very old jerseys. They had to stay in those clothes for days, plodding frequently to the station to see if the luggage had turned up. Of course we traced it as quickly as we could, but it must have been a bad beginning to their honeymoon.

Nowadays, with the stream of Bond Street shoppers diminishing to a trickle, we often notice people hovering round our sign-board pretending to be staring at the shop window next door. We have no idea how many toy with the idea of walking in and then lose their nerve and go away, but we often recognise clients who come to the office as somebody we saw walking up and down outside when we went to lunch.

Whether it is a compliment to us or just a reaction after having taken the plunge and come in nobody knows, but the way they pour out their life story when they do arrive is rather surprising.

Having appeared once they are usually no longer shy about coming again, but we did have a woman client who did not like visiting the office in case her friends saw her. She used to call for her introductions (we were never allowed to post them) but instead of coming in she stood in a doorway opposite and made our secretary run across the road and give them to her when no-one was looking.

Not long ago we were trying to form a record of reasons why people sometimes fail to attract the opposite sex. We selected a number of clients at random, and sent them each the names of four people they had met, asking them to say why they turned them down. So in case these might be useful reading for anybody who wants to get married, the following are some of the replies:

A retired stockbroker of 59, with £700 a year, met:

Miss — (an independent spinster of 42). 'She has a charming personality, but does not seem particularly fond of settling down to a quiet home life and that is what I want.'

Mrs — (a widow of 57 with £3,000 a year). 'The story of her past life depressed me. Her pessimistic outlook and her contempt for the middle class disgusted me. She completely forgot she once owned a pawnshop, but did not let me forget for one second that she has £3,000 per annum. Above all, her snobbery infuriated me.'

Mrs — (an attractive widow of 45 with £1,500 a year). 'She appeared to me most suitable as a wife. Eventually, having met her a few times, I spoke to her about marriage, but she told me that she did not think me a suitable partner.'

Mrs — (an attractive widow of 45 with about £1,000 a year). 'Her conversation re clothes and amusements displeased me, so did her gushing manner, and her siren-like voice grated on my nerves.'

A spinster, 30s, with a four-figure income, met:

Major —. 'Nice, but had no sense of humour. Too short, and too army.'

Mr —(a retired manufacturer). 'Too old. Bad breath.'

Mr — (a film magnate). 'Common. Not used to my class of friends. Was shy with them. Wore ready-made clothes.'

Major — (retired). 'Very nice. Old and staid for his age. Too many relations. Too fond of country life, and he lived too far away from London.'

An architect of 49, with £650 a year, met:

Miss — (who owns a fruit shop in Manchester). 'Too peroxided.'

Miss — (a small, dark secretary of 27). 'Too gushing.'

Miss — (a schoolmistress of 30). 'Too schoolmarmy.'

Miss — (in a Government office). 'OK, but she didn't like me much.'

A spinster of 29, with £300 a year, met:

Mr — (a manufacturer earning about £1,000 a year, aged 36). 'We spent a pleasant afternoon and I enjoyed his company immensely. We appeared to have many interests in common, and I regret that I have not heard from him since.'

Mr — (optician, early-40s, with about £800 a year). 'His very high opinion of himself was shown in all his letters, and the very fact that he addressed me by my Christian name in his second letter told me he lacked breeding.'

Major — (a cavalry officer in his 40s). 'He took me out for tea, and his shyness made me feel most uncomfortable and embarrassed, although his manner was charming.'

Mr — (a film director with about £3,000 a year). 'His loud check overcoat dazzled my eyes. His bowler hat (at least two sizes too small) and purple socks, would not lend themselves to my quiet taste in wardrobe.'

A young parlour-maid met:
Mr — (a caretaker at a girls' school). 'Quite nice, but his children got in the way. Marrying him would include a ready-made family.'
Mr — (a tanner). 'He was quite nice and we shall remain good friends. But I couldn't contemplate marriage with somebody who doesn't like country life.'
Mr — (an optician). 'Definitely a football-fiend. He told me he was the goal-keeper of the local team.'
Mr — (a railway clerk who came all the way from the Orkneys to see her). 'He was inclined to be mean and rather too fond of neat whisky.'

An Army Major of 42, with £1,500 a year, met:
Miss — (about 28). 'Insufficient brain. No taste in dress.'
Mrs — (a vivacious young widow). 'Oldish. Talks too much.'
Miss — (an independent spinster of 32, and very attractive). 'Didn't like me. Attractive woman.'
Miss — (somebody we didn't see, and who said her age was 26, but when this man met her she was over 40 and had to be helped out of the taxi). 'Said she was much younger than she was. Very blue stocking.'

A welfare worker of about 30, met:
A schoolmaster. 'Too domineering.'
A commercial traveller of 35. 'His one idea of life is dancing and cards. He wouldn't be able to settle down to everyday life.'
A secretary of 42. 'His political outlook was the reverse of mine. He couldn't understand my outlook any more than I could understand his.'
A soldier of 37. 'Too affectionate. He embarrassed me in public.'

A young divorced woman of 27, who lived on a houseboat, met:
A Major. 'He proposed, but I turned him down as he expected me to keep him after he retired.'
A food king of 40, a widower with two children. 'He was very attractive, but on second thoughts he didn't want to marry me as I have a daughter of two.'
A solicitor of 33. 'I would no more marry him than fly to the moon. I disliked him the moment we met. He has no manners and his looks and lack of charm put me off.'

A widower of 51, with £750 per annum, met:

A spinster from Brighton (rather buxom and a very nice type). 'She is too serious for me. A good type of woman but not my type.'

A 25-year-old games mistress. 'I like her very much but she is too tied up with her family.'

A spinster in her 30s. 'I like her very much too, but she didn't like me.'

A spinster who sold arts and crafts. 'She is too well dressed. It makes her seem hard.'

Sometimes clients write long letters to each other, saying how they failed to please. And in this connection one woman gave us a copy of a letter she sent to a young man explaining why she did not want to meet him a second time. As we thought it rather illuminating, I should like to quote some extracts from it:

Your ideals about marriage are almost perfect, and I confess that the thought of being loved as I believe you *could* care is very attractive. That is why I am sorry so much potentially fine material is being wasted as you are wasting it.

Keep your ideals by all means, because one day they will glorify someone's life, but at the same time I think you are looking at the question from the wrong angle. Instead of saying to yourself, "I should be a different man if I had someone to care for *me*," make it "I will *be* a different man before I ask any woman to share my life."

We both agreed we wanted only the best, didn't we? Are you offering your best? Have you the right to place such a burden on a woman's shoulders from the outset, because burden it would be, I assure you, if she had to become engaged to a man before he got an incentive to live. Personally, I want a *man* for a husband, not a grown-up child who is always crying for the moon without trying to get it...

I have hit hard, I know, but I am doing it because I believe there *is* a man underneath that layer of self-pity – a man I, or someone else, could be proud of.

I should imagine you have a very fine mother, but I think she has been *too* fond of you in letting you foster that habit of pitying yourself so much. I realise this means a lot to you, and you would probably be a different man if you had hope, but life has some hard knocks for all of us, and it is the way we face up to them which makes character.

I do not know the full circumstances, of course; therefore perhaps I have no right to judge, but have you really done all you could to get friends, or get a job with an income which will enable you to keep a wife? I repeat, have you a right to expect *any* woman to become engaged to you just to give you an incentive, when you have no idea when you are likely to give her a decent home?

You will say here that your lack of a job has prejudiced me; this is not entirely so, but it has in the sense of the effect it has apparently had on your character.

There is another thing, too, I *must* mention, and that is your personal appearance. I have formed the opinion that if you altered this, your whole life would change. Look at yourself in the mirror and try to see yourself with a woman's eye. You were kind enough to say you liked my green outfit; I put this on because I desired to pay respect to you, even though we had never met, but had *you* done anything to make yourself attractive in a woman's eyes?

I feel like a cad writing like this, but you need a stimulant now – not milk-and-water pity. Why not try the effect of buying a few smart ties and collars to match your shirts and suits (I should always insist on my husband looking his best when taking me places!) turn down the collar of your coat, wear a neat muffler and gloves if you are cold, square your shoulders and walk as if you are going to conquer the world – I am sure the effect will be electric.

For the moment I do not feel I want to meet you again, but if, say in three months' time, you are still unfixed, you might like to write and say "if only I had someone for whom I could care and protect ... I have a job and in a few months' time could offer a home," then if I also am still unfixed, I should count it a privilege to meet you. Until then, however, I feel we must both be free.'

Chapter XV

Some married couples.

"Yes, but what happens after they are married?", "Do you ever get anyone coming back and saying what a frightful wife you've given them?", "How do they get on afterwards?"

Heather and I are forever answering these questions. We wonder why anybody should think that just because a couple met in a rather practical fashion, their marriage is bound to pursue an erratic and spectacular course quite different from any other marriage. That it should be perfectly normal and harmonious seems beyond belief. And that in the whole two years of our career we have not, so far, had a complaint from one of our nine hundred and thirty-two married couples seems to them equally incredible.

We like to keep in touch with clients after they are married to find out whether our judgement was good. And, like anybody who has taken much painstaking care over a piece of work, we naturally want to see the result. So whenever a couple are nice enough to ask us to go and see them afterwards we always accept...

Henry and Dorothy had been married five months. They lived, as planned, in a small modern house in the suburbs, with a brightly painted front door. There was a bell, a knocker, a very correct letter box and an elaborate affair for scraping mud off your shoes. The step was a line of yellow that compelled one to stride over it without leaving a footmark – a stride which took you to another door-mat inside like an oasis in the shining linoleum of the hall. It was a very newly-married house, and clearly belonged to somebody in the first flush of house pride.

Dorothy took me up to the spare-room, explaining that I was their first visitor and the black-out was not yet fixed properly.

I trod warily up the staircase, which had narrow carpet oddly roped off from the varnished cream paint on the stairs by pieces of string. "Don't you think it's a good idea of mine to keep people from walking on the paint?" she said. I struggled with a sudden inclination to stray off the carpet, which I felt was entirely induced by the presence of the string.

She showed me all over the house, and I followed her round feeling gratified at her delight in it. I felt as if, having given someone a present, I was watching them unwrap the parcel. At frequent intervals she referred with equal pride to "my servant," not one gathered, that the servant had any particular merits. On the contrary she was prone to leaving most things undone, but she was part of this glorious new thing, "a home of my own."

Henry got back from the office about half-past six. "You remember he's in shipping," said Dorothy rather grandly, in the way people usually refer to one of the directors, and I remembered he had an administrative job in a small steamship company.

He had lived with his parents in the same neighbourhood till he was thirty-seven, was earning £800 a year, and had covered himself with glory by running the local tennis tournaments and dances for Spitfire funds. Then he calculated he could marry and set up a home and add to his local laurels by importing a good-looking wife from Town.

Dorothy was just what he wanted. She was nice-looking and strikingly neat, with the stamp of perfect housewife about her strong, capable, unvarnished hands. She wanted just the kind of little home he wanted.

When Henry arrived he unlocked a cupboard full of all kinds of bottled, ready-made cocktails and waved his hand towards them for me to take my choice. At dinner they very touchingly brought out their champagne, while 'my servant,' decked in starchy muslin frills, handed round a very good dinner.

Twice there were telephone calls for him in the middle of the meal and he went off straightening the collar of his blue shirt, saying, "Pardon me, will you, I expect it's my boss ringing from Liverpool."

"I do wish we'd never had the telephone put in," said Dorothy, when he was out of the room, her eyes shining with pride at the luxury of having it beside her bed.

It was encouraging to see how much they were enjoying themselves, and how thoroughly devoted they were and pleased with their lot. As we sat at the dinner-table I could not help comparing them with the same two people who first came to the office...

He, perhaps, had only changed one comfortable suburban life for another. But it was Dorothy I thought of most. I remembered her as a receptionist in one of those dreary London houses that call themselves flatlets, and which are really a warren of ill-adapted single rooms with a wash-basin, a divan bed and a Yale lock. They are usually occupied by impecunious young bachelors, thrifty stenographers, retired Army men, and spinsters with library subscriptions.

Dorothy's flatlet house sought to achieve a hotel atmosphere by having her sitting behind a large desk with a bowl of flowers in the hall, and an array of key-hooks for the occupants to hang their door-keys on when they went out. She had to be there until 10.30 at night, in the swirl of draughts from several long, bare passages, answering the telephone and listening to complaints from the tenants about other people banging doors.

Except for one night off a week and several hours each day, she had little time to meet people, and after trying a few times without success to get another job she had given up. She came to us on a sudden impulse after getting frightened that she would be there for the rest of her days.

Now she asked nothing more from life than what she had, for it was *exactly* what she told us she wanted when she came into the office to put her name on the books.

We find our married couples never tell their friends they met through the Marriage Bureau. These two had not told a living soul, and I was amused to see it was almost as though they had even convinced themselves that they met at a party instead of through us. Evidently they did not give our office a thought any longer, and if I spoke about it they behaved as though it was something they only remembered very dimly and which had really no connection with them.

Cuthbert and Jane had stopped the clock.

Any day now Cuthbert would be called up, but until it happened they were living an idyllic existence in one of the most attractive country houses I have ever seen. The fact that they were living on borrowed time did not worry them because they were too happy to think about anything else.

At thirty-nine, with three thousand a year of his own, and complete leisure, Cuthbert was quite unspoilt. He was tall, with an aristocratic, outdoor face, an athletic figure and an obviously genial disposition. And at twenty-four Jane had been chosen by him out of fifteen well-born country girls to share this delightful house which had been his before they married. She met five other men before she got engaged to Cuthbert. She was pretty, with dark, curly hair, rather heavy legs, a lovely skin and a sweet expression.

At first they were both a little embarrassed at meeting me again, perhaps because although they each saw me a good deal before they got engaged, this was the first time they had seen me when they were together. They kept looking shyly at me and then at each other. There were long silences, when I would keep asking for another cigarette or a drink which I did not want. With typical perversity of circumstance all I could think of to talk about was the Marriage Bureau, and obviously that would be calculated to make the next silence last forever. So till they recovered themselves I wandered round the room admiring it.

We were in a big, low-ceilinged lounge with cream-washed walls, navy blue and white patterned chintzes on the deep arm-chairs and a white rug in front of the open brick fireplace. There were shelves in the brickwork round the fireplace, adorned with gaily coloured old china pot lids, and the few pieces of furniture were lovely antiques, perfectly chosen.

When we went over the rest of the house all shyness was forgotten. It had the most inconsequential architecture, full of odd alcoves and quaint blind alleys in the passages, and in each of these unconventional spaces there was something nice to look at. An old corner cupboard, stripped of its varnish and holding china, with concealed lighting underneath the carving at the top; a little bureau, or just a table of flowers with an invisible beam shining on their petals.

There were lovely Grinling Gibbons overmantels on some of the fireplaces, and prettily dressed window-seats in all the rooms, while their bedroom was pale green with a rich, plum-coloured carpet and hangings, and limed oak woodwork.

They were rather sweet together when they were taking me round. "Not so bad? Humph?" Cuthbert would say with a modest attempt at concealing his pleasure when I admired anything very much. And Jane would murmur quietly, "I like it." So that he gave her a devoted little glance because she was pleased with his choice.

Later we had dinner in a plain panelled dining-room at a long refectory table, with the candlelight shining on old silver, and distant gunfire jingling the spoons and forks on the crooked oak surface.

It was an ordinary, comfortable English home, and no less vulnerable to enemy action than any other. Yet I felt as if I was in a real bastion of peace. This had nothing to do with it being in the country. I should still have felt an illusion of complete sanctuary were it in the heart of London or Manchester. It was just the atmosphere of the house, and the happy couple inside it, that were enough to dispel any grave thoughts which might have come into one's mind with the gunfire.

Jane had been living in the country with her parents, who made her help in the house and play the devoted daughter to a very binding degree. There was not too much money, and her only changes consisted of visits to former school-friends who all seemed to live as remotely in the country as she did. She scarcely met anybody, and that was why she came to the Marriage Bureau.

Her mother knew she had joined, but they told all their friends and relations that they met 'through friends.' All curiosity they parried with extreme vagueness, because they always meant to arrange a stock story, but forgot to settle on one. They told me this just after Jane said some people were coming for cocktails on Sunday evening.

"You won't mention the Marriage Bureau, will you?" she said apprehensively, "because nobody knows except my mother."

I assured her I would do nothing so tactless.

Conversation revolved round golf, bridge and gardening, and the friends who played golf and bridge with them. They took me round the garden next morning and followed the war-time fashion of showing off their vegetable garden. It was all tended by a couple of gardeners, except for two little rival patches, side by side, which they each gardened themselves like children.

"Look, now they *are* coming up. By May you'll be put hopelessly in the shade, darling."

"Did you keep the packet or can you remember the name?" he asked mockingly.

"Don't be inquisitive. Anyway, I didn't have to write it on a wooden stick and leave it in the flower-bed."

"You would if you'd thought of it in time."

Jane laughed good-naturedly and did not deny that whatever came up in her garden would be news to her.

While they were talking I remembered about Cuthbert being called up, and realised they had blissfully forgotten that he would not be there to see the two little rival gardens in bloom.

Love is probably the only thing that stops the clock in war-time.

"My dear, I can't even boil an egg."

The voice that made this exaggerated statement was rich and low. It came from somewhere inside an opulent high-backed arm-chair, from whence the owner was too lethargic to tilt herself forward and look at me.

From the side I had a view of tapering dark-red fingernails holding a cocktail glass, and a length of very shapely leg. They belonged to a good-looking girl of twenty-eight who was now a Marriage Bureau bride.

She used to live by herself on a not very imposing dress allowance, in a flat where I felt she must have boiled many eggs in between going to night clubs. Her own particular circle of friends, who were mostly smart night-lifers, evidently thought she was too much of a good-time girl to want to get married. Probably she pretended she was against the idea, for she had a very cynical line of conversation, but whatever the reason, she asked us to find her a husband.

He was somewhere at the other end of the room, mixing cocktails. Forty and good-looking, rich and in the Army, with not too many brains and an amiable disposition. I felt he was the kind of man who would refer to his wife as "a very fine filly."

They did not mind talking about the Marriage Bureau, and they talked about themselves rather as though they had each picked up a bargain at the bloodstock sales.

She was certainly very good-looking, with a taste for clothes, and he had adorned her with all kinds of lovely jewellery from rings to regimental badges. But she was one of those young women who cannot talk about a bed or a dog without making other women blush. In fact, her conversation was well sprinkled with *risqué* remarks, which I personally found a trifle embarrassing.

They had hired and expensive-looking furnished house in the West Country, near where he was stationed, where they kept a batman and two young maids who giggled at the batman. Amongst other things the husband had given his languid lady a sun-ray lamp, with which she occupied her mornings, basking naked beneath it on a large white sheepskin rug in her bedroom.

"Can't get any brandy – it's such a stinking price," cooed the voice from the chair.

"Disgusting sum; thirty-five bob a bottle. Matter of fact, a feller round here said he'd sell me some cheap, then went and sold it to a wine shop at a profit. Rotten shame I call it," said her husband, holding the shaker up to the light to view his result.

"Crashing bores, all the people round here," remarked his wife. "They simply don't speak our language."

"Do you see much of them?" I asked politely.

"Nothing at all, my dear. We vegetate. It's paralysing without brandy."

"Mind you, that's not a bad little bit of something who lives at the Monastery," said her husband, coming over to the fire.

"Oh, darling, you really don't know. You've only seen her in electric light."

He was always told he did not know, a treatment which he weathered good-humouredly every time. I began to wonder if he liked being patronised, and that she had divined it as being the right way to treat him.

I left after half an hour's visit feeling they were well matched. At least they spoke the same language.

Somewhere in a maze of streets behind Chiswick I found a row of little semi-detached red houses. I counted my way along to No.12, where I rang the bell and waited. The front door looked as though it had never been opened, and the windows, which were all shut, had heavy lace curtains that hid any sign of life there might have been inside.

No-one answered the ring and I began to wonder if anybody was at home. Next door a small boy of less than four in long trousers, with a comforter in his mouth and a face rather like old wax, stood squarely by the fence and stared at me as though I were some strange animal that had woken him in the middle of the night. Beneath the stare I almost imagined I was doing something quite outlandish in calling there, and as the minutes dragged on I began to feel a complete fool.

Having waited long enough, I lifted the large brass knocker and gave it a resounding *rap* that echoed down the street.

"Oh, there you are, Miss. Isn't that lovely of you to come along."

I looked round and saw Emily, who had emerged wreathed in smiles, from somewhere round the side of the house.

"Do you mind coming this way, if you'll excuse it. We never use the front door and I think Dad must have the key in his pocket."

I followed her round the corner along a narrow cinder path and she led me into a bright kitchen ornamented with calendar backs of half the views in England.

"Come and have a little chat in the front room," she invited.

We continued into the room behind the lace curtains, which was filled with photographs and china ornaments that covered every bit of space on the walls and furniture.

"I did want to hear how you were getting on, as I haven't seen you since your wedding," I said.

"Oh yes, ever so well, thank you, Miss. And the wedding all went off all right. My sister at Clapham lent her house and we had a lovely cake and Dad made a speech."

Emily's eyes shone happily in her honest round face, as she sat with her hands folded in a billowing lap and described her marriage. It was quite touching the way she called her husband 'Dad', and I could vividly picture him making his speech next to the large flat wedding cake, the glasses of port and sandwiches, and the fifteen guests. And I could see Emily in her black chiffon frock with her bouquet (I dissuaded her from a bridal preference for pale blue) blushing and smiling after the toast.

"Who'd have thought it!" she finished.

What she meant was, who would have thought she would be a bride for the first time at forty-three, when she thought she had been passed by for life.

But Emily had the comeliness of kindness, and even if she could have parted with two or three stone without loss, she made a delightful companion and a capable wife.

'Dad' was a quiet, pleasant-faced railway man of fifty-four, a widower with a grown-up family, and he soon took Emily off our hands to revive his home for him. Apparently the sister at Clapham approved him first before she accepted, and they talked openly about the Marriage Bureau; all their friends and relations knew how they had met.

"Dad's ever so nice, but what I like best is having a little home of my own and not to be looking after someone else's," she said, for before she was married Emily worked as a cook-general in Hampstead.

"And the neighbours are ever so friendly," she continued. "We see them for a chat now and again, and every Saturday evening we go to the cinema, and Dad has his Rotary Club and fire-watching two nights a week. My sister at Clapham thinks I've done very well, because being a railway man he gets a pension when he stops work, and we'll still be very comfortable. Her husband hasn't got a Government job, so there won't be a pension and it's hard to put by in war-time with prices so high. I think she's really quite envious of me. And you know, Miss, Dad and I are really very grateful to you for introducing us."

"I'm so glad, and I should think you make him a very good wife," I remarked with sincerity.

Emily smiled as she got up to put the kettle on for tea. "Well, I try and keep him comfortable," she said modestly. "Men don't want any extra troubles these days."

A tall, grey stone house right on the high street of a mining village in South Wales. When you opened the front door a faint smell of ether, mingled with antiseptic, clung about the hall, and suggested that the miners' doctor had his surgery in the house.

What might have been a comfortable lounge was the waiting-room where the patients filed in and sat on benches, jabbering in sing-song Welsh voices while they waited for their consultation. Heavy boots tramped along the passage during those crowded hours when the surgery was open, and when it was not, there was always a ringing telephone or an urgent door-bell. Then the front door banging and the car starting, and meals waiting in the oven, congealing and being abandoned.

"I wish I'd married anyone but a doctor," said Mildred, having given me this picture of her bridal home.

We were having lunch in London when she was up for a week's shopping not long after she married.

"But you knew what a doctor's life was like," I replied gently, trying to conceal any reproach.

"Yes, but I didn't think it would all be so much on top of me. Never having a moment's peace. I couldn't believe people would be so fond of going to the doctor as they are in that place. It's like the cinema, the way they come flocking in."

She was seriously discontented about it. I felt very concerned and hoped she was not being unkind to the silent, overworked little doctor whose career was getting on her nerves.

Had she been a younger woman she might have idolised his work, or if she had a motherly disposition she might have rejoiced in taking care of him while he was so over-burdened. But she was forty-five, and she was not motherly but domineering. She had approached marriage rather as if she was going on a cruise, and she was prepared to criticise if it did no come up to her expectations.

It was not so much her age (though that was fairly disadvantageous) that made her a problem client when she was on our books, but her domineering character. Although she was good-looking and quite smart and had £1,000 a year, she had dozens of introductions without any success. I think she treated the men rather as if she was shopping in a bargain basement, where the goods must be studied critically in case of flaws.

When the doctor came along his wife had been dead a few months, and he said he wanted somebody who would take charge of him, so she seemed to be just what he wanted. He was obviously a very mild, easy person to live with, and we would have been afraid of putting two domineering people together in the same house, so he seemed to be the solution for her, too.

"How do you like your step-daughter?" I asked, to stop her dwelling on the smell of ether.

"She's away at her job in the daytime, but it's like a herd of elephants in the house when she comes home and brings her friends. It's high time she grew up, and I think the best thing would be for her to get a job in London and have a small flat of her own. But Harry thinks she's too young and wants to keep her at home."

"She's only eighteen, isn't she?" I said, remembering that she was the pride of the little doctor's heart.

"Yes, but it's still time she grew up."

I seemed to have found a fresh flaw, and I began to feel very apprehensive as to how this match was turning out.

Meanwhile I changed the subject again and she was soon engrossed in telling me about the things she had bought. Among them, I was surprised to find, were many attractive things for the deplorable antiseptic house. She was even impatient to install them and see what the doctor thought of them.

"Gracious! I'll have to fly for my train," she said, suddenly catching sight of the clock in the restaurant. "But I'll be up again next week. Harry's coming up for a meeting at the Medical Society to do with his special miners' sanatorium. You know, he's really doing wonderful work down there, and he says it's been such a help since he married me because I've taken all his other worries off his hands, and he can attack his work so much better."

As we parted on the pavement outside, and the smart capable figure vanished into the crowd, I was feeling quite happy again. I had remembered similar grumbling before she was married, and realised they were not the outpourings of an unhappy person, but merely her particular form of amusement.

An afternoon's grumbling, to some people, is as refreshing as a game of golf. I was only glad that I, and not the doctor, had partnered her in this particular round.

Chapter XVI

Second birthday party – The wallflower comes back
– News of some of the others – Ending.

On April 17, with the dust still unsettled from the ruins of the worst raid on London the night before, the Marriage Bureau had its 2nd birthday.

A few yards away there was a gaping tear in a familiar side-street, where the work and hopes of several more people were now reduced to a mountain of rubble sprawling across the road. Further down Bond Street were other gaps from earlier raids, since tided up and waiting for peace and a new building. There were many more windows without glass, and buildings that stood up with their contents churned into demoniacal chaos.

It was the kind of day when a sleepless night and the fate of others were enough to make one feel a futility about troubling with something that might fall in the next hour of destruction. But our office walls were lined with greeting telegrams from happy couples, and the people who picked their way across the broken glass were mostly men and women who had found in each other something precious that shut out all the ugliness and fear of war.

At no time in the history of any generation could they have needed love and companionship more than now, and we had helped these once lonely people find it, and thus equipped them with the best armour against all the terror raids that might happen.

And so, even if the Marriage Bureau offices are razed to the ground in the next 'blitz,' our work would not be just a memory with a monument of rubble. There would be living, breathing testimonies to it all over the world in those nine hundred and thirty-two married couples, and the two hundred and fifty-odd people who were just engaged.

Of course it was worthwhile, I reflected, much more so than it ever was in peace-time; as I looked at the faces round us and remembered the lives we had re-fashioned, I drew fresh encouragement to carry on.

Now, just after our second anniversary, with the war increasing in intensity, we are as busy as ever, and seeing an average of thirty-three new applicants every day, apart from the more timorous hundreds who write in. Except for a famous naval and military tailors (who anyway have been bombed and had to move their premises) we can claim to be one of the few really thriving concerns in Bond Street that war-time conditions have not affected adversely.

We still have our problems. Many of the original ones are with us yet...

Hope springs eternal in Mr Dewlap, the Bureau wallflower, who has lately put sanitation in his garage to add to his charms.

Fanny, our loveable, middle-aged butterfly, has almost found a resting-place with a retired business man who lives in a coastal resort. She has asked us not to send her any more introductions as they are getting on very well, and he has written glowingly about her to us. But her destiny is still not quite settled, and he has hinted delicately that Fanny is rather fat. Meanwhile, as they are both so pleased with each other, we are goading her into a more drastic slimming programme, which is already bearing fruit.

The mother with the child in the similar clothes rates herself high, and frightens everyone away with descriptions of her first husband's private aeroplane and the landing-ground in the garden. She has scared off several £5,000-a-year men, and we are trying to impress on her that this particular line of build-up is unseasonable in war-time.

At last the industrial widower with his seven children and plush settees has persuaded a gay young widow to become his bride. Shortly after the wedding the gloomy mansion was burned to the ground, antimacassars and all. Luckily no-one was hurt.

And our church mouse has, I am proud to say, made a very good marriage with the agent of a big shooting estate in Scotland, who was enchanted with her. 'She is charming, and just the person I have been looking for, for I dare not say how long,' he wrote. We hear they are very happy, and incidentally he was the recipient of the startling snapshots that fell out on my desk.

In spite of the fact that so many of our clients either overrate themselves or demand perfection – which doesn't exist – in others, approximately one-third get engaged within three months of receiving an introduction from us, and only about five per cent have failed to find a mate at all.

One client, an American engineer, wrote a very nice description of our work in one of his letters:

"In constructional engineering every thought goes into the smallest detail to ensure stability and unity. Yet in the majority of cases so little attention to detail is given to the finest machines in the Universe – Man and Woman – to enable them to achieve unity and give the best results.

That, Miss Oliver and Miss Jenner, is why your Marriage Bureau caught my attention. You, in a sense of the word, are engineers. You want to get together the right material, see that the 'specifications' coincide; then you are reasonably sure that your 'constructions' can weather severe conditions and tests."

The severe conditions and tests are certainly there just now, so we hope we are good engineers.

Mary Oliver – date unknown

Afterword: Happy Ever After?

If the Blitz couldn't stop Marriage Bureau, nothing could. In the following decades it went from strength to strength, and by the time Heather Jenner wrote her own memoirs in 1954, she said 10,000 people had found their marriage partners through the Bureau.

And it wasn't just about quantity. After 20 years in the business, the Bureau wrote to 1000 couples and got 800 answers; of these, only three couples had divorced.

For Mary Oliver, though, it was a more complex story. There is a real ambivalence in her descriptions of British life, and the truth is, she never really felt at ease in the UK. Although she loved her work at the Bureau, she often felt strangely detached from England. Perhaps rule-breakers never do feel comfortable, which is why they have to shake things up.

In 1947 she left the UK and sailed west, crossing from Canada to the USA at Niagara Falls on July 17th. Her visa says she was 'unaccompanied', that her occupation was 'secretary', and that the purpose of her visit was to 'reside permanently'.

From that point on, her records become very scanty. She made an occasional visit to the UK, but it's clear from her letters that Mary Oliver found her true home in the United States; it was there that she could breathe freely.

She married a man with a wooden leg, and settled in Philadelphia; then in 1979, aged 65, she married a second time in Florida, where she ended up managing *Louis Tussaud's Museum of Wax* on St Petersburg Beach.

Intensely private, Mary never had any children of her own, and finally, aged 74, after a life of chain-smoking, she died of cancer.

But even in her last will and testament, Mary's sharp, inscrutable voice cuts through: *"the personal representative of my estate shall arrange for the cremation of my body. I do not want any services, and I want my ashes scattered in the Gulf of Mexico."*

Back in London, Heather Jenner continued to grow the business, eventually bringing her daughter in to run it with her. By 1967, Heather had become enough of a celebrity herself to feature on Desert Island Discs; even the age of the permissive society couldn't dent the Bureau's appeal.

It's hard to pin down exactly when Marriage Bureau closed its doors for the last time. It was still advertising as late as 1978, but it seemed to get swallowed up in the wave of dating agencies that swept through Britain in the 1980s.

Reading through Mary Oliver's private correspondence, and talking to her relatives, a picture emerges of a difficult woman; for someone who helped so many find happiness, it seemed to constantly elude her. But Mary's legacy is much, much bigger than her own personal happiness.

The Tinder generation take being in control of romantic destiny for granted, but someone had to break the shackles of tradition.

And that someone was Mary Oliver.

Care to Compete?

Other titles by Hal F. Rosenbluth and Diane McFerrin Peters

• •

The Customer Comes Second:
And Other Secrets of Exceptional Service

Care to Compete?

Secrets from America's Best
Companies on Managing with
People and Profits in Mind

· ·

HAL F. ROSENBLUTH and
DIANE MCFERRIN PETERS

PERSEUS BOOKS
Reading, Massachusetts

ISBN 0-7382-0135-9
Library of Congress Catalog Card Number: 99-64873

Perseus Books is a member of the Perseus Books Group

Cover design by Bruce W. Bond
Text design by Diane Levy
Set in 9.5-point Stone Serif by Argosy

1 2 3 4 5 6 7 8 9 10– –02 01 00 99

Perseus Books are available at special discounts for bulk purchases in the U.S. by corporations, institutions, and other organizations. For more information, please contact the Special Markets Department at HarperCollins Publishers, 10 East 53rd Street, New York, NY 10022, or call 212-207-7528.

Find us on the World Wide Web at
http://www.perseusbooks.com

This book was originally published in hardcover with the title *Good Company: Caring as Fiercely as You Compete*.

We dedicate this book to our friends around the world.

Praise for *Care to Compete?*

"*Care to Compete?* contains many excellent examples of how to manage a company during times of rapid change. I recommend it for anyone trying to improve performance by increasing employee morale, improving productivity, and strengthening the bottom line."

— *Craig R. Barrett, President and CEO, Intel Corporation*

"Hal Rosenbluth is no dewy-eyed optimist. He survives (nay, thrives) in a merciless industry, yet he has become *the* evangelist for doing the right thing by people—and for the bottom line. *Care to Compete?* is the long-awaited antidote to the shriveled 'philosophy' of lean-and-mean thinking."

— *Tom Peters*

"*Care to Compete?* is a treasure of practical business advice compiled from the workplace ecology of thriving organizations large and small. The authors' unique access to such diverse organizations makes this a compelling read. Executives and managers looking for the best practices in leadership will find substantial evidence that grace and consideration for employees is the first ingredient to manage change successfully."

— *J. Lawrence Wilson, Chairman and CEO, Rohm and Haas Company*

"*Care to Compete?* is a great way to learn from other successes. I have led six major companies through change and really wish I would have had this book to help me each time. Focusing on people and helping them be successful is the only way to create sustainable change. *Care to Compete?* is a wonderful roadmap to helping leaders lead!"

— *Jerre L. Stead, Chairman and CEO, Ingram Micro Inc.*

"Rosenbluth and Peters have the guts to say what many feel but few articulate. You can be a fierce competitor and still be nice. In fact, it's the key to preeminence, and *Care to Compete?* shows how to do it."

— *Scott McNealy, Chairman, President, and CEO, Sun Microsystems, Inc.*

"*Care to Compete?* says the best companies to work *for* are also the best companies to work *with*. I couldn't agree more! This book underscores how Hal Rosenbluth's focus on employee satisfaction in the workplace is such a winning formula. If you want to profit from the experiences of others, read this book."

— *George M.C. Fisher, Chairman and CEO, Eastman Kodak*

"A must for any manager who wants to create a great place to work. *Care to Compete?* is loaded with insight from Hal Rosenbluth's own remarkable company. But it also is illustrated with dozens of the best practices from a handful of the nation's preeminent employers. Highly recommended."

— *Robert Levering, coauthor of The 100 Best Companies to Work for in America and founder, Great Place to Work Institute*

Contents

Preface

Since this book was first published in 1998, we have heard from readers around the world who are grappling with the very same issues we set out to explore, such as how to find, attract, and retain great people and how to hold fast to core values in the face of searing competition and unprecedented change. Each e-mail, letter, or call brings its own unique spin, and it's been fascinating and gratifying to see that the issues and the potential application of these ideas are truly universal.

Our readers have been most drawn to the story of our own company's redesign based on the unlikely model of the family farm (chapter 2). We've had calls from companies asking us to consult for them as they embark on redesign initiatives, and the media doesn't seem to be able to get enough of the story. It's rewarding to spread the word about something that produces exceptional results.

The farm model is a study in honesty, in stark contrast to the atmosphere of mistrust that has been permeating the business community in recent years. This mistrust comes between employers and employees, between companies and their partners, and between companies and customers. It's not hard to see where the mistrust comes from.

Today, image is a powerful force. People's tolerance for hype is heightened every day, which only sets the stage for disappointment when faced with mere reality. When hyped claims (like promising results that can't be achieved or deadlines that can't be met) are put to the test, they naturally fail, and trust is broken. That takes the fun out of business. Yes, fun—that's what business should be if you're doing it right.

The beauty of farming is that it has nothing whatsoever to do with image. **You can't fake farming.** There's nothing to hide behind. Your crop either grows or it doesn't. If you tend to it, make sure it gets its nourishment and the proper amount of water, and pull the weeds before it's overtaken, it will flourish. However, if you ignore it, abuse it, or otherwise mistreat it, it will wither and die.

Why do companies feel compelled to hype themselves into the danger zone? Perhaps it's competitive pressure. Possibly, the need to win at any cost overwhelms them. Or maybe it's just a rat race they can't seem to escape. In *Care to Compete?* we reveal companies that dare to be different—companies that have long since blown past their competition and aren't stopping to look back. These are companies that are doing the right thing and are being rewarded for it.

The tight job market is a good example to illustrate this point. People today recognize that they can chose where they want to work. Companies late in realizing that people are the differentiator between companies that survive and those that rule, scramble to find and keep great people, causing costs to skyrocket and performance to suffer. By comparison, companies like Rosenbluth and our fourteen friends in *Care to Compete?* never lost their people-focus.

When it was fashionable to expend people for the sake of profits, we knew that valuing our people was the only long-term means of being profitable. We're pleased to report that we are enjoying record profits, and our people are profiting, expanding and using their knowledge, and enjoying support as they seek balance in their personal and professional lives. The trust and loyalty we have earned rewards us every day.

The formula for preeminence found in *Care to Compete?* is deceptively simple—easy to understand, but hard to execute. Yet it *is* possible, and the fifteen companies who open their doors to you here are proof. We hope you'll benefit from the stories of their journey and that their advice will help you in your own.

Care to Compete?

1
....

Burning Issues

Business can have an overwhelming effect on our lives, perhaps more than anything else except our family and loved ones. But does our family life impact business as significantly as business impacts our family life? Business can contribute to our happiness, but it can also make our lives miserable. In Care to Compete?, *we demonstrate that companies not only can positively influence lives, they have an obligation to do so. This is not to imply that this book is soft on people; it's not. Companies have every right to expect the very best from their employees, but only when they create an environment worthy of it. People will never care because they have to; but because they want to. And when they do, it's magic.*

Care to Compete? *will lead you into the heart and soul of a company built on friendship, a company where people fight for success because they care so much about each other. They know they are part of something really special, and they want to protect it and make it grow. There's no substitute for that scrappy, survival instinct permeating a business. Combine that with heart, and you truly have* a company that cares as fiercely as it competes. *When a company is in that "zone," nothing can stop it.*

In Good Company

We wrote *The Customer Comes Second: And Other Secrets of Exceptional Service* in 1992, because we were receiving a lot of requests for information on how our company grew and how we built our culture. Those requests pale in comparison to the flood of queries we have received since then, regarding how we managed the changes of the '90s, and how we plan to lead our organization into the new millennium. Our answer to those questions is *Care to Compete?*. Fifteen world-class companies share their thoughts in the coming pages on what gives them their competitive edge.

Friends from the 100 Best

In 1992, when Rosenbluth was selected for inclusion in the book *The 100 Best Companies to Work for in America* (Robert Levering and Milton Moskowitz), we were humbled because we consider it to be among the highest of honors. We've always believed that the best companies to work for were also the best companies to work with. That was confirmed when we began to build friendships with our peers from the top 100. We learned that each of those companies has its own strengths and its own creative solutions to challenges. We realized we could learn a lot by sharing ideas with them, and we were right. Shortly after *The 100 Best* was released, we held a symposium for all of the companies—and we have been meeting every year since.

At those annual get-togethers, we talk about challenges we face, share solutions, and discuss emerging issues. We thought our readers would benefit from a look into this unique think tank, so we asked a select group of 100 best companies, with whom we have worked closely, to comment on some key issues for this book. They graciously agreed to share their strategies with us.

The following is a brief overview of the 15 participating companies. Chances are, you will be familiar with most of the organizations. You'll find their answers to today's burning questions as you read on.

- ALAGASCO (Alabama Gas Corporation) is a utility company that distributes natural gas. It has 1,350 employees, all in Alabama, and their sales volume is more than $362 million. Birmingham, Alabama, headquarters.

- BE&K is a construction and engineering company, specializing in the pulp and paper industry. They have annual sales of $1.6 billion and employ 8,800 people in 13 countries. Birmingham, Alabama, headquarters.

- BETH ISRAEL DEACONESS MEDICAL CENTER employs 8,599 people in Massachusetts. With an annual sales volume of $600 million, the health care provider was formed following the merger, in 1996, of two academic hospitals, Beth Israel and New England Deaconess. Boston, Massachusetts, headquarters.

- ERIE INSURANCE is a property/casualty insurance company with annual sales of $1.9 billion, and 3,200 employees in nine states. Erie, Pennsylvania, headquarters.

- FEL-PRO is a $500 million-per-year manufacturer of gaskets and other sealing products, with 2,700 employees in seven countries. Skokie, Illinois, headquarters.

- GREAT PLAINS SOFTWARE is a $57 million financial software developer, whose products are distributed in 12 countries and sold in more than 50 countries. Great Plains employs 600 people. Fargo, North Dakota, headquarters.

- HALLMARK CARDS is a greeting card company with interests in television programming and artists materials. The company has nearly 20,000 employees worldwide, and distributes its products in more than 100 countries. Sales volume is $3.6 billion. Kansas City, Missouri, headquarters.

- HEWITT ASSOCIATES is a global management consulting firm specializing in human resource solutions. More than 7,500 associates in 30 countries account for revenues of $709 million. Lincolnshire, Illinois, headquarters.

- LANDS' END is a direct merchant of clothing, accessories, domestics, and other products, with 5,700 to 8,400 employees (depending upon the season). Lands' End has operations in four countries and annual sales of more than $1 billion. Dodgeville, Wisconsin, headquarters.

- MARY KAY INC. is a global manufacturer and marketer of cosmetics, skin care, and personal care products. Its sales volume is $1.2 billion wholesale and $2 billion retail. Mary Kay operates in 27 countries and employs 2,500 people in the United States plus 1,250 internationally. Dallas, Texas, headquarters.

- NORTHWESTERN MUTUAL LIFE offers life insurance, disability insurance, mutual funds, and annuity products. The company employs more than 3,500 people and has annual revenues of more than $13 billion. Milwaukee, Wisconsin, headquarters.

- SAS INSTITUTE INC. is the world's largest privately held software development company, with revenues of $750 million. The company has more than 5,000 employees in 50 countries. Cary, North Carolina, headquarters.

- SOUTHWEST AIRLINES is a major U.S. airline, with 26,000 employees, operations in 26 states, and annual operating revenues of $3.4 billion. Dallas, Texas, headquarters.

- USAA is an insurance and financial services company with $6.7 billion in annual sales, employing more than 18,000 people. USAA serves its customers around the world out of seven U.S. locations and two abroad. San Antonio, Texas, headquarters.

And now a bit about Rosenbluth International, because, for the most part, we don't have walk-in locations, so we may not be a household name to you. Founded in 1892, the company today has the second largest global presence in travel management in the world. Our business is 98 percent corporate travel. We answer the phone 60,000 times a day (that's 15.6 million calls a year) and issue 20,000 tickets a day, 400,000 tickets a month, or about 5 million tickets a year. We have 5,000 employees (we call them associates), and our annual sales are approaching $4.3 billion a year. Our world headquarters is in Philadelphia, Pennsylvania.

Across the 15 companies in this book, the key business drivers and critical issues were remarkably similar, from which eight major themes emerged. We introduce those themes here and explore the approaches to managing these issues in the chapters ahead.

Change: The Only Constant

The past five years have been some of the toughest yet most successful in our company's history. We probably learned more in those years than our predecessors did in the first 100. But these days, everyone seems to have that "Toto, we're not in Kansas anymore" feeling, and so that you don't think you're the only one reeling from all the upheaval, let's review some changes we and our peers have lived through. We'll start with our company. In the past five years, Rosenbluth International has:

- More than tripled its size, from $1.2 billion to $4.3 billion.
- Shifted from alliances to wholly owned operations overseas.
- Expanded to own its own locations in 28 countries around the world.
- Completely redesigned itself, decentralizing into business units.
- Moved from a 100-year, no-layoff policy.

- Redesigned its approaches to training, human resources, and sales.
- Faced an industry turning point: commission caps.
- Shifted from paternalism to personal responsibility.

Our friends have had their share of change too. Alagasco's CEO, Mike Warren, tells us "Alagasco is a 142-year-old utility company that is living proof of the adage 'Old habits die hard.' The company spent its first 125 years or so resisting change, or at least being very satisfied with the status quo. And frankly, in the heavily regulated, slow-changing natural gas industry, our management style worked very well. Utility mentality suited us just fine, thank you. But inevitably, change reached even the gas utility business. We realized we had to look at old things through new eyes."

Here's a sampling of the types of changes other companies have faced in recent years:

- Lands' End made major changes in senior management, including the CEO.
- Weather-related disasters dealt a blow to Erie Insurance.
- Southwest Airlines faced new and costly regulations; safety/security requirements; and federal, state, and local taxes and fees imposed on airlines.
- Alagasco lived through deregulation of the natural gas industry.
- Great Plains Software went public.
- Mary Kay transitioned to a new leadership team as its founder fell ill.
- Hallmark went through a major restructuring.
- Beth Israel Deaconess survived a merger.

Rapid Growth

All of the companies we talked with have grown tremendously over the past few years. As SAS Institute put it, "Growth, whether in terms of staff, revenue, customers, products, or geography, has been the single largest change in our company over the past five years. Managing our current staff of about 5,000 in over 85 offices in more than 50 countries is very different from managing the staff of 2,600 in fewer than 40 offices in 25 countries that we had in 1992. One of the biggest challenges that came with that growth is responding to the needs of such a large staff and meeting the business needs of the company, while maintaining the corporate culture that has allowed us to attract and retain quality people."

Our friends at Hewitt Associates said, "Our biggest challenge in recent years has been our explosive growth, driven by the changing business environment and our clients' demands. In the past five years, we've doubled both our revenues and the number of associates in the firm."

At Rosenbluth International, we are winning business at the rate of nearly $4 million per day. That number is mind-boggling, when you consider the highly customized approach we take with each client. And a sale isn't a transaction; it's the beginning of a long-term partnership that requires constant nurturing.

Tougher Marketplace/Intensified Competition

The folks at Erie Insurance summed it up for us all when they said, "Our competitors have downsized, emerging as more cost-efficient rivals. In an industry that has always been price-competitive, we were suddenly faced with even fiercer price-based competition. And it didn't end there. Other, nontraditional rivals have entered the marketplace, to make this current era one of the most intensely competitive we have ever seen."

Fel-Pro noted that company consolidations and fewer, larger competitors have intensified the competitive landscape in the sealing products industry. We know that's the case in the travel industry too. The folks at Southwest Airlines added, "In an effort to contain our costs, we have asked our people—who have always been our competitive edge—to work harder, faster, and smarter."

Intensified competition brings out the best in us all. Alagasco's Mike Warren asks, "As a relatively small fish swimming in an unfriendly, competitive, and rapidly changing sea, can Alagasco use the strength of our employees and our new legacy as a great place to work to reform itself again so that we can thrive in this new world? As that famous 'philosopher,' Yogi Berra once said, 'The future ain't what it used to be.' At Alagasco, we say, 'Thank goodness!'"

Globalization

Rosenbluth International is a very different company from what it was just a few years ago. Today, it operates in 45 countries around the world—we're on every continent except Antarctica and our associates speak twelve languages.

The point is, the world is the marketplace. Whether a company is global or not, it should *think* globally in order to capitalize on opportunities, prepare for emerging competition, and pursue growing markets. In SAS Institute's view, "Employees of tomorrow will need to understand other cultures and speak different languages as the sociological barriers of the world crumble and new doors to business open."

Design for Speed

A majority of the companies we spoke with have some combination of "business units" and centralized service functions. Beth Israel Deaconess has a combination structure, and reports, "We tend to think of ourselves as a highly decentralized organization. This means that while philosophy and objectives will be commonly understood across the organization, how these are put into practice may vary in different departments. This allows individual units to tailor solutions to the work and [to] the subculture of that particular unit. This structure is supported by an organizational emphasis on collaborative decision making. Work teams are used extensively, both within and across departments."

SAS Institute adds, "In our flat organizational structure, ideas can be introduced, responded to, developed, and implemented in a more timely—and more creative—fashion, thus allowing the company to continue the practice of meeting customer needs."

Shift from Paternalism to Personal Responsibility

The folks at Hewitt Associates summed up the challenge to reach a higher degree of personal responsibility when they said, "Like most businesses, we've struggled to outgrow the paternalist family/entitlement focus of the past, and now prefer to think of our employment relationship as one similar to friendship. Friendship is a relationship that is harder to hold on to than family. It requires voluntary commitment and loyalty that has to be constantly earned. Keys to friendship are respect and sharing—a shared responsibility for the relationship."

Most companies had something to say on this subject. It has been a major focus at Fel-Pro over the past five years, where the family-friendly programs they offer have increased internal costs. To be able to do the types of things that "best" companies do, they needed employees to share the responsibility. For example, in the past, Fel-Pro employees considered their bonus part of their salary, which they received around the holidays. Now they understand they will be sharing the risks along with the rewards. President, OE Sales & Marketing, Paul Lehman says, "Two years ago, we didn't have as strong a year, and employees saw a smaller bonus. We kept them informed, and they were paid less than 100 percent of target. The following year, they got 124 percent. They could feel in their wallets what risk and reward meant."

At Alagasco, when the first edition of the *100 Best* was published, making the list became a corporate objective. They achieved that objective in 1992, and an interesting thing happened. Between 1993 and 1996, Alagasco employees began to get comfortable. When an employee attitude survey showed a shift from a "we" to a "me" focus, they considered it a wake-up call. Alagasco now places a high priority on "having employees act like owners." They've changed a number of benefits to include more employee decisions, flattened their organization, and empowered employees to take more control of their own careers. Alagasco's method of strategic planning, performance appraisal, and compensation (including incentive pay) all send empowerment messages.

Mary Kay feels so strongly about this issue that HRVP Doug Mintmier developed a thesis on "the valued employee paradox," which he presented at the 100 Best Companies Symposium in 1996. There was resounding agreement on the paradox. The concept is simple: "The better you treat employees, over time, the less they appreciate it, and begin to display feelings of entitlement." His thesis explores tendencies of employees at high-touch, people-oriented companies to take their good fortune for granted. In some cases, employees may even lose perspective over time and shift from appreciation to expectation to entitlement. Doug says, "This is a high-class problem to have, but it's critical that it be addressed."

Tough Employment Market

Virtually all of the companies talked about how increasingly difficult it is to find the right people. In fact, several of them cited it as their primary challenge for the future. Mary Kay believes, "Growth potential of all businesses will be limited by the number of good people they can attract and retain. Two types of companies will be able to hire qualified workers: companies with an established reputation as an 'employer of choice,' and companies that don't provide a great place to work but are willing to pay dearly for qualified workers."

Mary Kay also believes that employers who pay top dollar but do not value their employees will not succeed in the long term, and that the solution is for companies to strive to be great places to work. We agree, and we think it will be increasingly important in the future.

There is a human resource drought, and one cause is the healthy economy (low unemployment). Another cause is less likely to fluctuate: heightened company expectations. Everyone is filling multiple roles today, and doing a lot more work than ever. SAS Institute says, "Tomorrow's shrinking workforce will be thirsty for employees who are not merely computer-competent but who can empower technology to do great and wonderful things."

An article on the creative magic of Disney in *USA Today* (June 18, 1997) profiled the creative duo that masterminded big hits such as *Aladdin* and *The Little Mermaid*. The article read, "The real secret of their success is actually one of the oldest Disney tricks in the book: 'plussing.'" Ron Clements, half of that creative team, says, "Everyone on a movie isn't just expected to carry out an assignment, but to 'plus' it and find a way to make it better."

Northwestern Mutual has a tradition of taking extra steps to ensure that customers receive all benefits to which they are entitled. They shared several examples with us. One deceased policyowner never married and had no children. An assistant controller at the company actually compiled a family tree in order to search for a beneficiary. After a long search, he found two distant relatives. In another case, a student pilot's policy excluded benefits during his flight training. When he died in a plane crash during training, his family assumed he would have no benefits. But after his log book was found in the wreckage, Northwestern Mutual calculated that during the flight he had reached the 100 hours required to become a standard risk. They paid the benefits to his family.

"Plussing" will be a requirement for the future. Only those people and companies that practice it consistently will thrive in the changing marketplace.

Holding Fast to Values

Each of the 15 companies expressed in some way the need to be able to change swiftly, yet hold fast to core values. No less than half of the companies specifically named living the golden rule as the key to their success.

Great Plains Software's Group Vice President Jodi Uecker-Rust tells us, "We recently started positioning our business evolution in terms of the paradox, 'dramatic change, with no change at all.' At the heart of this philosophy is the belief that although our business and financial strategies have changed dramatically as our industry has evolved, the Great Plains mission statement, shared values, frameworks for decision making, and our corporate style remain anchors for how we do business. And as long as they do, we can meet any challenge the industry presents."

What's Ahead

Those are the eight critical issues that companies will need to address for the future and that are woven throughout the coming pages. You'll read more about people than you will the bottom line, because people are everything. They *are* the bottom line.

Here's a quick overview of each chapter. In Chapter 2, we discuss corporate redesign—our company's and several of our peers' organizations—the catalysts, steps, and results. Chapter 3 addresses the new strategic role of human resources and its key areas of focus. In Chapter 4, we explore the new field of human capital management and take a look at how companies are maximizing their knowledge assets. Chapter 5 covers learning—today's higher standards, innovative approaches, and use of resources. Chapter 6 is dedicated to leadership, ways to instill and strengthen it. Chapter 7 is a window into the unique cultures of a number of leading companies, along with how they nurture their work environments. In Chapter 8, we take an honest look at the challenges of becoming a global company and outline steps to getting there. Chapter 9 sums up the overriding issues and ideas in words of wisdom from visionaries who lead the companies participating in the book.

Let's Get Started

We chose organizational design to lead off with, because it affects everything else. Have you ever watched birds flying in formation, able to change direction in an instant, as though they were one? Companies need to perform like that today, and to do it, they need the right design—and sometimes a new perspective. Consider Picasso's response to his biographer, who noticed that a Renoir hanging over the fireplace in the painter's apartment was crooked. Picasso said, "It's better like that. If you want to kill a picture, all you have to do is hang it beautifully on a nail and soon you will see nothing of it but the frame. When it's out of place, you see it better."

2

Design for Speed

At a meeting held by Philips, one of our long-time clients, I was asked to discuss what makes for a world-class supplier. I began by saying that for a company to be world-class anything, it must first become a world-class employer. That will allow it to attract, retain, and develop world-class people, who are the foundation for world-class performance. Unfortunately, I continued: "World-class employers beget world-class people. World-class people and world-class leadership create and live world-class values. This makes it a world-class company, enabling it to be a world-class customer and world-class supplier. I think I just exhausted myself and now I have a world-class migraine."

In short, a company's people are its differentiator and only sustainable competitive advantage. The wrong organizational structure can inhibit people, whereas the right design can elevate them to greatness.

Management gurus, top-dollar consultants, business professors, and executives all chase the ultimate in corporate design. The fruit of this endless search lies not in some convoluted business formula, but in nature, where people have worked in harmony through the millennia. I have found what has proven to be the ultimate in corporate design for our company, and it can be applied to any organization.

In 1992, I became obsessed with designing our corporate structure into one that was a step ahead of the change curve. Outside factors were undeniably penetrating our business. The economy was suffering. The Gulf War had a lasting effect on international travel. Our clients were restructuring and downsizing, and that, too, meant far fewer travelers. We needed to make a preemptive strike on these pressures before they affected our company.

I knew we could no longer guarantee employment for life, but I also knew that virtually the same results could be achieved by ensuring long-term corporate success and growth. I was determined to replace guarantees with opportunities. I also knew the new structure would require a level of organizational speed I had never encountered anywhere. It would mean a company so in touch with the external and internal forces driving change that we could predict it, prepare for it, and capitalize on it, for our clients and our associates. I knew we would have to be swift, nimble, strong, aggressive, intuitive, and brave.

To begin, I read all the books I thought might hold the answer. I canvassed the country's business leaders. I tried all the traditional sources of inspiration. Nothing. I decided to take a break, to get a new perspective on things. I went where I always go when I need to sort out my thoughts, to my ranch in North Dakota where I raise cattle and horses. Each morning I'd fetch my horse, Spud, and ride across the plains to check the animals. Out on the trail, I spent many long hours praying for something to come to me; but it didn't. I wasn't going to settle for just anything. Corporate changes are difficult and take their toll on people. This change had to be right.

At the end of the trip, it was time to take my calves to market, so I went to round up the little doggies with my friend and neighbor, Dave Bauman, who has been a family farmer his entire life. Our ranches border each other, so we keep our herds together, moving them from one pasture to another, from spring until fall.

One night, after sorting the calves by sex and weight, Dave and I stood outside his barn, ankle deep in cow piles (preferable to the corporate kind). I asked Dave if he and his wife, Kathy Jo, wanted to fly back to Philly with me for a Monday night Eagles-Cowboys football game. The words were barely out of my mouth when I realized what a stupid question it was. Dave's ranch is his living, and to join me he would have had to leave the ranch work unattended for several days. So I was amazed when he said yes.

Little did I know, I was about to discover the organizational design I had so desperately been seeking. I asked, "Who's going to look after the ranch, feed the beef cows, and milk the dairy ones? Who'll run the tractor, and who's going to fix it if it breaks down? Who'll haul the hay from the fields?" Dave looked at me as if I were as dumb as one of the cows, and then he answered, "Wayde." I said, "Wayde? He's only eight." I got the dumber-than-a-cow look again, but I continued, "How does Wayde know what to do; and what would happen if he runs into trouble?" Another look, and then Dave said, "Jaime will help him." I persisted, "Jaime's only 10." Dave saved me from

another look, and said, "There's always Billie Jo. She'll keep 'em straight."
Billie Jo was 11. I asked how they'd know what to do, and Dave's reply was
short and to the point, "They've been doing everything with me since they were
old enough to sit in the tractor." My lesson was just beginning.

Later that evening we went back to the ranch house for dinner, and there my
lesson continued. While Dave and I were tending to the cows, a leak had developed in some plumbing in their house. Kathy Jo explained the problem and how
she had fixed it. This was really advanced stuff for me. I would have called a
plumber immediately. Unfortunately, out where we ranch, there aren't any
plumbers for over 35 miles. Everyone in Dave's family chimed in as to how they
would have fixed the problem. I was amazed that Dave, Kathy Jo, Billie, Jaime,
and Wayde all knew what to do. My mind drifted back home to Philadelphia,
and I had visions of a family scramble to find the Yellow Pages.

The next morning my lesson continued while we hayed. I raked and Dave
baled. We were making good headway when a belt broke on the baler. I suggested we ride to town to get a new belt. "Nah, too expensive," Dave said.
"We'll fix it ourselves." I asked how much a belt cost, and he said, "Hundred
bucks." I asked why it cost so much, and his answer held a wisdom with
direct application beyond the ranch, "Cause they gotta pay for the store, the
people, the electricity." But I was also concerned that if we didn't finish hay-
ing that day, our Monday Night Football jaunt would be out. I asked what
would happen if he couldn't get the hay up in time. He said, "Oh, I'll call
Max," (his neighbor). I asked how much Max would charge to help and he
said, "Nothing, you city idiot, he's my neighbor!"

After supper that night, Dave asked if I wanted to take his magazine from
KEM Electric on the flight with me. I declined, saying I hadn't caught up on the
latest edition of The Economist. But I asked what KEM Electric was, just to be
polite. He said, "It's the electric cooperative around here. We all own it and it
helps keep prices down; plus we get a say in how it's run. The magazine covers
the newest techniques in farming." I was on familiar turf now and muttered,
"Kind of like best in class or best practices forums," but it sounded so pompous,
so textbook, compared to the purity of the lessons I had learned that week. All
the pieces had fallen into place.

- Lesson 1: Team members able to fill in for each other on a moment's notice
  (Wayde, Jaime, Billie Jo running the ranch).
- Lesson 2: Well-rounded team members able to do whatever needs to be
  done (the entire family capable of fixing the plumbing).

- *Lesson 3: The inherent and needless expense of corporate overhead brought on by the perpetuation of towers of expertise at headquarters (Dave electing to fix the belt himself as opposed to supporting overhead in town).*

- *Lesson 4: A spirit of friendship and teamwork among teams (Max helping his neighbor whenever needed).*

- *Lesson 5: The beauty of a "cooperative" network throughout an organization, not just to share information, but to give everyone a say in how things are run.*

I had found the perfect model for our corporate structure: the family farm, the best, most efficient, friendly, honest, team-oriented business structure in the world.

A feature article on Rosenbluth International in the February/March 1997 issue of Fast Company *magazine asked and answered the obvious questions one might raise about the family farm as the right business model: "Before you dismiss the family farm as an endangered species, more suited to coping with the business climate of the last century than with the next one, consider Rosenbluth's argument. Farming—like travel services and plenty of other businesses—is all about merging cutting-edge technology and down-to-earth people. The demands are the same: to survive on razor-thin profit margins, react instantly to unpredictable changes, control resources meticulously, and come up with new ways to sell a commodity that, at first glance, seems indistinguishable from the other guy's product."*

And for those who say the family farm is dying out, I point out that more businesses fail each year than family farms. But the point isn't to debate the success of the family farm. It is to take its best traits and put them to work in businesses. Like anything else, well-run farms are as successful as well-run businesses, and vice versa. The model makes perfect sense; the key is in the execution. Let's look at how the model is built.

Every member on the family farm is multifunctional and multifaceted. Each learns from the other, without a formal training department, and is privy to the best techniques from on and off the farm. Each learns through participation, observation, explanation, and the chance to jump in and *do* everything. Each debriefs the others on what happened during the day, and all have input on how to do things better. Everyone pitches in. In business lingo, one could call it a "business unit," but with several unique twists.

"Town" (corporate headquarters) should exist only to serve the farms. It's the most expensive place to run and the least profitable. If costs aren't driven down, the farmers won't buy anything. The services that town "stores" (corporate departments) produce (or sell) must meet the needs of the farms, or those stores will cease to exist. Areas such as marketing, communications, and accounting become keenly focused on the needs of the field, rather than on building and protecting vertical empires—as is the case in so many corporate functions in the typical company.

The "cooperatives" (shared services) help the communication and learning processes. On this front, one of the most sophisticated telecommunications networks in the world links all of our farms (business units) together so that calls can be shifted seamlessly and instantly, enabling one farm to help another during peak times, without generating additional cost structures.

From a learning perspective, with the decentralization of our training function (to be explained later in this chapter and again in Chapter 5, on learning), each business unit designates "leaders in learning," to ensure the learning needs of each farm are met. As with true co-ops, our farmers (who are closest to the crop) have critical input into what they need, what to invest in, and how things are done.

Most important, there's the "crop" (our clients). If they're not tended to, provided the right nutrients, and cared for each day, they won't flourish. If a farm doesn't have a crop, then there is no farm. If a business unit doesn't retain its clients, there will be no business unit. If the business unit doesn't grow its client base, there will be no growth for those in the unit. It's self-motivating, self-perpetuating, self-pruning.

There you have it. A company built of business units made up of multi-functional people, designed around its customers, communicating best-in-class procedures, practicing continuous learning and improvement, backed by just the right amount of overhead needed to best address the clients' needs—all linked to produce the finest customizable service, at the lowest cost. It sounds like a corporate wish list, but at Rosenbluth, it's reality.

Moving to Green Acres

Getting from here to there is no easy task, but the steps we took can be followed, and companies can learn from our successes and failures along the way. The change was made quickly, and not without casualties—217 people were let go in the first layoffs in company history. Nobody said farm life was easy. But today, Rosenbluth International operates well over 100 thriving, growing business units around the world, making what is a very large organization behave like a fully integrated collection of small, fast, fiercely entrepreneurial companies. (Rosenbluth International provides major corporations with sophisticated programs designed to lower their overall travel costs. For example, by creating travel policies; analyzing and negotiating airline, hotel, and car discounts; utilizing proprietary technology to find the lowest fare; and providing clients with detailed reports for budgeting and assessing spending.)

The bottom line underscores the power of the model. Our company saved $7 million during just the first year of operating under the farm design. But the benefits extend far beyond that. Our clients are thrilled with the new design. The underlying lesson of the farm model is that you can't fake farming. The results of your hard work (or lack of it) are evident at harvest time. Our results speak for themselves. Getting there was the trick.

Planting the Seeds of Change

Following the revelation at the ranch, we called together the officers of the company to discuss the new design. We all agreed on the benefits of the model, but we knew that implementing such a redesign would be a monumental undertaking. We had some serious planning to do.

Each year, our top officers meet in strategy sessions to create the future. We hold them at least twice a year, and have done so for more than a decade. There was only one item on the agenda for the planning session held shortly after our initial discussion of the farm model: whether to implement the model, and if so, exactly how to go about it.

We began by laying down some important rules. A change as sweeping as this affects all areas of the company, and true progress is cut off at the knees when people focus on just their own piece of turf. The rules were simple: personal feelings were kept out of our discussions; everyone wore the CEO hat; and when an area was under discussion, the vice president over that area had to keep quiet until everyone else had given their input.

Our goals were to create a design that would bond us closer than ever with our clients, increase our efficiency and drive down costs, and improve the lives of our associates. We were determined to ensure that our goals, not our structure, would drive the company.

Our structure at the time was typical of most corporations: designed around functional areas. As we grew, our organization had become so steeped in structure that it had become a barrier to the flow of information and ideas; it took weeks for any new understanding to make it up or down the organization. For example, we had corporate travel reservations associates reporting to senior reservationists, reporting to lead reservationists, reporting to reservations managers, reporting to area directors, reporting to directors, reporting to vice presidents, reporting to an executive vice president. It was a communications quagmire.

A Farm Raising

We weren't certain what the new design would look like, but we were sure what it wouldn't look like. We began at the center of our universe—our clients—and we worked from there. We wanted to bring the different functional areas together, close to the client, to enable fast, customized solutions and spontaneous communication. We decided to set up business units (which we of course called "farms"). Visually, the old design might have resembled a series of towers, while the new design looks more like a bunch of octopuses with tentacles reaching to each other. (It's not pretty but it works.)

We knew we would still need some functional expertise, so we agreed that corporate support departments, such as accounting, training, or communications, would evolve as necessary to support the new farm structure. In keeping with the farm model, we referred to them as "stores." Further, we decided to let the farms decide what they needed, and let those needs dictate the design of the stores. If a store wasn't providing what the farms needed, it would quickly find itself out of business. Farms would be empowered to go wherever they felt offered the best services to make their farms successful, be it inside or outside the company.

Next, we designated "fences," guidelines to ensure consistency throughout the company in some crucial areas. Examples include salary guidelines, benefits, certain training programs (like our orientation), service standards, and our culture.

Then we set out to select a small team of key leaders to complete the design and implement it. These leaders were critical to the success of the redesign, so we put them through a rigorous selection process. Our top officers selected a group of our strongest leaders from all areas of the company, and offered them the opportunity to apply for a spot on the team. They were asked to compose essays based upon hypothetical leadership issues, explaining what their responses and actions would be. We told them we would be evaluating their judgment and decision-making strength, their vision and leadership, their knowledge and communication skills.

From their responses, the strongest candidates were selected for the next round in the process, in which internal references were consulted. An executive assessment was conducted for each finalist by our corporate psychologist, complete with intelligence testing, extensive interviewing, personality profiles, and other key indicators. (The day-long process is applied to candidates for most of our top leadership positions. Most candidates find the process really interesting. And though it's rigorous, it's also comfortable, to enable us to get a good read on the candidate's style and fit for the role.)

The assessments contain written and face-to-face portions, which include some commercially published instruments as well as some proprietary tools developed by our psychologist, to get at the root of a candidate's career interests and personality. For example, the proprietary Career Development Questionnaire asks candidates to list things that would excite them if it were on their calendar tomorrow.

FINDING THE BEST OF THE BEST. Diane recalls going through the process. She completed the battery of written tests over about a half a day, which required her to dig deep into her values, priorities, and leadership style. She recalled one test in which she was asked to piece together some oddly shaped blocks to match a design she was given on paper. Throughout the test, our consulting psychologist held a stopwatch and took copious notes. On the surface it might appear that time-to-solve was the measurement of success, but he explained that speed was just one factor.

Following the test, Diane asked our psychologist what he had been writing and he shared with her that the most important determinant of the test had been her approach to problem solving. Did she ask questions? Was there method to her steps? Did she lose her temper? (He shared stories of executives getting so frustrated that they threw the blocks and said they didn't have to do a silly exercise like that.) Did she have a sense of humor? Was she interested in finding out, at the conclusion of the exercise, what would have been the most effective method?

In general, these tests tell us a great deal. In preparing for our redesign, this process helped us to come up with a short list of top candidates for the team of four who would lead the change. The final step was a panel interview with a team of top officers. Following the interview, the officers brought their individual areas of expertise to the table, and evaluated each candidate accordingly. Our consulting psychologist then joined the panel with the results of the executive assessments, and they reached a decision based upon the combined analysis.

These were the tactical champions of the redesign. The officers of the company stayed out of the way unless their support was needed. The team reported to no one, though each of the four was assigned two advocates among the VPs. The advocate role was strictly to clear paths and remove any obstacles that might hamper their progress.

The team locked themselves in their planning room 16 hours a day for two solid weeks, existing on caffeine, take-out food, and the knowledge that they were creating the future. The joke among the officers of the company was that these four were *running* the company, and to a certain extent that was true. I went in to visit them once, about halfway through the two-week planning process. Except when they asked for help, they were on their own.

They discussed at length the pros and cons of the various options for determining the business units: by geography, by client, by industry, and every other possibility. They determined that the best possible solution was to develop a customized approach, taking each client in mind.

For some clients, the best solution was a dedicated business unit. For others, it was a small geographical grouping of clients sharing the resources of a business unit dedicated to them. Before matching clients with business units, the team met with clients to discuss the options, and consulted the associates who had the most involvement with each account.

After outlining the farms, our team began to call in our support departments one by one, to bring them on board, explaining how dramatically their roles would change. Each meeting began with an extensive overview of the new farm structure, the goals, and what was needed from their particular area. For example, one of the first areas consulted was human resources. The new structure called for a complete redesign of the company's job descriptions. Each farm needed a general manager to run the business, account leaders to work closely with the individual accounts, and other positions that didn't exist in the current structure.

The new positions called for an entirely new skill set, combining several roles that had previously been specialized, such as operations (day-to-day service functions) and client services (determining and communicating client needs). This required new training programs and new compensation systems. The business unit structure called for a redesign of our financial systems, P&Ls, and other measurements, since each unit would be, in effect, an individual business.

The changes didn't stop there; they rocked the company from head to toe. Literally every area of the company had to reinvent itself to support the new structure. But it was worth the effort and temporary chaos, because the entire structure was built around our clients, not our roles or areas of expertise. We took a quantum leap to a higher level of performance.

Calling All Farmers

Finding the right people to run these farms was of paramount importance. One primary goal was to make the organization as flat as a pancake. The implementation team of four were named Directors of Business Development (DBDs), and theirs was to be a temporary role: to get the business units up and running. The next layer was that of General Manager, (GM), the "owners" of these entrepreneurial businesses. Each account had an Account Leader (AL), to be the expert on that particular account. All other associates in the business units were designated Travel Services Associates (TSAs).

Having only four layers to the CEO meant fast action and no red tape. Almost immediately, our productivity (measured in transactions per associate) jumped by 13 percent. But the results reach far beyond numbers. Our GMs are given full autonomy and decision-making power to run their "farms" in the best interest of our clients, and that means stellar service. Clients need only call one person when they have a request or a question.

Southwest Airlines: Lean Leadership

Southwest is unique among airlines on many fronts, including structure. Director of Customers Kathy Pettit says, "We employ 26,000 people, and are 87 percent unionized, which surprises many, given our historically (and notoriously) favorable labor relations. Southwest has an extremely thin management layer in comparison with other companies—airlines in particular." In most locations, Southwest employees have just a supervisor and a location leader.

To find the best possible people to fill the critical GM role, we opened the opportunity to everyone in the company, and executed an intense selection process. Our team of DBDs, working closely with experts from Human Resources, developed job descriptions for each of the three afore-mentioned positions: General Manager, Account Leader, and Travel Ser-vices Associates. Then, they began their search for the ideal GMs.

First they made the opportunity known to everyone in the company. Those interested sent in cover letters and resumes. From those applicants, the most highly qualified were interviewed over the phone by human resources leaders. The strongest candidates were then given written assignments that included, for example, a question about why the appli-cant felt the redesign would benefit our clients and our company.

The strongest to emerge from the written assignments were then asked to provide internal and external references from their leaders, direct reports, and of course, clients. Those passing the reference checks with flying colors were interviewed by a panel of experts, including a vice pres-ident, DBD, and a human resources leader. From these extensive inter-views, our final selections were made. Then the GMs conducted the selection process for their account managers, in a similar process.

Once the GMs were selected, they were divided into four groups assigned to the leadership of a DBD. They were given the opportunity to submit a prioritized list of preferred business units in advance; where pos-sible, these were fulfilled. A number of GMs had to relocate to their new business units, but after the dust settled, everyone was pleased with their new assignments and roles.

Immediately after the assignments were made, each DBD held a confer-ence call with their group of new GMs. The most important step was next: meeting with each client to discuss the new structure, introduce the leadership team, and ensure their full understanding of client priorities.

Back at the Ranch

With this clear understanding of where they were headed, the GMs met at our executive ranch and conference center in North Dakota to map out the journey they were about to begin. This meeting marked a turn-ing point in our company; it was a roller-coaster ride. The highs were embarking on amazing new career opportunities and learning experi-ences for our GMs, and significant performance improvement for our clients. The tremendous low came when we acknowledged that our new efficiency would uncover unnecessary positions throughout the company and that, for the first time in over 100 years, we would have to lay off associates.

The planning meeting began on a Sunday and ran through Friday; we began by 7:00 A.M. each day and wrapped up around midnight each night. The bond-building, energy, and creativity that marked that event were incredible. That's the way of pioneers.

To begin the meeting, the DBDs explained the new world the team was about to enter—the structure of the business units and the work that lay ahead. They told their new GM team that they were presenting a "half-baked" plan, and that the other half was the GMs' to determine. This instilled the kind of ownership necessary to make the redesign work. The result was a complete organizational design and a detailed implementation plan created in less than a week. Each GM returned home with a specific business plan for his or her individual business unit, with short- and long-term action items.

One of the most striking results from the meeting was the "whack 'em" list, which itemized the redundancies, rework, and inefficiencies the group uncovered. Teams of GMs discussed all the processes we went through in serving our clients, and each time a team uncovered one that would now be obsolete, they broke out in a chorus of, "Nah, nah, nah, nah, hey, hey, hey, goodbye." All over the ranch it sounded like the last minute of a sporting event, but 17 hours a day. If we'd had to pay royalty rights to the songwriters, we'd be out of business.

FACING THE INEVITABLE. Although uncovering redundancies was probably the most productive part of the redesign, it also turned out to be the most painful, because this is where the need for layoffs became evident. Anticipating the difficulty, an entire day of the GM meeting was dedicated to preparing for the inevitable. The new GMs were briefed by our human resources team and our corporate psychologist. They were coached on how to best communicate the changes, how people might respond, and offered suggestions as to what to say and do. There's no way to describe the pain we all felt that day.

The layoffs were initiated by a ripple effect. In selecting *one* leader for each business unit, we were combining primarily what had been two separate areas, Client Services and Operations. This meant we had approximately twice the number of leaders we needed in the new structure, all of whom were highly qualified. After selecting the best of the best for our GMs, the remainder of the candidates were considered for account leader positions, of which there were also about twice as many. Consequently, this still left a number of leaders from both areas without a leadership opportunity in the business unit structure.

In addition, there were supervisory roles that had become unnecessary in the new design. To a certain degree, the ripple of overqualification pushed outward. Those most qualified were given GM positions. The next most qualified were designated Account Leaders. The remainder of associates in each business unit were considered for Travel Services Associate roles. Leaders who did not wish to remain as TSAs, as well as the least qualified TSAs, were those who left the company.

A buyout was offered to all associates in advance. We were aware that companies typically run the risk with such a program of losing some of their best and brightest people—those who feel confident in their ability to quickly find employment elsewhere. But we knew how strongly our people felt about the company and decided to take the risk. (Actually, we adopt the same attitude each week in our new associate orientation program. Toward the end of the program, we always encourage people to decide whether or not this is the place for them. This company is different, and people realize that during orientation. The best time for them to leave, if they are so inclined, is before they start. We felt the same way with the redesign.) This marked a whole new way of doing business for us, and anyone who didn't want to be on board for it had the opportunity to leave, with our blessings.

We also offered outplacement services to all who were leaving the company, both voluntarily and involuntarily. We held seminars on change management for all associates to help those who remained to deal with the separation from colleagues and the stress of change.

Alagasco: Conquering Deregulation

When the natural gas industry underwent deregulation and subsequent enormous change, Alagasco was faced with a new, highly competitive marketplace. Cost control became imperative, and Alagasco turned chaos into opportunity. To begin with, the company offered a voluntary, early retirement option for salaried employees in 1995. According to CEO Mike Warren, "The change created a great deal of job movement and advancement opportunities. We began putting people in nontraditional roles, putting nonoperating personnel into operations positions, and vice versa. And we took the opportunity to place women and minorities into more strategic positions."

Not knowing which positions would be left vacant, yet wanting to uphold its practice of promoting from within, Alagasco notified all employees by letter that early retirement was being offered and that some job openings would result. They asked everyone to indicate their areas of interest and willingness to relocate. More than 250 employees responded, submitting their career goals. Ultimately, 40 positions were eliminated, and 65 employees were given new opportunities. This creative approach made a tremendous success out of a potentially difficult situation. Mike says, "One measure of how successful we are at filling a vacancy is seeing how many other people can be positively affected by the move—in other words, we use the domino theory."

Alagasco also changed their benefits significantly. Through their 401(k) and ESOP programs, they increased employee stock ownership from 1 percent to 11 percent. They invested millions of dollars in improving their work environments, in every operating division. And they now pay for performance with a new, formal compensation and performance evaluation system, in which "internal equity and fairness are the watchwords."

The Keys to Success

There were three primary keys to Rosenbluth's success in the redesign: fairness, speed, and communication. Let's look at each. First and foremost, fairness. Beginning with the reasons for the redesign and continuing through the implementation, fairness was at the heart of everything we did.

Playing Fair

Fairness began with our reason for redesigning. We sought to create the ideal structure to be the most effective for our clients. This was not a downsizing. We didn't decide to lay people off, then ask for each department to eliminate *X* percent of their overhead. The reasons were not economic, though one can't argue with the savings that resulted. This was nothing less than creating the future before the future came calling. We made the decision in the best interest of our clients, and our people, because nurturing our lifeline (our clients) and securing the future of our company is the best thing we can do for our associates.

People accepted the decision because they knew it was the right thing to do. It made us a stronger company, and it enriched our associates' lives. It gave the staff closest to our clients more authority, and it shifted the focus away from headquarters and into the field—where it belongs. Our motives were genuine, and that came across loud and clear to our associates. Motives always do.

Fairness extended to the implementation process. There were no shoe-ins for positions. *Everyone* had to interview, even if they had held a similar job for years. Though putting everyone through this rigorous process was unsettling, it was the only fair way to do it, and we knew that, through it, our strongest people would be leading the company.

Shortly after *The Customer Comes Second* was released, we began conducting companywide associate satisfaction surveys. The survey we conducted following the redesign had overwhelmingly positive results, which we found surprising, considering the upheaval that was generated by all the changes. Our people told us that the new design helped us to improve "walking the talk" about associate empowerment. They said they could feel the power of the contributions they were making, and feel a higher degree of satisfaction with their careers. No doubt they are working harder, but they're also growing and succeeding.

Moving at Hyperspeed

The second key to our success was speed. This is a company that operates in fast forward, and it always has been. The redesign, as far-reaching as it was, took place at warp speed. We made a deliberate decision to move quickly, for two reasons: to keep service seamless for our clients, and to prevent our associates from dwelling on the uncertainties of change.

Before we explain the impact speed had on the success of our endeavor, we need to describe the kind of speed we're talking about. The company design was created in two weeks. The GM selection process took two weeks. The GM meeting was held almost immediately after their selection. Two weeks later, the ALs and TSAs had been selected, and the redesign was complete.

The first two weeks of planning involved only our DBD team (and consulting departments, one by one), so there was really no disruption. We were very careful to keep the process under wraps until a design had been drawn, to keep rumor, speculation, and uncertainty at bay. So, in terms of potential effect on our associates and clients, the transition took just four weeks. As one DBD put it, "There were no toes in the water. We just dove in, and no one had time to dwell on it."

Speed was also critical because, unlike a manufacturing company that might shut down temporarily to retool, we have to be open 24 hours a day, 365 days a year for our clients all over the world. To our clients, the transition was nearly transparent, and the results have been indelible.

Speed contributed to the smooth transition, but our culture of excellence had more to do with it. Our people are committed to excellence, and we knew we could count on them to provide no less, even in such unsettling times. In fact, service was superb during the transition, because each person saw the company being designed completely around our clients, which served to reemphasize our priorities.

Of course, our clients are the best judges of how we did. Intel's corporate travel manager LaVonne Sovoda says of the redesign, "The business unit structure gave greater authority to the general managers, which really inspired a higher level of ownership. Service is customized, based on client needs. Rosenbluth's Intel team fully understands our account, and that's especially important for a company like ours, which is very demanding." She added, "The change was fairly transparent. It was clearly well thought out and planned. Everything ran smoothly, and there was really no impact on day-to-day operations. In fact, the new structure helped move us forward with regard to the future and strategy."

According to Ken Stateler, Director of Fleet and Travel Services at our long-time client, FMC, the change was very positive. He says, "It's a common-sense approach to managing business. It allows Rosenbluth to get extremely close to its customers." In some ways, FMC served as a pilot for the business unit structure. Ken discussed with us the merits of having a single point of contact between our companies at least two years prior to our redesign. He asked if we could try it and we did. We later told him we wished we had tried it sooner.

Ken says though he was pleased with his forerunner of our redesign, he saw even more empowerment for his general manager with the implementation of our companywide redesign. He says, "I used to call Rosenbluth headquarters all the time, and now I probably call once a year, socially." That's success.

The Lines of Communication

The third key to our success in the redesign was communication with our associates and clients. It was open, honest, frequent, and swift. We made sure that all associates learned of the changes at the same time. The farm analogy brought the concept home and made it something people could relate to. Textbooks or academic pieces about reorganizations tend to have a remote quality—they're more conceptual than real-life. The result is a more tentative, longer implementation process. Using the farm model translated the concept into something our associates could appreciate and believe in, because of our close association with rural North Dakota.

The farm concept can be used by any company. Almost everyone can relate to the ethic of hard work, cooperation, and overcoming obstacles that farming represents. But if there's another analogy that holds special meaning for your company, we can tell you from experience, it will help to ease the transition to any changes you make. No matter the design, communicating it to all audiences quickly, honestly, and compassionately is imperative to the successful implementation of any major change.

All communication at our company follows the following order of prioritization: associates, clients, external audiences (suppliers, media, etc.). We always inform our associates first, for two reasons: It's their company and they have a right to know first; and it's in the best interest of our clients that our associates be up to the minute on everything that affects the company. We never want an associate to hear company news from a client (or any other outside source). Associates must be informed and prepared for any implications the news might hold. Then they will be able to provide the kind of service our clients have come to expect from us.

A strong communication process is a lifeline in any organization. Employees must know that they will be kept informed. Here are some ground rules to follow:

1. They must be able to count on consistent communication vehicles (i.e., newsletters) that are credible, timely and honest.

2. Everyone must be included in direct communication because we all know how information gets distorted as it flows from one person to another.

3. Everyone should get the news at the same time, if at all possible.

4. People need to know what to expect next; for example, when the next communication piece will be released (and those schedules need to be met).

5. A communications plan should be developed for each important announcement/event, to ensure that all bases are covered, all audiences are addressed, interdependencies are considered, and all implications are thought out.

When a company can consistently follow these guidelines, a magical transformation occurs. People are free to concentrate on the work at hand instead of speculating and worrying about what's going on. People have the security and confidence necessary to achieve peak performance. The water cooler loses its power, and communication is accurate and true.

We carefully adhered to each of these ground rules when communicating the company redesign, and it was more important than ever at a critical time like this. Here's how the communication plan rolled out. We held our first strategy meeting to discuss the design in late December 1992. We spent the next two weeks reconfirming that we would make the change and creating the initial design. Then the communication began.

On January 13, the first official communication went to all associates, attached to their paycheck (a vehicle we reserve for very important information). It was a letter explaining the reasons for a redesign, introducing the farm metaphor, and outlining how the company would look in the new structure. It included steps that would be followed in the implementation, and even what details still needed to be determined. Finally, it told what and when the next communication about the design would be.

In fact, *every* piece of communication regarding the redesign began with a recap of what had taken place to date, and what was coming next, and when. This is vital in order for people to be sure they are in the know. For example, *KIT (Keep In Touch)*, one of our internal newsletters, featured a column every month from January to June 1993, dedicated to discussing the redesign. The January edition began, "With the January 15 paycheck, all associates should have received a letter from Hal describing some future companywide changes." It went on to recap the letter. The column ended, "Within the week, your office will be meeting to discuss the contents of the letter and any questions you may have. If you have any questions that are left unanswered by your leader, please call the hotline."

The reference to the hotline brings up an important point. Having vehicles in place through which associates can funnel their questions is of the utmost importance. We'll talk more extensively about these vehicles in Chapter 7, on culture, but for now, we emphasize that effective communication always takes place on a two-way street.

Following this first communication to associates came a steady stream of updates (memos and letters) along with overviews in company newsletters, on voice mail and in live meetings, to keep everyone fully informed. A series of special organizational redesign surveys went out to associates (in addition to our ongoing morale checks) to gauge the effects of the redesign, and to call for suggestions from associates for adjustments to the implementation plan. This enabled them to take an active part in the process.

> *It is always important with a significant change to make associates understand where they stand in the continuum of change. For example, in my second update letter to all associates, I wrote, "I want to emphasize that no decisions have yet been made regarding the selection of leaders for the business units." I went on to tell them what had been done (the selection of DBDs) and what was coming (the selection of GMs) and when. Attached to my letter was a complete outline of leadership opportunities available, position descriptions, the exact selection criteria and process, and the necessary forms to apply for those opportunities.*

Once the associates had a full understanding of the design and pending changes, we notified our clients. They received an initial letter from me, followed by calls from their local representatives, then ongoing updates via client newsletters, meetings, memos, and other vehicles. Before plans were finalized or changes implemented, our clients were fully informed and consulted. Furthermore, we deemed it essential that our clients be notified at the same time, so a combination of mail, fax, and hand delivery of the announcement letter was used, depending upon the location of each client. Of course, now that we have the business unit structure in place, communication with our clients has become much faster, more efficient, and customized.

After our associates and clients were fully informed, we next approached our suppliers and other key business contacts with the news. Templates for letters (for consistency of information) were provided to each vice president for customization and use in communicating to key contacts in their respective areas. Simultaneously, the media was notified of the changes; the public audience completed our communication chain.

Great Plains Software: Moving from Functional to Strategic

Great Plains Software evolved its organizational model in 1996 from a functional company to lines of business. Their reasons were (1) getting closer to customers, (2)speed to market, (3) increased opportunity for responsibility, and (4) better financial accountability. They organized into lines of business and numerous shared resources (i.e., finance, human resources, information systems). Each team has financial responsibility (P&L or budget), strategy/operational responsibility, a unique customer group, and is expected to deliver on agreed-upon goals.

Alagasco: Fewer Layers

Like Great Plains Software and Rosenbluth International, Alagasco operates support activities centrally (i.e., technology, finance, accounting, human resources, communication, etc.) while customer contact and operating activities remain decentralized. Alagasco reports that it is continually flattening itself, in order to push decision making out to the front-line levels. According to CEO Mike Warren, "We are deleting layers instead of adding them."

Farming Today

Here's a quick update on how things have progressed since Rosenbluth's redesign. Originally, the role of DBD was to be temporary, in place only until the GMs felt they had developed strong skills across all areas that were melded into their new role. But thanks to enormous growth, and new business units being continually added to accommodate new clients (the number of units has more than doubled in just four years), we have a constant flow of new GMs, so it looks like our DBDs will be around for a while.

We have raised the bar significantly over the years since our redesign in early 1993. The roles in the business units have grown. The skill level and performance of yesterday's DBD is that of today's GM, and today's account leaders are performing at yesterday's GM level. Our clients expect more and more, and it keeps us on our toes. We gain speed every day, and the result is much faster and better decision making, which benefits our clients repeatedly. They need to go to only one person for whatever they may need, and those people (in the field) control the resources of the company.

We thought we couldn't ask for a better design until recently, when we took the design just one step further. Four years after the redesign came the next logical evolution of our business unit structure. The initial redesign merged Client Services and Operations for single accountability. Next we combined Operations (the business units) with Sales and Supplier Relations, and then Marketing with Information Systems. These might sound like unlikely combinations until you examine them more closely. Sometimes the best way to ensure that areas that have strong cause and effect on each other are in synch is to combine them under single leadership.

United Fronts

A key role of the marketing function is, of course, to understand needs in the marketplace and fulfill them with the best possible products. A majority of the products we offer are technology-based. Therefore, the fulfillment of marketing's design for a product would normally be implemented by our IS group. Synchronization between the two areas is the key to product fulfillment and client satisfaction, so we named one person as vice president of IS and Marketing. In this way, a fully integrated team designs and delivers products as promised to our clients.

Likewise, the delivery of service sold to customers by our sales team is in the hands of operations (the business units). So we ensured seamless delivery of what was promised to customers by combining Sales and Operations under one vice president to head Worldwide Business Development. Not only is the fulfillment of the sales commitment important in the business units, but so is expertise in Supplier Relations. Our clients rely upon us for advocacy with the airlines and other suppliers, so naturally, this area has been rolled into the Business Unit operation as well, under single leadership.

I emphasize that this type of corporate fluidity is possible only in an environment where friendship counts for more than turf. It's the oldest principle of friendship—sharing—and something so often "unlearned" as people enter corporate life. I actively encourage a healthy disregard for territory. To that

end, every couple of years or so, I tell my leaders I'm declaring myself "dead"
and I ask them to reflect carefully on how well they work together, and chal-
lenge them to operate as though I weren't around.

These latest changes follow the path our company always takes—outward in. The first and most important changes took place at the front
line, followed four years later by changes at headquarters that further
supported the structure in the field, closest to our clients.

Organizational Redesign Wave

No two companies are structured alike, and much can be learned by
observing different designs. Here are some thoughts from our peers.

SAS Institute

The structure of SAS Institute is varied and flexible. It's designed to best
meet the business need, so some areas of the company are centralized,
while other functions are dispersed throughout different divisions. For
example, training occurs through several different areas such as Management Education Administration, Corporate Training, Training Services
(external), Research and Development Training, Sales and Marketing
Training. Each of these units is housed in a different division, based upon
content, and the function is carried out by a group of professional trainers from within that content area. In contrast, Human Resources, Legal,
and Finance are highly centralized.

According to Vice President of Human Resources David Russo, "The
strength of this approach is that it allows the company to operate in
whatever way works best for any given function or group of employees.
Talent in one particular skill set is not limited to one area of the company, so there are several resources available for meeting a single need.
This flexible structure also allows for more efficiency in meeting the
needs of the customer, both internal and external."

In the overwhelming majority of divisions at SAS Institute, there are no
more than four layers of management from front-line employees to the
president. One new employee remarked that she was surprised—and
excited—that only three people "stood between" her and the president of
the company. The Institute reports that their flat structure allows employ-

ees to feel they have a voice and can make significant contributions to the business process.

USAA

USAA underwent some profound changes when it decided to: (1) expand its membership base (potentially by a factor of seven) by offering insurance to a new audience, (2) establish a new line of business, and (3) build a state-of-the-art automated underwriting environment, which completely revised companywide processes. These changes were the largest in the past five years, and arguably in the history of the company. USAA has a long-established, strong, and highly successful corporate culture. Changing a piece of that culture was not easy.

The team's work began by identifying all personnel, from service representatives to senior management, who would be required to change behavior as they became part of the new underwriting environment. Then the team developed a change plan that coordinated a series of events, such as presentations, site visits, newsletters, articles, and manager hotsheets to deliver specific messages at specific times, to build buyin for the new underwriting philosophy.

Surveys and focus groups were used to measure the progress of the employees as they went through the change. Only after the majority of users expressed their support for the new way of doing business did actual training take place. The training included considerable use of a simulated business environment for the employees most impacted by the change.

Also incorporated into the transition plan was rigorous testing carried out by the project team. They examined every aspect of the new environment from component parts of the information technology system to full-scale process simulations. When the system was delivered, the employees were ready. The first day was a seamless event, with employees servicing a completely new market using the new systems and new work process skillfully, effectively, and comfortably. USAA senior executives consider it to be the smoothest large-scale new program implementation in the organization's history.

According to William Flynn, SVP, chief planning and analysis officer, "It means USAA can expand its membership manyfold, process millions of new members, complete membership applications online, select the appropriate level of coverage, correctly price that coverage based upon the individual's risk profile, and generate a written policy, all during the *initial* phone call."

The implementation of a system like this is key to USAA's modus operandi. Each day its employees process 350,000 phone calls and 16 million computer transactions. The company's automated call distribution system is the largest in the world. In fact, USAA is the nation's largest mail order company (by sales volume) and the second largest in the world. The company conducts its business entirely by telephone, fax, and direct mail.

Mary Kay

Any number of factors can generate the need for a company to redesign itself. In the case of Mary Kay, it began in 1996, when company founder, Mary Kay Ash, suffered a stroke in the midst of the company's aggressive global expansion. The company was making some organizational changes anyway to meet their expansion needs, but Mary Kay's reduced presence in the business meant even more changes. Most members of the senior management team were in place when Mary Kay fell ill. She had been grooming the corporate leadership, as well as that of her independent sales force. But her illness accelerated the transition process.

At corporate headquarters, Amy DiGeso was chosen as CEO to lead the company, with a team of top managers representing each division. Amy had joined Mary Kay as senior vice president of Global Human Resources, had gone on to serve in other key leadership positions, and was president of the international division at the time she was tapped to lead the company in January 1997.

On the sales front, the company worked with its independent sales force to assure that Mary Kay Ash's motivational genius continued to reverberate throughout. Efforts have been highly successful. The Mary Kay sales force was named one of the top 25 in America by *Sales and Marketing Magazine*—the same year as this transition.

Mary Kay attributes its success in this landmark period to four key elements: (1) preserving its culture, (2) strategically aligning communication, (3) providing ways for employees and sales leaders to get to know senior management members more personally, and (4) staffing global subsidiaries with high-performing employees who live the company's principles.

THE CULTURE. To preserve the culture, there was a renewed, strategic effort to integrate Mary Kay's vision into every aspect of the company.

Even decisions as simple as who would sign the birthday cards to the 475,000-member sales force were looked at with an eye to the right thing to do. The company didn't want to seem insincere by continuing to use Mary Kay's stamped signature when she was not in the office, but they discovered that the sales force didn't care; they wanted Mary Kay's signature on their cards, so Mary Kay's signature stayed.

One of the most daunting challenges was brought about by the sudden silencing (due to the stroke) of Mary Kay's powerful voice. She was a spellbinding speaker who rallied the company and its sales force at least a half-dozen times each year, in powerful presentations. To meet this challenge, initially, the communication focus was on her recuperation and updates on her health. For special events, video archives were used to capture Mary Kay's wit and wisdom through the years. When she couldn't attend the largest sales event of the year, Tom Whatley, president U.S. Sales, took the top 15 members of the sales force to visit her at her home. Word and photos of the meeting spread the spirit.

Eventually, Mary Kay was again able to appear at sales meetings. She began to communicate through brief, heartfelt written messages read for her by a member of the staff or sales force standing next to her. The messages have been very reassuring for the independent sales force and company employees.

COMMUNICATION. The vision of Mary Kay's new leadership was communicated clearly and immediately. In her first address as the new CEO, Amy DiGeso said, "We won't change for change's sake. We will not risk this culture in Boise and we won't risk it in Buenos Aires." Follow-up communication has been constant.

LEADERSHIP AND SALES PROMINENCE. When DiGeso became CEO, she made a promise to help employees and the sales force get to know the senior management team. This was critical because of the changes and the company's explosive growth. Senior leaders were profiled in company publications, and more in-depth profiles were sent to employees and sales force leaders.

Personal meetings were also conducted. When top sales directors met in Dallas to brainstorm, the management team hosted a dinner for them. And each executive manager visited a different distribution center (there are five in the United States) for interviews with members of the sales force. These meetings were critical to gain insight into what drives the business from the field point of view. In addition, independent national sales directors took over key roles traditionally reserved for Mary Kay. As noted, top directors stood beside her and read her messages to the sales force at meetings and made speeches to inspire the troops.

In July 1997, at the annual Seminar, the company's largest meeting, every member of the executive team was present, visible and accessible throughout the 15 days and nights of 5 seminars. Mary Kay veteran Rodger Bogardus, senior vice president of Global Research and Development, had never sat through an entire Seminar, let alone all five. As he left the convention center on day 15, he said the experience had given his usually analytical mind some new thoughts on his challenges to keep Mary Kay products technologically competitive worldwide.

SUCCESSFUL GLOBAL EXPANSION. To ensure its global expansion was a success, the company staffed subsidiaries with seasoned international talent, while sprinkling in current employees steeped in the Mary Kay culture. These employees played a key leadership role in the company's global expansion. For example, when the company needed someone to educate employees in Hangzhou, China, about the company and the value of quality, 12-year veteran Elizabeth Kraus Russell got the nod. She had been in a scientist role in Dallas. She developed new skills, and became a part of the company's global expansion. And where seasoned, international experience was needed, Mary Kay recruited new talent like Barbara Hyder. She joined the company as president of the Americas region, having been vice president of International for Maybelline.

Beth Israel Deaconess

In 1996, Beth Israel Hospital merged with New England Deaconess Hospital, to become Beth Israel Deaconess Medical Center. The task of blending the two cultures was enormous. But the company approached it as an opportunity to begin anew. They revisited practices and policies, to determine the best possible solutions for the current environment and the future. They also sought to preserve the traditions and practices that were important to patients and employees.

According to Laura Avakian, senior vice president, Human Resources, "In the period immediately after a merger is announced, there is typically a great deal of uncertainty and ambiguity. Employees at all levels have questions about the future, but many of the answers are not yet determined. At Beth Israel Deaconess, it has been important to identify concerns and rumors in the organization, and respond to them." For that reason, they held "town meeting" events led by divisional leaders; a highly-participative, 5-hour meeting of the top 200 leaders, to discuss strategy; employee focus groups; monthly managers meetings; weekly planning meetings; and a series of small-group coffees, hosted by the president. In addition to face-to-face communication, a weekly newsletter from the president (in three languages), a monthly organizational newspaper, question-and-answer memos, and e-mail broadcasts kept people informed.

Another means of alleviating uncertainty was to make management selections as quickly as possible. The selection of senior leaders was completed early, which enabled them to get the necessary planning done. They paid particular attention to creating a process for selecting department managers that was considered fair and respectful. Managers themselves helped design the selection process, through focus groups. Once the process was developed, it was widely published and then followed.

After the department managers had been selected, the training department sponsored "welcome breakfasts" for them. These events were designed to acknowledge the importance of their roles, and to provide a networking forum in which to share ideas and discuss experiences during this challenging time.

Beth Israel Deaconess worked with outside merger experts to offer extensive training on change management, as part of a program called Making Mergers Work. Their leaders learned about the typical stages and human reactions to a merger and what can be done to enhance effectiveness.

Another segment of the merger process was the development of a vision statement and a set of values for the new organization. These were developed in draft form by a cross-disciplinary committee, and then tested in the larger organization. In addition, they identified performance measures that together formed a balanced scorecard. They are currently creating a way to communicate the scorecard results to all employees on a regular basis.

Design for Speed: A Summary

• Look for your company's organizational design in unlikely places. Sometimes inspiration from nontraditional sources can be just the right catalyst for change. Consider Rosenbluth's farm structure or another model that has special meaning in your organization.

- Whatever the model, minimize focus on headquarters ("town" in our farm model). The emphasis should be on the field, where customer interactions are. That's the *real* world. Support departments should be just that—in existence solely to *support* the field. Let the front line dictate what they need.

- Emulate the co-ops found in rural America to provide a network for information sharing between all locations and departments in your company. Telecommunications networks, group software, and other tools are a good start, but giving the field a sense of ownership and a say in how things are run are the most critical factors.

- Set ground rules to encourage objectivity, *before* deciding on organizational design. As we noted earlier, a couple we've used are: Everyone wears the CEO hat; and when a particular area is under discussion, the leader of that area must keep quiet until everyone else has commented.

- All corporate designs should emanate from the center out, with clients or customers at the center. If everything else builds upon that, you'll always ensure a client focus. The fewer layers from client to CEO, the better.

- Make your selection process for key leadership roles an extensive one. Ours included written essays, internal and external references, executive assessments by a corporate psychologist, and in-depth interviews before a panel of top officers.

- A tight, tactical team should put the finishing touches on the design. Executives should stay out of the way, except to serve as advocates to run interference against any obstacles that may arise. To gain buyin, this team might try presenting a half-baked plan for midlevel leaders and front-line associates to complete. Their input will add an important perspective to the design.

- Don't overlook the opportunity to uncover "whack 'ems" in the process of redesigning. A new structure can render obsolete many of the processes in place today. Let them fall like dominoes. The rule should be: If no one misses it, stop doing it.

- We have found three keys to redesign success: fairness, speed, and communication. Regarding communication, a few ground rules go a long way: (1) Notify associates *first*. (2) Establish consistent communication vehicles your people can count on. (3) Include *everyone* in direct communication. (4) If possible, deliver news to everyone at the same time.

(5) Let people know what to expect next and when to expect it. A good way to ensure thorough communication is to develop a plan for each important announcement or event.

- Consider combining areas with strong cause and effect on each other under single leadership. We combined Marketing and IS, and merged Sales with Operations to do just that, and with great results.

- As a leader, ask your team to think about how they would operate without you. Ask them to work together to improve what would result if you were to step aside. If leaders throughout your company do this on a regular basis, it will strengthen teamwork, communication, and effectiveness.

- Make changes outward in. Begin where the highest impact will be—closest to your customers. Then reorganize headquarters to support the field.

3

Human Resources:
In the Boardroom,
Not on the Sidelines

The old saying goes, "Don't tamper with perfection." This is often good advice, but in the case of our human resources group, we didn't heed it. HR has always been a strength of our company, and like our philosophy and values, our emphasis on HR will never change.

But one spin-off benefit of our redesign was a metamorphosis in the role our human resources group plays. Always an invaluable resource for our people and our company, our redesign thrust them into a strategic role, one that fully utilizes their talents and expertise. We believe Human Resources should play this role in every organization.

In the earliest stages of the redesign, Human Resources was consulted for typical issues such as formulating job descriptions, designing and managing the selection process for the new roles, creating the separation packages and support programs, and others. But as the redesign began to touch every area of the organization, our HR team was called in to help redesign the company, department by department. In doing so, they became intimately acquainted with all facets of the company, and developed an in-depth understanding of each discipline, the current roles each department played, as well as its goals and needs for the future. These deepened relationships were extended through the redesign of the HR department itself.

Mining Our Resources

Our human resources team became a collection of consultants to the field, each assigned to work with designated business units and support departments (which we call Centralized Service Centers, or CSCs). In this role, they are actively involved in strategy and design, and are therefore able to accurately forecast future human resource requirements, and prepare to fulfill those needs. This has greatly benefited the company, in a variety of ways that will be explored in this chapter. And the key is to find the right people.

Mary Kay: A Visible Emphasis on HR

Mary Kay takes a view similar to Rosenbluth's of the role its human resources employees play. The company considers people its most important asset. That's why human resources executives regularly advise and counsel the CEO and other top executives on all aspects of the business. In fact, both the CEO and current president of International come from a human resources background.

SAS Institute: HR Partnerships

At SAS Institute, each division is assigned a human resources representative. Through these ongoing relationships, the HR representatives are able to become familiar with the needs and qualifications of their assigned division, which empowers them to effectively meet the needs of applicants and managers.

The changes in the HR operation have been primarily in six areas: (1) global thinking, (2) building a pipeline, (3) core competencies, (4) flexible work configurations, (5) heightened emphasis on work/life issues, and (6) diversity as a way of life. We're going to explain each of these new areas of focus because we believe they are universal in business of the future.

Global Thinking

Rosenbluth has radically expanded its global presence over the past five years. As you'll read in Chapter 8, entitled, "One World, One Company," not only have we reached more countries but we have also adopted a "wholly owned" approach, which means that those representing our company abroad are our own associates. This has dramatically affected the role our HR team plays globally.

Now, when making a decision, our HR team (like the rest of our company) must stop and ask, "Does this make sense globally? If not, why not, and how could it?" This applies to benefits, policies, programs, and everything HR is involved in. Global thinking is the beginning; global support follows. This requires a whole new dimension of service.

For example, laws vary by country, but we have universal standards to uphold regarding issues to which we are committed, including equal employment opportunity, sexual harassment, and others. Not all countries have the same awareness or concern of these issues, and it's our responsibility to raise our associates' awareness in those locations. The laws don't drive us, what's right does; nevertheless, we need to be current on the laws in each of the countries in which we operate. This means a combination of U.S.-based HR associates spending a great deal of time abroad, and overseas-based HR associates working closely with them.

A Pipeline for Growth

The second change in our HR focus has been in the area of managing growth. Fortunately, our company has been growing by leaps and bounds. Also fortunately, we continue to be inundated with resumes from terrific people from around the world. We receive more than 30,000 unsolicited resumes per year. Publicity on our company and the success of our last book have had two very positive effects: More people apply to work in our company, especially from outside our industry, thus broadening our horizons considerably; and those applying more closely match our company, because they have greater understanding of what we're all about.

The challenge is finding the *right* people, particularly for leadership roles. Honestly, finding great leaders is getting harder, which surely isn't news to you. It's a challenge all businesses face, and it promises to become even tougher. Our explosive growth, combined with higher expectations on the part of our company and our clients, have made this a focus of vital importance. One of the ways we approach the challenge is by continually building a pipeline of potential leaders, people who can readily step in to fill leadership roles on a moment's notice.

You'll read in great detail about something we call our Accelerated Leadership Development Program (ALDP) in Chapter 6, but a brief explanation will suffice here. The program hires potential leaders into the company (as well as prepares current associates for leadership roles) and provides intensified, customized training to get them fully up to speed and ready to take on significant responsibility. The program is so crucial to maintaining a strong pipeline of leaders that we now have three full-time associates dedicated to recruiting and selecting the best possible people for this program—that's about 6 percent of our human resources team.

In addition to building a pipeline of future associates, it's imperative to focus on retaining the associates already on board. Understanding why people join a company and why they leave it are two of the most critical pieces of information a company can have in the fight to attract and retain the best talent. A new process has helped us to capture this key information.

We conduct 30-, 60-, and 90-day follow-up interviews between human resources associates and all new hires, to track their perception of the company from the day they join through those important first three months. The process is applied to those who depart the company as well, with the same 30-, 60-, and 90-day interview format, to gain clear information as to why the person left. Multiple contacts over time have proven to yield sharply truthful information.

Establishing Core Competencies

The third shift in HR has been an increased focus on core competencies. Of course, we have always sought people who had the right skills, but today we do it with a higher degree of science. We still rely upon intuition and our guts, but we back that up with a bit more discipline.

In *The Customer Comes Second,* we wrote about some very unusual interviewing techniques we've used over the years—such as analyzing driving habits and observing people in team sports. We still believe strongly in using peculiar methods to get to the heart of what a candidate is really about, but we match those up with strong analytical evaluations as well. These new tools help us to do more consistently what we were doing before, and that's important. Years ago, we formalized our culture (which we explained in our last book) in order to capture what was special about our company, to protect it, and to ensure that it was consistent throughout the organization. We've now done the same with our hiring processes, with the help of some tools to turn gut instinct into predictable results.

We began by defining the core competencies required for success in our organization. We called upon the expertise of The Hay Group, with whom we have worked for years. The goal was to determine the core competencies necessary for employment in the company, in general; leadership roles; and individual roles throughout the organization.

To do that, our team of HR leaders and their partners from The Hay Group interviewed people throughout our company whom we identified as outstanding at what they do, to help us define what skills and traits make them so. From those assessments, as well as from interviews with company leaders, a set of core organizational competencies for all associates were identified. They include the following: (1) results orientation, (2) flexibility, (3) commitment to continuous learning and development, (4) commitment to organizational values, (5) teamwork, and (6) client focus. Then we outlined detailed explanations as to what each of these competencies meant and why they were important. Under each were specific actions to gauge success.

We'll share an overview so you can see the type of foundation we are working from. These will not necessarily be right for your organization, though we suspect they would yield positive results in any company. However, the best course of action is to develop a set for your own organization, tailored to your goals and objectives. Here's an overview of our core competencies:

Results orientation—measured by the ability to:

- Work to meet company standards.
- Work through obstacles.
- Focus on the goal.
- Set personal standards.
- Align personal goals with company strategic objectives.
- Focus on long-term business impact.

Flexibility—measured by the ability to:

- Maintain composure.
- Seek to understand (i.e., ask questions).
- Respond positively under new circumstances.

- Support changes.
- Anticipate change.
- Initiate change.

Commitment to continuous learning and development—measured by the ability to:

- Demonstrate enthusiasm for learning.
- Understand strengths and developmental needs.
- Actively pursue development opportunities.
- Share expertise and learning.
- Ensure expertise and knowledge are applied organizationally.
- Stay abreast of future requirements.

Commitment to organizational values—measured by the ability to:

- Demonstrate professionalism.
- Act in accordance with organizational values (i.e., act with respect and integrity).
- Actively support company values.
- Look for ways to integrate company values (i.e., introduce culture to new associates).
- Act as a role model for company values.
- Take a leadership role in ingraining values

Teamwork—measured by the ability to:

- Willingly cooperate.
- Place team objectives first.
- Share relevant information and learning.
- Value multiple perspectives.
- Actively support team (i.e., offer help and guidance to team members).
- Bring conflict out in the open.

Client focus—measured by the ability to:

- Follow through.
- Maintain clear communication.

- Take personal responsibility.
- Act to make things better.
- Address underlying needs.
- Apply a longer-term perspective.

These core competencies need to be mastered by all associates throughout the organization. Beyond excellence in these six areas, leadership calls for additional core competencies, which we identified as strong ability in the following: (1) lead a team, (2) develop associates, and (3) hold others accountable. Again, we'll share the criteria we use.

Lead a team—measured by the ability to:

- Treat team members fairly and objectively.
- Clarify roles and expectations.
- Promote team morale.
- Capitalize on associates' unique abilities.
- Communicate a team vision.
- Actively involve others in vision creation.

Develop associates—measured by the ability to:

- Give clear instructions.
- Provide behavioral feedback.
- Openly encourage associate development.
- Tailor coaching approach to associate circumstances.
- Proactively target learning opportunities.
- Strategically plan for long-term development of associates.

Hold others accountable—measured by the ability to:

- Give directions.
- Communicate expectations clearly.
- Set parameters.
- Expect high performance.
- Hold people accountable for their performance.
- Take action to ensure high performance.

Once the company and leadership competencies were outlined, a model was developed for each area of the company, which includes specific competency profiles for each position within our business units, and for each functional area in our CSCs. This helps us not only to find the right person for each and every position within the company, but to use the competencies in performance management as well, ensuring that we measure what really counts.

Another key benefit of the competency profiles is that they serve as a career guide for our associates. The profiles are automated, and associates can log on to PCs to see what competencies and skills are required for a specific position or area in which they wish to work. They can measure their skills against those required, and work to close any gaps. This is an important resource, because it enables associates to manage their own careers.

Tools of the Trade

When it comes to hiring, it need not be said that it's a competitive world. Companies are utilizing a wide variety of new tools to find the best people. Here are several examples of innovative practices from among our peers, including everything from matching people with competencies to being aggressive about attracting good candidates.

ERIE INSURANCE. Erie Insurance created a management competency model from interviews with a number of their successful managers. They believe these competencies keep their culture alive; in essence, they are delineating the behaviors they consider critical to their success. Here they are:

- ACHIEVEMENT GROUP: (1) entrepreneurial drive (vision, innovation, product enhancement), (2) action orientation (taking risks, tenacity), (3) efficiency orientation (setting goals, planning), (4) diagnostic orientation (research, analysis, problem identification).

- MANAGEMENT GROUP: (1) directing and delegating, (2) employee development, (3) positive expectations (instilling self-esteem, providing challenges, and introducing change).

- LEADERSHIP GROUP: (1) team effort, (2) influencing/persuasion, (3) organizational and interpersonal sensitivity, (4) concern for company values and reputation.

- PROFESSIONALISM GROUP: (1) self-confidence, (2) objectivity, (3) communication skills, (4) self-assessment and development.

Erie Insurance is one of the prime employers in their area (Erie, Pennsylvania). Keith Lane, vice president and manager, Corporate Communications, says, "For the most part, we haven't had the need for any unique recruiting strategies. We do offer bonuses for referrals for certain positions; for example, $1,000 for referring a life sales specialist. And perhaps our most unique hiring practice is nepotism. We're a firm believer that 'the apple doesn't fall far from the tree.' Since we call ourselves the Erie Family, what better way to illustrate that family spirit than by hiring other good family members?"

Erie uses a tool in the hiring process called the AVA (Activity Vector Analysis). It measures a candidate's behavior profile, and aids the company in matching a candidate's behaviors to those required for a specific job.

MARY KAY. Mary Kay is highly consensus-driven in its hiring practices. "Each vote really counts here," observes Tim Wentworth, president of International. "On the way in, you've got to meet a lot more people at Mary Kay than you would at most companies."

The "vote" Wentworth refers to doesn't necessarily come only from senior level executives. One potential candidate with sterling credentials was taken out of the running on the basis of how he treated the driver sent to greet him and the administrative staff member who scheduled his interview trip.

The company also uses a tool called the Mary Kay Human Resource Planning System (HRPS), which comprises several management tools, including a leadership profile that spells out clear expectations of what it takes to be successful in the company. The system was developed by HRVP Doug Mintmier, in conjunction with an outside consultant. It was created through in-depth interviews with top company leaders and refined through evaluations by a team of a dozen carefully selected, high potential, midlevel employees. Of the system, Doug says, "There's no doubt that the HRPS further transforms the human resource function at Mary Kay into a world-class business partner." That's exactly how HR must be viewed in the company of the future.

SOUTHWEST AIRLINES. When it comes to recruiting, Southwest Airlines is in the catbird seat. In the year following its appearance in *The 100 Best* (as one of the top 10), Southwest received more than 150,000 unsolicited applications and resumes. While they consider this a blessing, it has created three burdens on the company, the first of which is sheer administrative overload. To ease that burden, Southwest invested in a new application and resume-scanning software package. Fitting the company's style, they call it STAARS, for Southwest's Totally Awesome Applicant Resource System.

According to Kathy Pettit, director of Customers, the second challenge is "culling those applicants, through the screening and interview process, who are focused on fun and adventure, but are not at all interested in working as hard as Southwest, a cost- and productivity-conscious corporation, expects and needs for them to work."

The third challenge is identifying people with the "upbeat, team-oriented and customer-friendly personality traits that fit Southwest's organizational profile." This challenge has become so great that the company has been gearing its advertising and job descriptions toward upbeat, fun-loving applicants (while being very careful to include a blurb about "being prepared to work harder than you ever have in your life").

FEL-PRO. Fel-Pro has toughened their hiring standards. They require all shop floor employees to pass basic math and reading tests. They administer drug tests and conduct background investigations. Not surprisingly, their selection process takes longer. They hire only about 5 percent of the people they consider, but they say it's worth the extra effort. Consequently, Fel-Pro needs a high number of applicants to find the right people for their company, and that calls for creative recruiting. According to Arlis McLean, vice president of Human Resources, though being in *The 100 Best* draws potential employees to Fel-Pro, the company still must be proactive and aggressive in pursuing candidates.

To that end, they are putting together an employers council with other manufacturing firms in their geographic area. The first order of business will be to help high schools, technical schools, and community colleges shape their curricula toward what companies need. Fel-Pro figures that if 8 or 10 companies unite, they will have the critical mass necessary to effect change. They also plan to increase internships, co-ops, and job-shadowing programs.

Fel-Pro currently has a partnership with four area high schools to shape curriculum. And according to Arlis McLean, "I think we will see a trend toward increased partnerships with community colleges in the future. They are a good source for local talent, and are more flexible in directing curriculum for the needs of area businesses."

GREAT PLAINS SOFTWARE. When it comes to attracting talent, Great Plains Software isn't shy. A March 31, 1997, article in *Fortune* magazine entitled "Beating the Odds" tells a story about the determination of Great Plains founder and CEO Doug Burgum. "Burgum, it seems, will stop at nothing to get the people he wants. Vice President Scott Lozuaway-McComsey took a rather odd road to his post. A New Jersey native and a graduate of Amherst College, he knew Burgum from their bachelor days in Chicago. When Lozuaway-McComsey quit his job to ride a motorcycle cross-country for a few months, he stopped in Fargo for lunch one day. 'Doug asked me if I wanted to see Great Plains,' he recalls. 'So I arrive in my leather, and he has job interviews set up for me.' A year later he returned in a moving truck."

Great Plains also relies upon their employees, who make referrals and recruit their friends and family to work there. The company's employee base includes 35-plus couples and many siblings. Their people-friendly approach permeates their recruiting. When advertising for employment, they have found that ads including employee photos have the best results.

Their sales ads have the same homespun feel. One shows a rolling prairie meadow with a white picket fence and a barn in the background. In front of the fence are several pairs of faded, worn blue jeans hanging on a clothesline. Alongside the jeans is a pair of pinstripe suit pants. The caption reads, "Fargo, North Dakota. Home to a financial software company that combines new technology with good old-fashioned hard work."

LANDS' END. Lands' End enjoys the status of employer of choice in Dodgeville, Wisconsin, and surrounding communities; nevertheless they have some added incentives to attract employees. They provide busing for students from a local university town. And because their best recruitment source is their own employees, they make it worth their employees' while to help the company find good people. Lands' End offers a $35 bonus for referring a temporary employee and a $500 to $1,000 bonus for referring a full-time employee.

They also sponsor some unique events. For example, they draw names, out of the referrals, for tickets to a Green Bay Packers game. The company buses all the winners to the game. They also have cash drawings where employees can win jackpots of up to $1,000. Such activities work for Lands' End. They increased their 1997 application flow by more than 1,000 above the previous year, even though unemployment was an historically low 2.5 percent. And even though they are located in a community of only 3,800, they employ 4,500 at their main location. To meet the needs of their peak season, they need to recruit an additional 2,600 people each year.

BETH ISRAEL DEACONESS MEDICAL CENTER. Beth Israel Deaconess Medical Center has an innovative program to address hard-to-fill positions. They provide skills training in the two categories that are hardest to fill: surgical technicians and secretaries. For both these groups, demand far exceeds supply of available candidates, so Beth Israel Deaconess trains to create what they need.

The training is open to both current employees and members of surrounding communities. Through formal, didactic training, current employees are given the opportunity to grow into these positions, and it's also a great recruiting tool for external candidates.

HEWITT ASSOCIATES. Hewitt Associates depends heavily on its Associate Referral Program to find strong people. In 1997, over 35 percent of the company's new hires were referred by current employees. Another Hewitt success tip is their stubbornness about quality: "We first focus on whether a candidate shares our values, then look at what skills and competencies they possess—judging their ability to learn today and into the future. We look for potential to learn. We're very selective in our hiring process, and we won't compromise our standards even when pressed by business need."

Hewitt also incorporates the use of videoconferencing in hiring. One HR associate says, "With our new videoconferencing abilities, we were able to interview a candidate in Asia from our Lincolnshire, Illinois, offices. We then followed up with a phone interview, and could make an offer, which the candidate accepted."

SAS INSTITUTE. SAS Institute's greatest source of external applicants is current employee referrals. Although the Institute doesn't have a formal referral program, and employees are not rewarded for making referrals, according to Vice President of Human Resources David Russo, "The employees of the Institute are committed to the company and have a positive feeling about the work environment, so they are motivated to invite and encourage others to join the team."

The SAS Institute Human Resources team regularly reviews applications to look for trends in employment history and referrals. They use this information to make decisions about future advertising and recruiting efforts.

Bending without Breaking

In recent years, we have opened our company to a world of talent by adopting flexible work configurations. We certainly didn't invent the concept; in fact, I consider us to be a late entrant into the market. Perhaps that makes me a good source for an objective look at the benefits. I fought the idea for some time and, I believe, with some sound reasoning. In an editorial piece I contributed several years ago to a trade magazine, I took a negative stance on incorporating home-based workers into the company. Here were my primary concerns: (1) lack of positive cultural influence, and (2) lack of an immediate support network.

I feared that associates working out of their homes would miss the camaraderie and inclusiveness that are a major part of our company and have such a positive effect on our service to our clients. And to a certain extent, off-site workers do miss some of the day-to-day aspects of our culture. But through the vast array of communication vehicles we have available to us, they manage to stay up to the minute on the latest developments, and to stay in touch with their fellow associates. Periodic face-to-face meetings also help to keep them in the fold.

I also worried that telecommuters wouldn't be able to lean over to the person nearest them to ask for help, or to pop into someone's office with a question. But I've learned, through our farm structure and the ability for one office to come to the immediate aid of another across the country, to trust that help is just a phone call away. It's people and their willingness and ability to help their colleagues that count, not where they are located.

The ideal location for our associates to work still is in a Rosenbluth International location, surrounded by associates and friends, but we're not going to let some terrific talent slip past the company in order to maintain that ideal. And this has added a new dimension to our human resources initiatives. True, as more people work from virtual offices, it presents challenges. But our HR group is on top of those issues, ensuring that far-flung workers are very much a part of the company.

Currently, Rosenbluth has about 90 people telecommuting (2 to 3 percent of our workforce) on either a part-time or full-time basis. Some associates telecommute part of the time and work in the office the rest. When someone switches to a telecommuting role, his or her salary, benefits, obligations, and conditions of employment don't change. He or she is treated the same as any other associate of the company with respect to these issues, as well as to opportunity.

If someone wants to telecommute, he or she is responsible for submitting a proposal to his or her leader, who ultimately makes the decision as to whether or not it makes good business sense. The requirements are straightforward. Associates must provide a proposal, agree to and sign a telecommuter's agreement, and have a "fully proficient" or better performance level. During work hours, they can't be the primary caregiver of any children, adults, or elders.

Telecommuters can use either their own equipment or the company's. We outline hardware and software standards, which helps facilitate support, reduces cost, and enables us to keep an eye on new technologies that will support growth. We have an asset management database to account for off-site equipment. From a telecommunications perspective, our satellite associates can use a calling card, dial into our network via a toll-free number, or we can install additional phone lines, depending upon what makes the most sense.

For companies considering telecommuting options, it's critical to outline all aspects of the arrangement (e.g., responsibilities, expectations, reporting specifications and frequency, measurement criteria, and reimbursable expenses) in advance of allowing someone to telecommute.

There is considerable expense in setting up a telecommuting site, and for that reason, we have established a sliding scale of cost-sharing with our associates who work from home. If they utilize the site for over a year and a half, we pick up the entire implementation cost. If they telecommute for less than six months, they assume the set-up costs.

Our leaders with telecommuters on their teams are careful to review goals, manage by results, and keep the lines of communication flowing, using e-mail, voice mail, conference calls, faxes, and company mailings. We require telecommuters to attend staff meetings and recurrent training. Additionally, both leaders and off-site associates participate in a five-hour workshop on telecommuting, created by our learning and development group. A follow-up program is used to address any issues that emerge after the group begins telecommuting, and is an effective way to gather input for future off-site associates.

To help telecommuters and their leaders, a multidiscipline team developed a 25-page telecommuting guide, which includes everything from policy to equipment standards to ergonomic guidelines for work comfort, even netiquette (network etiquette). The guide also features a telecommuter relocation checklist to help us ensure we've covered everything.

Flexibility: Watchword of the Future

While we were venturing into alternative work configurations, so were our peers. Here are some of their experiences.

LANDS' END. Flexibility is the name of the game at Lands' End. They offer almost unlimited options to their employees, including 23 start times; the option to select their hours between 6:00 A.M. and 6:00 P.M.; a reduced workweek option for salaried staff, and two different compressed workweek options. In addition, Lands' End gives their people the opportunity to work on short-term projects in different areas, or to work between two departments (more than 1,000 people work two part-time jobs in two departments). They have remote work options (for the 1997 holiday season, more than 35 sales agents worked out of their homes).

Lands' End also offers some 1,400 fully benefited part-time jobs. This benefits package is exactly the same for full- and part-time employees. Recently, they added several benefits for their flexible part-time (seasonal) staff, such as a catalog discount, educational assistance, use of the company's activity center year-round for their families, and the opportunity to purchase medical insurance at a reduced rate.

ALAGASCO. Alagasco has had a flexible work plan in place since 1996, and many employees take advantage of flexible hours or the sharing of expanded work time with other employees. Supervisors and department heads are given the authority to work out these flexible arrangements with their employees without any higher level of approval.

BETH ISRAEL DEACONESS MEDICAL CENTER. Beth Israel Deaconess Medical Center's Senior Vice President of Human Resources, Laura Avakian, says, "We believe strongly that the care for our patients is enhanced when employees have been given help dealing with personal hassles that can affect their ability to focus on giving freely of themselves." To that end, a number of departments at the medical center have instituted part-time, work-from-home, and job-sharing programs. Work-at-home arrangements are typically made when staff are easing their way back from a leave of absence. The nature of the work is generally clerical.

Beth Israel Deaconess also has an in-house, temporary pool for clerical and administrative jobs that allows employees to have flexibility in both the type of work and hours of work they do. And, like a few of the companies we talked with, they have extended most full-time benefits to employees working at least 36 hours.

NORTHWESTERN MUTUAL. Having offered variable working hours for several decades, Northwestern Mutual Life recently extended employee flexibility by starting a voluntary Alternative Work Schedule (AWS) program in departments needing expanded business hours. This provides improved service for customers while offering employees greater flexibility and more personal time.

Some 150 employees are currently on alternative work schedules, with compressed workweeks being the most popular option. For example, Barbara Mosley, a service associate in the company's New Business Department, says that in addition to giving her more time with her husband and their two children, AWS also lets her help her husband in his career as a self-employed computer consultant.

Another Northwestern Mutual employee, Bret Blizzard, a senior disability benefits analyst, says, "My wife Cindy and I have two young children, and like a lot of other young families, we view spending time with them as the best investment we could possibly make. Three years ago, Cindy left her job in importing, which required long hours and extensive travel, to take a part-time clerical position, so she could be with our kids more. We moved to an older, smaller house, closer to our families; pared expenses to just the essentials; and simplified our lives. But now that I was the family breadwinner, I spent a lot of my time working and picking up overtime. I also had an hour commute each way. I rarely had time for other things.

"As soon as it became feasible, I opted for an AWS of working four days a week. I've designated my day off as 'Dad's Day.' Last Friday it was a movie and McDonald's. This Friday is a trip to Green Bay for a Packers practice (I hate it when that happens!) and to an amusement park. My kids are constantly asking me, 'Is it Friday yet?' AWS has given me a much better balance between my work and family.

"I've had no difficulty fulfilling my job duties, and my customers have adapted to my schedule just fine. They have options for assistance when I am out, and my West Coast clients know they can (and do) call me late in the day. As you can see, AWS is working well for me, from both a personal and professional standpoint."

ERIE INSURANCE. Erie Insurance has had employees working out of their homes for many years. They find it means employees are closer to their customers, and helps them provide quicker, more efficient service. In fact, today, approximately 30 percent of Erie's employees work out of their homes.

HALLMARK. Hallmark Cards' Work and Family Services Department facilitates alternative work arrangements for Hallmark employees. Hallmark works hard to keep part-timers fully integrated in the staff. Parents can job-share until their children are of school age or longer, and then return to the full-time workforce with their careers in full throttle. Several of Hallmark's unit directors came from the part-time ranks, and Chairman Donald Hall is supported by a job-sharing team to fulfill his secretarial needs.

SAS INSTITUTE. A SAS Institute employee, interviewed for a 1997 television news story on the company, said, "We're not rigidly held to certain hours. If you have an appointment in the middle of the day, it's very flexible, and people are on the honor system to make up any time that they miss."

Employees can choose to begin their workday as early as 7:30 A.M. or as late as 10:30 A.M. The lunch "hour" can be extended, so people can take advantage of the fitness center and still have time to eat lunch in the cafe. SAS Institute employees can adjust their hours to meet changes in their personal lives. Debbie, a 13-year Institute employee, began working part-time in the fall of 1997, so she could pick her child up after school, and be there for homework, piano lessons, and soccer practice. When another long-time employee, Denise, adopted a third child, she changed from full-time to part-time. Now that her youngest child is older, she has returned to working full-time.

In addition to the opportunity to modify work schedules to meet personal and family needs, employees can take a leave of absence to return to school or complete a degree program. Work arrangements are set on a case-by-case basis.

Some Institute employees in the regional offices are home-based, and employees in all offices take advantage of remote-access technology from time to time, allowing them to work on projects when they can't be in the office.

HEWITT ASSOCIATES. At Hewitt, associates consistently indicate, through surveys and other feedback mechanisms, that increased workplace flexibility improves their personal satisfaction, as well as their work contribution. In addition, the complexities of their business (global, 24-hour service) require them to consider more flexible, adaptive ways to meet their clients' needs. The answer is not only a more flexible work-place, but a carefully planned one.

Hewitt Associates has had much success by following these princi-ples: (1) Business needs drive the decision-making process about flexi-ble work configurations. (2) An associate's performance history must be strong and clearly demonstrate maturity (a minimum of one to two years' experience required). (3) It is the associate's responsibility to develop a business proposal that accounts for the firm's business needs and his or her individual needs. (4) It is the manager's responsibility to determine whether the proposal makes business sense for the work area and the practice/region.

One Hewitt associate shared her personal experience: "At my previous employer, employees were treated as expendable assets—'use them up and throw them away.' When I had my fill of that environment, I contacted a search firm and said, 'I don't care what I do, I just want to work for an employer that treats its people with respect.' She immediately suggested Hewitt. I stay here because Hewitt lives up to its reputation. I've been here nine years, and Hewitt has been extremely accommodating in allowing me the flexibility to work part-time, at home or in the office, at hours that are convenient for me, while still giving me all the responsibility I want."

Balancing Act

We won't be the first to tell you that the public mood has shifted over the last decade, especially the last five years. However, once again business lags behind the shifting public mentality. Futurist Faith Popcorn predicted a values shift toward emphasis on the quality of life. As she predicted, both the baby boomers and generations X and Y are increasingly preoccupied with fulfillment, relationships, and other "softer" issues. That carries into their choice of employment, their values on the job, and their attitude in the workplace. The overwhelming success of Dilbert, symbol of the back-lash against corporate abuse, points to this transforming public direction.

The Dilbert Zone Web site gets more than 1.5 million hits per day, and Dilbert's creator, Scott Adams, receives 300 e-mail messages on an average day, according to *Newsweek* (August 12, 1996). In the *Newsweek* article on the phenomenon, author Mike Hammer (*Reengineering the Corporation*) says, "It's not a comic strip; it's a documentary—it provides the best win-dow into reality of corporate life that I've ever seen." The cover design carries the title "Work Is Hell" and features Dilbert with a caption that reads simply, "Help."

This is how too many people feel coming to work every day. The primary culprits are workplace pressure, and a lack of respect and basic kindness and consideration on the part of employers. We address this in Chapter 7, on culture. Another aspect of workplace misery is the inability of companies to address the very real and growing stress our nonwork life has on us, in the workplace.

Great Plains Software: Finding Balance

When Great Plains Software conducted its first employee survey, people said they needed better balance between their work and personal lives. One of the ways the company addresses that need is through a course entitled First Things First, created by the Covey Institute, and based upon Stephen Covey's book of the same name. Great Plains Software trainers have been certified to conduct this course in life leadership for all of the company's employees, and it has even been extended to family members.

Our HR group has been monitoring and addressing this growing trend for well over a decade and has had solutions to address it for as long. The group has seen an increasing number of people who made a lot more money elsewhere join our company because they sought meaning and balance. We look at our associates in a whole-life context. We realize that it's ludicrous to believe they can check their personal lives and responsibilities at the door when they show up for work, so we help them address those issues and provide support wherever we can.

At the same time, we have seen a trend toward people taking on greater responsibility within the company, as well as in their personal lives. So it's not enough just to offer support. Companies have to worry about their people and proactively address their potential overload.

Our HR group works with a variety of outside companies to provide a number of helpful resources to our people anywhere in the world, at no charge to the associate. For example, associates receive newsletters addressing childcare and parenting issues, eldercare and health issues, and helpful hints for achieving better balance. They have access to toll-free numbers for advice and resources on a vast array of issues they may be facing in their lives.

We also have a Work/Life Station, which includes a listing of available materials to help associates. It is housed at our corporate headquarters; associates from around the world can receive information via fax. We intend to expand the program globally. At our companywide meeting in August 1997, a Work/Life Station was set up for all associates to visit, to ensure they were aware the resource was available to them, and to encourage its use.

These initiatives take time, focus, and money, but they are well worth the investment in our most precious asset—our people.

Hallmark Cards: Achieving Peace of Mind

Hallmark Cards' Work and Family Services Department was established in 1990, with three primary areas of focus: family care assistance, counseling and education, and alternative work arrangements. The underlying principle behind the program is to help employees achieve peace of mind at home, so they are free to concentrate on their work while at work.

The company publishes materials to help employees fully utilize their benefits, for key events like marriage, births, home-buying, and caring for aging parents. They hold Lunch and Learn brown bag seminars on life issues, and parents who work at Hallmark can schedule on-site, one-on-one consultations with a child behavior specialist through The Doctor Is In program to discuss child behavior and development issues.

Hallmark's Moment's Notice program accommodates employees' children on school "snow days" or when they are ill. The company works with a local day school, which keeps spaces open for Hallmarker kids, and Hallmark subsidizes part of the cost. To provide care for sick children, the company struck a partnership with six area hospitals to care for the kids. The first day is free, and the cost of the remaining days is split between Hallmark and the employee.

One of the company's nicest perks is take-home dinners for employees, available at an on-site deli. Diane has a sister who worked at Hallmark for 11 years, and the two used to eat those Hallmark dinners several times a week; they can personally attest to what a terrific benefit it is.

FEL-PRO: ADDRESSING PERSONAL NEEDS. Fel-Pro also has a number of work/life benefits for its employees. Like Hallmark, they offer care for ill children of their staff. The service, through an outside resource, sends a trained caregiver to the employee's home for up to five days per year, so the employee can return to work. Fel-Pro pays for the majority of the care, asking employees to pay only a portion.

Fel-Pro also offers a "brown bag" seminar series, at lunch and after work, on parenting topics; an on-site day-care center, subsidized by the company; tutoring services for employees' children with special learning needs; and counseling for older children on how to choose a college.

One of the most unique work/life benefits at Fel-Pro is Triple R, the company's 220-acre nature and recreation center. Triple R is available for use every day of the year, and employees can each bring up to nine guests. Two terrific programs at Triple R include an eight-week summer day camp for employees' children and individual "mini-farms," where employees are provided a 20' × 20' tract of preplowed land and gardening tools to create their own farm. (Of course, we like that idea.)

Valuing Diversity: A Way of Life

My children, 5, 6, 7, and 14 years of age, play and go to school with children of all races, religions, and ethnic backgrounds. If I mentioned the word "diversity" to them, and the need for it to flourish and be celebrated in business, they'd probably look at me as if I were nuts. Fact is, I'd have to spend the next two years explaining to them why business isn't diversity-rich to begin with, and why business must understand and embrace those who look or think differently.

Why would all this seem so strange to them? Because the kids they play and go to school with are friends. And that's that. The other stuff (race, color, religion, etc.) doesn't influence their decisions; they don't use it as criteria for friendship and inclusion. They must think businesspeople are weird.

The key word is friendship. If businesses treated their people like friends, diversity and all its beauty would shine, giving companies a competitive advantage for their people, customers, and all who were touched by it. I've always felt kids could make great business decisions. Now I know it's true.

In a 1996 "state of the company" letter to my associates, I wrote about diversity. The letter read, in part, "An area of the company that I feel we must always focus on is diversity. This is not just because it is the right thing to do, and it is, but because it will make us a greater company. I know our hearts and minds are in the right place; we just need more action.

"Rosenbluth International is committed to creating and supporting an environment conducive to valuing and optimizing differences and similarities among our associates and clients worldwide. Our global diversity initiative encompasses three primary focal points:

- *Linking diversity to our corporate objectives and success measures.*
- *Ensuring that our corporate processes, practices, training programs, and communication reflect our commitment.*
- *Offering diversity awareness and skills development programs for all associates."*

"Diversity is not a program—we see it as a way of life, the way we do business—and thus, the principles are consistently instilled and maintained in our daily operations and interactions."

To achieve our diversity goals, Rosenbluth has set some key objectives:

- Establish and support a climate that values and promotes diversity.
- Define and communicate our diversity position to our associates, clients, and partners.
- Raise awareness and offer tools to help our associates work effectively in and manage a diverse culture.
- Equip our leaders and human resources personnel with the skills and tools necessary to model and promote a diverse environment.
- Demonstrate our diversity commitment, top down, and ensure that communications, policies, and business objectives reflect our commitment.
- Ensure that diversity is reflected at all levels in our organization.

Though diversity is the responsibility of every associate in the company, its leadership rests on the shoulders of our director of Cultural Diversity, who reports directly to me. She has a number of initiatives under way that address diversity management from a variety of perspectives.

Diversity Programs at Alagasco and Hallmark: Valuing Differences

At Alagasco, the company's diversity initiative is one of the most popular with employees. It includes four key elements. The first is a workshop entitled Valuing Differences. This two-day program is held off-site, for 25 people at a time. All company employees will attend, and nearly 1,000 have completed it so far.

The course is designed to make employees aware of and appreciative of the unique contribution each employee can make toward the company's success. It also promotes understanding and acceptance as a vital part of working in teams.

The second element of the initiative is a day-long class called Managing Diversity, which is taught to management and supervisory staff. Its role is to remind those with leadership responsibilities how important the differences are that each employee brings to the table. While the Valuing Differences course teaches awareness and appreciation, Managing Diversity takes that a step further, toward making diversity a strategic strength for the company.

Alagasco's third major diversity initiative is its Diversity Council, made up of employee volunteers, who review business-related diversity issues. The council meets regularly with the president of the company to discuss these issues, which also serves as a good sounding board. Approximately 15 employees serve on the council for a specified term.

The fourth element, the Diversity Grant Program, is designed to let employees identify issues in their work areas and then develop a program to address them. Programs selected for implementation are supported by cash grants, and are run by the employees.

Hallmark Cards has had a corporate diversity department since 1992, and the company addresses all forms of diversity, from the traditional (ethnic, gender, age, etc.) to the less often addressed (geography, employment status, and thinking style). In 1993, the company formed a Corporate Diversity Council, made up of senior managers from each division, and upon which the chairman of the company sits.

This council determined nine inaugural initiatives: (1) education and training (managers are trained to teach courses in their divisions); (2) communication (including managers' packets to facilitate discussions);

(3) executive action (leaders setting the right example); (4) employee career development planning (including mentoring); (5) management style (leaders must be able to work with diverse groups); (6) HR policies (including compensation and benefits); (7) commitment to the business rationale (committing the resources to make it a priority); (8) developing assessment tools; and (9) employee involvement (including task forces, a multicultural exchange group, and networking groups of employees with common interests). In addition, the company has an Ethnic Business Center, which creates products for minority markets.

We broadly define diversity to reflect both primary factors (race, age, gender, abilities, sexual orientation) and secondary factors (education, economic status, geographical region, job title, etc.). As we continue to expand globally, the issue of diversity becomes a prism of dimensions. We are learning about different cultures, and we need to raise awareness of potential biases. Initiatives such as mentoring, training, communication, and measurement become even more critical. (Details on our programs can be found in Chapter 8, on global expansion.)

Our director of Cultural Diversity has a team of "diversity ambassadors" whom she has trained to know as much as she does about diversity issues and opportunities. She says, "Ultimately, the diversity role should be drawn into the culture—absorbed the way quality has been. Eventually, we see everyone as ambassadors, but to get there we need change agents, so we put together a team to lead the way."

Though we have always been a company dedicated to equal opportunity for all, and an organization that celebrates diversity, we know we need to be more aggressive. We aspire to create and maintain an environment with no glass ceilings and no glass walls. This goal has the priority status it deserves and we'll be a much richer company for it.

Human Resources in the Boardroom: A Summary

- The Human Resources role should be a strategic one. It belongs in the boardroom, and not on the sidelines. The more involved HR is in strategy, throughout a company, the better equipped it will be to recognize future needs and fill them.

- To ensure that you're hiring the right people, the first step is to staff your HR team with role models. These are the first contacts potential employees have with your organization, and they serve as ongoing advocates for your employee base.

- Define the major areas of focus for your human resources team. Ours are (1) global thinking, (2) building a pipeline, (3) core competencies, (4) flexible work configurations, (5) heightened emphasis on work/life issues, and (6) diversity as a way of life.

- To maintain a global focus, everyone in the company (particularly HR) must continually ask, "Does this make sense globally?"

- One of the most effective ways to build a pipeline of future leaders is to institute a rapid leadership development program that encompasses intense, real-world experience. To keep our Accelerated Leadership Development Program brimming with outstanding talent, our HR team dedicates 6 percent of their staff to finding highly qualified candidates for the program.

- Keeping current associates is probably more important than finding new ones. Our 30-60-90-day follow-up program for new associates and those who depart the company further strengthens our retention. Through it, we learn how we are measuring up to our new associates' expectations, as well as why people leave the company. Repeated intermittent checks yield sharply truthful information.

- It's critical to define the core competencies required for success in your organization, and to spell them out clearly for all associates. We worked with an outside consultant to outline ours for (1) employment in the company, (2) leadership roles, and (3) individual roles in the organization. Each includes specific ways to measure success. These competencies can be used for hiring, performance management, and career planning.

- Be open to flexible work configurations. It may not always mean the ideal work setting, but insisting upon traditional work arrangements limits a company's access to some terrific talent. Managed in the right way, a flexible program can increase productivity, lower overhead, and reduce the stress levels among your workforce.

- As employers, we must face work/life issues head-on. These issues are here to stay and like it or not, they affect the way people work. Human resources staff can call upon the services of a growing number of outside firms specializing in providing assistance and resources to support your associates in their personal and professional lives.

- Diversity should be approached not as a program but as a way of life. For the growing global company, geographical and cultural issues should be addressed along with traditional diversity issues (race, gender, etc.). To ensure progress, diversity should be linked to corporate objectives and success measures. Corporate processes, practices, training programs, and communications must reflect a company's commitment. Diversity awareness and skills development programs must be offered to all associates.

4

Maximizing Brainpower

There's a Cinderella story to be told in all businesses today. Not the one you think. It's not about a small company making it big overnight. It's not about a once-unnoticed employee quickly rising to the top, although that's closer to what we're talking about. This is the story of hidden assets and unfulfilled opportunities being discovered within the corporate world through the science of human capital management. It's probably more often referred to as "intellectual capital management," but as an organization, we tend to focus on the human side of things. So we call it "human capital management," and it's changing the way we work.

It's estimated that anywhere from 50 to 90 percent of a company's value is in its intangibles—employees, ideas, customers. Yet how many companies have a true reading on what those assets are, or a plan to protect and maximize them? At Rosenbluth, we are particularly interested in harnessing the creativity and potential of our people—every last one of them—sharing it with all of our associates and clients, and growing more of it.

Exactly what are we talking about here? We're talking about *really* understanding what skills exist throughout the company, who has them, and making sure each of those skills is fully utilized. Getting the right people in your organization isn't enough. The strongest skills from all areas of the company have to be put to work on the right projects, regardless of job description or department. The point is, those skills must be treated as fluid, not static, assets. Skill sets are constantly changing. Initiative and opportunity enable some to move ahead of others in specific areas and, in general, companies just don't keep tabs on what each individual's current capabilities are.

There are myriad cases of people joining companies in an area where there happened to be openings, even though they possessed expertise in another area. That expertise is wasted. In the typical company, the person's current manager will want to keep that brainpower within his or her department, and not necessarily where it truly belongs.

Or there's the person who has been diligently pursuing courses in a given discipline, but has been pigeonholed into the area in which he or she currently works. Any newly acquired knowledge is not being called upon. Or perhaps a person's work with a volunteer organization, community group, or place of worship has broadened his or her skills in a given area significantly, but that person never gets to use those new skills in the workplace.

The United Negro College Fund (UNCF) slogan is a classic: "A mind is a terrible thing to waste." That waste is epidemic throughout corporations, so this chapter is about the potential to maximize the intellectual riches within organizations. It tells our company's story (our journey into the intellectual capital discipline, the creation of our human capital role, its current programs and plans for the future) and includes a look into the human capital initiatives of other 100 Best companies.

Intellectual Capital 101

We stumbled upon the concept of intellectual capital management before we even knew what it really was. Around 1992 we began using the tagline "The thought leaders in travel" (which we still use). We knew instinctively that our power came from the minds of our people, and that their brainpower was responsible for everything we were able to accomplish. We recognized it, and valued it, but we didn't have a science to perpetuate and maximize it. Then, we ran across a study entitled "Perfecting the Labor Market: The New Social Contract at Leading American Corporations," by The Corporate Leadership Council (a private research organization in Washington, D.C. that talked about the importance of focusing on the real value of a company: knowledge, skill, expertise. We looked at our ability to gauge these assets, and decided this was an area that warranted serious attention.

This study made the point that there were effective labor shortages in selected areas of companies because technology, product cycles, and marketplaces had become so accelerated in nearly all industries, while employee capabilities had changed slowly. The study also talked about a "no-resting-spots" policy, reducing the "stickiness" of jobs, letting talent flow to where it's most needed. Therein was the basis for human capital management—the maximization of resources.

An article in the June 3, 1991, issue of *Fortune* magazine read, "Most companies are filled with intelligence, but too much of it resides in the computer whiz who speaks a mile a minute in no known language, in the brash account manager who racks up great numbers but has alienated everyone, or in files moved to the basement. Or it's retired and gone fishing." This same article addressed the enormous advantage intellectual capital affords: "The U.S.-led victory over Iraq—the most lopsided war between big armies on record—was a direct result of the intellectual supremacy of allied arms and doctrine, not superior numbers of troops or tons of TNT." In the end, what counts is not necessarily the amount of resources an organization has, but how they utilize those resources.

Managing Human Capital

To harness brainpower and put it to work, you have to know where it is. Every company needs a process by which to measure it, along with a plan to maximize and share it throughout the organization. Without that, it's like money in a mattress. Time and inactivity eats away at knowledge the same way inflation chips away at money. And there's always the danger it will leave the organization.

A lot of scientific jargon can be heard in the halls of human capital management, but two very commonsense lessons are at its core: It's important to not "lose the recipe," and storytelling is a great way to spread knowledge. We were reminded of these lessons when we sat down to write this book.

Our organizational redesign was one of the most significant, most effective, and most memorable events in our company's century-plus history. But when we began to gather information for the chapter on it, to our surprise, we found our files, records, and official accounts of the event sorely lacking. The best information came from swapping stories, handwritten notes in files, and pages from daytimers. The personal accounts explain it best, and if we hadn't written this book, those stories might have been lost forever. How many companies are in this position? Probably most. We're too busy *making* history to record it, and therefore, we run the risk of losing the recipe.

We see great potential in intellectual capital, and so have designated resources to pursue it. Our new human capital function is separate from human resources, though they work closely together. The new role helps us keep up to the minute on changing skill sets throughout our associate base of more than 5,000, and direct those skills to where they can make the strongest impact. This keeps the company fast, fresh, and working to its maximum potential.

The Human Capital Agenda

The degree and direction of activity varied widely among our peers in *The 100 Best,* with regard to human capital management. Here's a sampling of what they're up to.

ALAGASCO. Alagasco uses an interesting metaphor to describe their approach to human capital maximization. According to CEO Mike Warren, "Instead of employees climbing up the ladder in their particular area or department, we are doing a lot more 'scaffold climbing.' We now look at the organization as a scaffold, with employees moving laterally throughout. This enables them to learn more about the entire organization. We are trying to put people where they will be the most productive, and we are aligning personal compensation with corporate performance." (The company's 401(k) and ESOP plans have paralleled employee long-term interests with long-term corporate success.)

BETH ISRAEL DEACONESS MEDICAL CENTER. Beth Israel doesn't have a human capital department, but since their late-1996 merger, they have created new structures for knowledge sharing. For example, teams report success stories and innovations at monthly managers meetings (story swapping is a key component of human capital management), as well as in the medical center newspaper and the president's weekly newsletter. Problem-solving ideas are discussed in focus groups and department retreats. A hotline and an e-mail box have been set up for cost-savings and other ideas.

USAA. Like Beth Israel Deaconess, USAA doesn't have a formal "human capital" role, but it does have a number of initiatives to maximize knowledge. According to Bill Tracy, senior vice president of Human Resources, its lineup of activities includes business process reviews (extensive self-evaluations to seek improvement) and best-practices reviews (visits to outstanding companies seeking ideas on the best possible use of resources).

MARY KAY. Mary Kay's new Human Resource Planning System (explained in Chapter 3) is the cornerstone of the company's human capital management initiative. Their HRPS helps identify current and future talent needs, and directs the company to where human resource investments are needed. Similar to Rosenbluth's associate database, Mary Kay's HRPS is designed to provide companywide data on employees' desired career paths, desired locations, and other information that helps the company place people in the best possible roles.

SAS INSTITUTE. After much research on the subject, SAS Institute elected not to have a formalized human capital management program. And their approach works for them. Here are two stories that illustrate strong idea-generation and brainpower at work.

A new division, Business Solutions, was the direct result of employee innovation. SAS Institute employees in human resources and finance saw a gap in appropriate computer tools for their segment of the organization, so the company responded by creating packages to fill that gap, internally and externally. This created an entirely new division and growth area for the company.

Similarly, an engineer in the Institute's video production group went to the company president with an idea for taking multiple streams of video and manipulating them via computer, to create a feeling of walking through, for instance, an office or building. This technology allows the designer to create a three-dimensional effect using video rather than generating it with graphics. Thus, SouthPeak Interactive—a business unit dedicated to developing the newest generation of computer games—was born.

NORTHWESTERN MUTUAL LIFE. Maximizing each individual's contribution is what drives the human capital effort. At Northwestern Mutual Life, it has been a long-standing tradition to give current employees a shot at "Cinderella" jobs, as evident in the following account:

Mike Miller, a long-time employee in the company's food service operation, had a passion and a gift for photography. When a job opened for a company photographer position, Mike made a pitch and gained an interview with Bill Drehfal, the head of the Creative Services Division. Bill remembers that the "portfolio" of photographic samples Mike showed him was a collection in albums, frames, and cardboard boxes. But Bill saw real talent in that collection, and so did Communications Vice President Ward White.

Mike joined the photo unit, and literally went from stockroom detail one day to photographing company President James D. Ericson the next. He is now in a position where he can be highly creative every day. In addition to being a great opportunity for Mike, it sent an important message to other employees in the company who thought they might never stand a chance at a different career path.

HEWITT ASSOCIATES. Hewitt Associates views knowledge management as "a combination of strategies, behaviors, and systems to capture, share, create, and leverage the intellectual capital of the firm." They recognize that as a service firm, their only real assets are their people, knowledge, and skills. Their approach is to "value each individual for the experience and knowledge they bring to the firm, and entrust them with powerful information tools to help them share that knowledge and experience with others." One of their strategic tools is access to Lotus Notes databases firmwide. They share what they know across practice, office, and geographic boundaries.

One associate illustrated the power of these tools. "A client in Switzerland needing an update on plan costs for their new Hong Kong flex plan called and e-mailed me. They called me around noon and needed an answer by the following morning—their time. I wasn't in the office at the time, but got their message by voice mail and by e-mail on my laptop. It was already midnight in Hong Kong, where all the information was. I sent an urgent e-mail to another associate who was in Beijing but happened to be on Notes on his laptop when I sent my message. He worked on it for a while and had a spreadsheet to me a couple of hours later. We made modifications back and forth over the next few hours. I e-mailed it to the client. They had it by 4 A.M., their time. I figure that file traveled 40,000 miles in several hours. A true example of how we connect globally."

LANDS' END. Lands' End has identified human capital management as one of the company's six initiatives upon which its senior management team will concentrate. They tell us, "There probably aren't too many things our senior group can spend their time on that would be as important to the company as this."

A number of activities support this initiative, including (1) quarterly meetings where the CEO shares with employees how the company is doing and what's ahead; (2) monthly communication meetings with the CEO, CFO, or COO, where people are chosen randomly to hear what's going on and to share ideas to make Lands' End better; (3) "Down the Road" presentations by the CEO that focus on where Lands' End wants to be in the future (the two-hour talk has been given to all departments); (4) "Farm Agenda," an off-site meeting (several days) for key merchandising and creative people to discuss "who Lands' End is" with the company's founder and previous and current top management.

Getting Started

At Rosenbluth, human capital maximization was launched by creating a new position, director of Human Capital Management. We felt strongly that an organization of our size and scope that places its people (and therefore, their contributions) as its top priority required a full-time, dedicated resource. (If that doesn't suit the profile of your organization, explore it as a project, utilizing a short-term, temporary, or part-time resource.)

In March 1996, our director of Human Capital Management commissioned a study by the aforementioned Corporate Leadership Council, entitled "Identifying and Developing Key Value Creators." Researchers conducted extensive interviews with companies across a variety of industries that were leaders in the human capital field. From it they concluded that key responsibilities of the human capital role should include leadership, development of metrics for intellectual capital, mapping information flow, and aligning organizational competencies with business purposes.

We decided to focus our efforts on the *human* capital aspects of the field (as opposed to the structural, i.e., patents, processes, and trademarks). Depending upon the industry you're in, your priorities may differ from ours. Our director of Human Capital Management is involved in an organization called the Intellectual Capital Management Network (ICM Group). He finds that most members are from the legal or engineering areas of their companies, because their initial focus is on their structural assets, such as patents, whereas ours is clearly on our human assets.

The way we see it, probably 90 percent of the value of the company goes home each night and on weekends, and we have no guarantee that they'll come back. A lot of companies try to capture the benefits of their brainpower by putting legal boundaries around it. But this creates a tug of war over ideas and intellectual property.

Certainly these issues are important, but the real value is in the annuity factor—not just today's idea but tomorrow's and all the ideas to come in the years ahead. So we focus on taking stock of where the brainpower is, making sure it's being used in the right places, nurturing it, developing more of it, and ensuring that its benefits are shared throughout the company.

Our human capital plan includes the following elements: (1) an associate skill database, (2) a project prioritization process, (3) a business-planning database of client needs, and (4) a team to forecast the impact of trends. Beyond these four building blocks is a wide range of ideas we plan to explore. We'll explain our plans and progress in each of these areas.

Measuring Brainpower

The first step we're taking is to create a tool that will pinpoint where knowledge is, so we can put it to work in the right areas, study it, and learn how to grow it. We set out to build a database of associate skills, throughout the company, around the world. To do that, we determined what we wanted from it, purchased the best possible software to house it, and jumped in with both feet.

The database includes basic demographic/administrative information, background and educational information (including majors of study, etc.), work experience (both at Rosenbluth and elsewhere), and specific skills (such as foreign languages, technology, and certain skills unique to our industry).

For phase two, we are considering rolling our competency assessments (as mentioned in Chapter 3, on strategic human resources) into the database. Future applications might include adding performance assessment information, incorporating a succession-planning process to identify future leaders, and tracking more intangible skills such as creativity, communication, leadership, interviewing, motivation, and others.

Our database can be used in many ways, for example, to find the right person for an open position within the company. Let's say we need someone in our office in Frankfurt who speaks fluent German and has good programming skills. We can look in our database to see who fits the bill. That enables us to utilize resources from within the company. It's good business and it's good for morale.

The database is also an important addition to a standard internal job posting process, because for the most part, the only people scanning posted opportunities are people looking to make a change, not necessarily the person most qualified for the opportunity (in this case, the person who speaks German and knows programming).

Another nice aspect of the database is that it puts associate skill on an even keel, and takes self-promotion ability out of the equation. No longer do the opportunities gravitate toward those who are good at getting noticed; now they point clearly toward the person who has taken the time and effort to develop the right skills.

The database can also be used to identify the right person or team for special projects; to measure bench strength; to develop succession planning, restructuring, and other important events. We can use it for purposes as disparate as assessing our learning and development needs as a company to studying demographic information to align our benefits with the needs of our associates, and to monitoring the strength of our diversity.

We recommend building a database as the first step in taking stock of a company's intellectual assets. It can uncover valuable sources of expertise and identify areas of needed improvement. Utilized fully, such a tool can keep a company moving forward, by assessing where it stands today and where it needs growth, either through training or targeted recruitment. Bringing the human capital function full circle, it can be used to ensure that key assets are being used to the fullest advantage of the company. And this benefits our people because it's human nature to want to exercise our skills.

DATABASE CONSTRUCTION AND IMPLEMENTATION. Now that we've talked you into what a great tool the database is, let's talk about how to build it and apply it. First, we decided what we wanted it to do. To accomplish this, our director of Human Capital Management sat down with leaders throughout the company, both vice presidents at headquarters and, most important, general managers in the field, those closest to our customers. Based upon that feedback, we prioritized what we wanted it to do. We couldn't do everything at once, and we knew we needed to jump in somewhere. After that process came the design (hire a database consultant or outsource).

Finally, we developed a questionnaire for all associates to complete, to capture the demographic, educational, employment experience, skill/knowledge, and career interest information we needed. In addition to the usual questions, we asked which project teams associates had been a part of in the company. We inquired about their mastery of different programming languages, if and where they might be willing to relocate, which outside training programs they had attended, and which areas of the company interested them, careerwise.

Our Human Resources area administers the database, and access to it is limited because of the proprietary and confidential nature of the information it contains. As we further develop it, we will open parts of it to leaders throughout the company so they can directly assess resources available for their needs. It will also be available to associates to assist them in charting their careers.

Identifying Needs

The second step in our human capital initiative was to identify needs within the company. Though this transcends the database project, the needs assessment is built into the database, so we can match the resources we need with those we have. To inventory our true needs, we created a prioritization process—which was no small task, and not a particularly pleasant exercise, but critical.

No matter how in tune a company's people are with each other, no matter how tight the top leadership team is, everyone is bound to value their own area, placing it near the top of the corporate priorities. There would be something wrong if they didn't take that kind of pride in their work, but it does make the process of agreeing on a prioritized list of corporate projects challenging. We all have lists of things we want to accomplish, and they're always at least twice as long as what's possible. We knew we had no shortage of ideas for projects, so what we needed was a realistic handle on those resources (especially time) that would be available for those projects, and which to tackle first, second, and so on.

BUDGETING TIME. We developed a process by which, twice per year, each leader submits a "time budget" of exactly how time is being spent in his or her respective area. This is a tedious but extraordinarily valuable exercise. It reveals exactly what's happening in each area of the company, who's working on what, where there are redundancies, and where our focus really is day to day.

To create this budget, each leader needs to know exactly what each of his or her people is doing every day, in terms of ongoing responsibilities, special projects, and repeated "interruptions." The idea for the process was the brainchild of our director of Human Capital and our corporate psychologist. Having this information gives us an incredible advantage. What an eye-opener it is for everyone to see where time and resources are *really* spent.

After gathering the information, it's important to put it in a consistent format, across all areas of the company. We have it presented in terms of hours per month spent, and we insist that it include all working hours. A 40-hour workweek is a thing of the past. We need to know how many hours are being invested in the business and how they're being spent—whether it's checking voice mails from a hotel room, reviewing correspondence on a flight, or meeting a client for breakfast.

Individually, we've all been amazed at reality versus our perception of where our time was going; as leaders, seeing the collective results and trends has been fascinating. But the real benefit comes when we meet to review the results across the company. Our team of vice presidents meets at our corporate ranch during our semiannual strategy sessions, where they report on their areas. There are three primary goals: (1) to find things to stop doing; (2) to find ways to streamline what we are doing (or perhaps outsource it, if it makes sense); (3) to prioritize what does need to be done.

The cumulative results are:

- From the prioritization process, we know exactly where we should be concentrating our efforts.
- From the database, we know where the expertise for those priorities lies.
- From the time accounting process, we know where the resources are available.
- We can make sure the right people are working on the most important things at all times.

It sounds so commonsense, so natural, but how many companies can say with assurance that they are accomplishing these four goals? This process affords that assurance—for aligning human resources with corporate priorities—and it can be implemented by any company.

Incorporating Client Needs

Of course, the key consideration in our prioritization process is client need. Our company design is built upon our clients, centered around understanding and fulfilling their needs. But as busy as we and our clients get on a day-to-day basis, sometimes, realistically, long-range planning can take a back seat to today's priorities. And long-range planning is a critical ingredient to prioritization, maximization of resources, succession planning, and all the other key components for a successful human capital management program. So we developed a process to ensure that our clients' long-term needs were part of the process.

We hold joint business planning sessions with clients to forge two-to-three-year plans tied to the client's strategic objectives as a company.

These meetings normally take place over two full days, and are facilitated by our director of Human Capital Management and our vice president of Business Development.

From these sessions we gain a clear understanding of where each of our clients is headed, so we can ensure that we have the right resources to be where they need us in the future. Looking at the results across multiple accounts gives us a world of information on emerging trends. We are getting a clear picture of where we add the most value and what skill sets are most important going forward. The collective information charts a road map for our future, and raises our awareness of the implications today's events have on the coming years. There is no better input than that of our clients for ranking our own objectives.

A Prognostication Team

The final component of our four-step process to prepare for the future is our Strategic Human Resource Development Advisory Team. Created in August 1997, it's made up of 10 leaders (half of whom are vice presidents) from different areas of the company. They meet one morning each month to discuss what's going on—in society, our industry, the world—that could have a long-term impact on our company. In short, it's a think tank. Attendees don't make decisions about solutions; their role is to stir up thought. Based upon their input, our human resources and learning and development areas sit down to examine what needs to be done to prepare for the coming changes.

The team examines possible scenarios within the context of different time frames (the next 6 months, 6 to 12 months, 1 to 2 years, and beyond 2 years). They talk about the potential impact coming changes might have, based on a variety of possible outcomes. For example, how the rise in telecommuting will impact support issues, or how we nurture our culture.

One secret to their effectiveness is that they don't try to take on the world in any one session. They key in on one subject at a time, and cover it thoroughly. For example, in one session, they addressed technology. Our CIO talked for almost a half-hour on emerging technologies, and the group took it from there.

In addition to reporting their findings to the HR and L&D team for action, the team periodically issues white papers to the entire company so that each area can plan for the future accordingly.

Endless Possibilities

Beyond our four initial steps (taking stock of our intellectual assets, assessing and prioritizing our company's needs, incorporating our clients' strategic objectives, and forecasting trends), we have a whole lineup of ideas we want to pursue in the area of human capital management. Here are just a few we are investigating.

We are intent upon identifying some very important intangible assets, things we have long tried to inventory intuitively, but now believe call for a bit more science, to bring consistency to the process. For example, we want to pinpoint the people in the company to whom everyone seems to turn for help. We've always used this as an unofficial sign of leadership skill; unfortunately, identifying it consistently is difficult. Our goal is to do so accurately. We realize these are the people who know how to get things done, people who are resourceful, possess a broad range of knowledge, and who care about the success of others in the company. Otherwise, people wouldn't gravitate naturally to them. We need to know who they are, what draws people to them, and how we can recognize, maximize, and, most important, replicate their assets.

There is software available to help with this, and we are looking at some packages. Usually referred to as "organizational network mapping" programs, they are designed to help define the *true* networks within a company (not the network as defined by organizational charts). Companies are typically pretty good at instituting standard information flows across official reporting lines, but unforeseen or unacknowledged barriers cause people to find alternative avenues for finding out the information they need. For example, the person from whom they are *supposed* to learn something may be on the road or may constantly have his or her door shut. So that person's staff are drawn like magnets to people who *are* accessible, informed, and willing to share information.

We call this a "trust network," and it can be among a company's strongest assets. These "go-to" people should be the leaders of teams, the captains of change, and other important roles that call for inspiring and motivating others. And they are not necessarily in those roles. We've always found them throughout the ranks of the company.

Mapping these assets can be really revealing. Some people are so pivotal to the success of the organization that little gets done among their trust network when they're gone. Everyone is so accustomed to turning to them for direction that a few vacation days can slow things down tremendously. Think of the cost of losing someone like that. And that is the point of identifying, recognizing and emulating those assets.

Next at Bat

Continuity planning is essential to the future of every organization, but it's one of those areas that can easily slip off the plate at a busy company. As individuals, working on a plan to replace ourselves is not normally among our highest priorities. Ironically, though, it is only when we have someone to fill our shoes that *we* can advance.

There are a number of components to successful continuity planning, and they fall into three basic categories: (1) commitment, (2) tools, and (3) culture. First, commitment. Companies must commit to developing and deploying a standardized process by which to plan for their future. They need to know who will lead them into the coming decades.

The process must incorporate monitoring mechanisms to ensure that progress is being made, and it must transcend any continuity planning efforts individual leaders provide within their own departments. This ensures cross-pollination of resources and is a good safeguard against natural insecurities over preparing one's replacement.

In order to keep themselves in shape for the future, companies need to continually reshape the responsibilities of individuals and departments throughout their organizations, to verify that the right things are being worked on and the right skills are being honed.

The second component for successful continuity planning is the right tool set. As you might have guessed, the first tool we recommend is the database we've already discussed in this chapter. It can be used to measure a company's bench strength as well as to track skills needed for the future.

The second tool we endorse for succession preparation is a career planning support process. People need direct access to information that will enable them to manage their own careers. This information must include a breakdown of all roles in the company, along with the qualifications or competencies required for excellence in those positions. This enables each associate to match his or her own skills with those needed for another post.

To answer this need, we developed what we call our Career Enhancement Guide. It was unveiled at our companywide meeting in August

1997, during which we encouraged our associates to "tap into the CEG." It's a PC-based tool that also comes in binder form; currently it is only in English but is being translated into a variety of languages for our associates around the world.

The CEG includes the following: (1) core competencies for the company as a whole; (2) an overview of each area of the company, including areas of responsibility, sample positions in each area, and competencies required for those positions; (3) a self-assessment tool for each area, to help figure out what development might be required to work there; (4) career options, complete with stages that must be reached (this section even shows when it might be necessary to take a step backward in order to move forward in a given area); (5) resume writing tips; (6) interviewing tips; and (7) a directory of associates to consult in each area for informational interviews regarding that department.

USAA: A Commitment to Workforce Development

At USAA, support of academic education, professional development, and leadership and human skills training has always been of paramount importance. In 1996, to help employees further manage their personal development and prepare for the future, the company implemented a Workforce Development Program to enhance this support. Additionally, employees can now receive one-on-one consultation with workforce development consultants for skills assessment and action-plan development. Resource centers, located in all major offices, are open 24 hours a day, 7 days a week for self-development. USAA offers a 4-hour class on self-reliance, conducts mock interviews, and offers help with resume preparation, networking, informational interviewing, and a host of other skills.

At Rosenbluth, pairing our associate database with the Career Enhancement Guide brings continuity planning full circle. Through the associate database, the company identifies those skills we possess collectively and those we need to reach our goals. Using the guide, our associates take stock of the skills they possess in reference to those they need to reach their individual career goals. That way, we can ensure that we're moving ahead as individuals and as a team.

The third component for effective succession planning is the right culture (covered extensively in Chapter 7). For now, it's enough to say that without a culture of trust, a company has to be naive to think that people will make an honest effort to create a plan to replace themselves. The best-laid plans of corporations rely heavily upon the foundation that the right culture provides.

Pinch Hitters

Every team needs people who can step in to fill a need as it arises, and in today's lean environment, few companies can afford the luxury of padding their staff to accommodate those sporadic needs. To meet those needs, we are investigating the "critical talent pool" concept; its premise is to form a stable of associates with skills high in demand upon which departments can call on an as-needed basis.

This would be a centralized talent pool of full-time associates who would contract out internally to business units or departments throughout the company. These internal consultants would be employed by the talent pool, and not any one department. Although there are several obvious benefits to the concept, we have some concerns as well.

First, the benefits, to both the company and to the associates who participate. The most obvious benefit to the company is having "just-in-time" resources available to smooth peaks and valleys that inevitably occur in every business. This, of course, enhances service and contains expenses. But there are more. Because these are company associates, there's no need for orientation or training. They have virtually no learning curve. Departments or business units that call upon these associates benefit from the wide variety of skills and experience they bring to the job, in addition to their full understanding of the company.

What's more, there's a cross-pollination aspect to a program such as this that facilitates the sharing of ideas from one area of the company to another. This helps develop a more cross-functional workforce, communicates best practices, breaks down barriers, and helps identify and develop associates to fill future full-time positions.

The benefits to companies are clear, but how about to individuals? Being a part of a critical talent pool provides them an opportunity to explore different areas of the company to gain vast experience. This makes them more valuable, inside the company or if they choose to pursue careers elsewhere. It's not for everyone, but for the right people, it can offer variety of work and greater control over their own careers. Finally, it can provide the opportunity to build a strong network of contacts throughout the company, which expands their future career options.

No doubt, there are many benefits to both companies and associates adventurous enough to try such a program, but I do have my reservations. In fact, the first time the concept was proposed to me, I rejected it. My concerns parallel those I had initially with satellite associates (as explained in Chapter 3 on human resources). I worry that associates in the pool might not feel part of a team. I worry that they will feel less secure in their roles with the company than those in traditional positions. I worry that they could be viewed as potential targets for cost-cutting. These are issues we are grappling with, and perhaps the answer lies in a phased approach.

Alagasco: A Study in Cross-Utilization of Resources

Alagasco has had success with cross-utilizing people's skills within their company. CEO Mike Warren says, "At times, projects inside the company allow us to assign people across functional lines. This has enabled us to stretch employees and create the flexibility needed to successfully manage in an ever-changing environment. For example, our 25-year-old customer accounting system was replaced in 1996 following an 18-month, $15 million special project, which involved approximately 20 people being assigned full time to this effort. The team had separate work space, unique work and dress rules, and its own bonus plan. Its work involved interfacing with more than one-third of all company personnel, and it provided numerous opportunities to celebrate interim successes. This effort really became a culture within the larger corporate culture. The same approach is currently being used on a smaller but similar project for our human resource information system."

Alagasco has also used a Temporary Reassignment Program (TAP) for several years. With TAP, employees are asked to do jobs or projects different from their normal duties, with a definite beginning and ending time for each assignment. Also on a regular basis, Alagasco practices nontraditional job replacements and rotations. Mike Warren says, "Putting employees in jobs where others may have never seen them has proven to be very motivating and successful. For example, we have found that putting a communications/media spokesperson in a market-ingrepresentative position provides a chance for new skills to be brought to the job. Others working around that nontraditional employee learn, too; we have found it to almost always be a win-win situation."

We plan to begin testing the waters by brokering talent through our associate database, matching skills with needs, and shifting resources temporarily as needed. The next logical step would be to share resources between departments that require the same skill sets. From there, if the demand warrants, we may begin to build a critical talent pool.

A recent program has had promising results and may be just the springboard we need. A new "floating assistant" position gives us a permanent pipeline for strong administrative skill. We began the program when we saw that most temporary associates were used for administrative assistant positions. This is a difficult area to keep filled in our company, because so many from there are promoted to other positions. And temporary help isn't an ideal solution; not only is it difficult to ensure quality with temporary help, you also lose value time and again training temporary associates, only to have them leave with that knowledge.

Through our floating assistant program, we always have fully trained associates with the right skills and complete understanding of our company, ready to fill administrative roles as they become available. Currently, we maintain three associates in the program, and are considering expanding it.

In some ways, a critical talent pool can support associates in reaching their maximum potential. Skill requirements are constantly changing, and that's a trend that's here to stay. While we hold fast to our values, we know that today's skills might be obsolete tomorrow. A big challenge companies face is how to keep people moving in the direction they need to succeed in the future, and not try to fill their days with activities that just match their current skills.

The critical talent pool can be a strong, up-to-the-minute barometer of which skills are in demand, so our associates can hone those skills. It also provides a way for associates who do possess cutting-edge skills to put them to work constantly, throughout the company, to keep them fresh.

> ### AT&T: Just-in-Time Talent
>
> AT&T is a pioneer in the field of critical talent pools. They call their pro-
> gram Resource Link,™ and in it they have more than 1,000 employees.
> AT&T's goal is to eventually have more of its workforce participate in the
> program, in order to accelerate the company's speed and flexibility.
>
> Resource Link™ began in 1991 as an in-house temporary firm, placing
> technical workers and managers in the company's business units, on a con-
> tract basis. These are full-time employees with standard salary and benefit
> packages; only their assignments are temporary. They are often used for
> short-term projects or to get new initiatives off the ground quickly.
>
> Since the program's inception, demand has skyrocketed to the point-
> where 60 percent of the requests for associates from the pool cannot
> be filled. AT&T has taken the concept a step further, forming what it
> calls a Talent Alliance™ with other companies. Through it, organizations
> requiring similar particular skill sets can share specialized resources.

There are any number of directions companies can take in an effort to
maximize their resources. Most important is to start somewhere, with a
few well-coordinated priorities. Here's a summary of our basic plan.

The goal is simply to maximize the impact of our current and future
associates. To do this, we are:

1. Defining our intellectual assets (determining core competencies, incorporating client feedback, performing internal assessments, and implementing a task/project prioritization process).

2. Identifying where the skills and expertise lie (building an associate
   skill database, and competency assessments).

3. Planning growth and development (targeted recruitment, development
   of current assets, continuity planning process, and career-planning
   tools, such as our Career Enhancement Guide).

4. Leveraging assets (continually realigning resources according to client
   and corporate priorities, utilizing our associate skill database, brokering intellectual assets across the company and, to some degree,
   developing a critical talent pool).

Probably the best place for a company to start is to designate a champion of human capital. New titles are popping up all around the world,

such as "chief knowledge officer," or "director of intellectual asset management," or several other variations on the theme of maximizing brainpower. There has to be a champion, and that champion must have access to the boardroom and to clients. He or she must also have a symbiotic relationship with the company's human resources and training areas.

Pursuit of the discipline of intellectual asset management, or as we call it, "human capital management," is a secret to becoming faster, fresher, and to working to maximum potential. It ensures the right people working on the right things, and there's nothing more powerful. But a company's knowledge assets need not be limited to its current employee base. There are alternative resources that can add incredible value.

Return Policy

No matter how deep people's feelings may be for their company, life events will take precedent over work, and that's the way it should be. Over the years, some terrific people have left our company for various reasons—the birth of a child, to enjoy retirement, even winning the lottery. One thread they all have in common is their lasting interest in and loyalty to the company.

We make it standard practice to leave the doors wide open to those who move on, and that has expanded our brainpower beyond our walls. People who leave stay in touch, and many have come back either on a full-time basis or to help us with projects. They say that Rosenbluth International reminds them of the Hotel California, in the Eagles song of the same name. "You can check out, but you can never leave."

We regularly call in former associates to tackle special projects that might otherwise drain the company of its core resources. This heightens our ability to get things done quickly, creatively, and just in time. We benefit from their expertise and experience, knowledge of the company and how to get things done. Meanwhile, they can put their skills to work without having to make a full-time commitment, thus enabling them to pursue whatever it is they left us for. We contend that fast companies will need to learn how to nurture relationships with star performers who leave, and draw them back for special projects.

To give you an understanding of the benefits of cultivating such relationships, and some guidelines to administering the process, here are a few stories of some associates who have come back to help us. We'll start with probably the most unusual story.

Life's a Gamble

It's always fun to speculate about what you'd do if someone handed you millions of dollars. Almost everyone says the first thing they'd do is retire. Well, it happened to a long time Rosenbluth associate. He's a little publicity-shy, so for purposes of this book we'll call him Jake Ducane.

Jake was, and then wasn't, and now is again an associate of Rosenbluth International. He has been through an awful lot, both good and bad. Jake joined our company in 1981, and over the next decade worked in a variety of leadership positions, most of them pioneering new areas for us. He was always ready to do whatever it took, wherever it might take him.

Once, when we were awarded an enormous new travel account, Jake unselfishly agreed to relocate his family, begin a new office to serve the account, and take on the role of its leader. His office was a model of excellence, and customers and associates loved him. In fact, our company was named Supplier of the Year by this very prestigious client.

Unfortunately, the client also believed in "riding 'em hard and putting 'em up wet," or, more bluntly put, "draining the blood from you until you die." And in this case, Jake almost did. At the young age of 40, he suffered a heart attack. It came out of the blue, with no warning. Jake found himself hospitalized in a strange town for some time. After he recuperated, he returned to work. Then one day, an amazing thing happened. Jake won a $13 million state lottery, and made one of the best strategic decisions of his career: He quit. Actually, he took a six-month leave of absence to decide what he wanted to do.

Everyone's curious as to what it would be like to win the lottery, so Jake indulged us and recounted the story he has told so many times. He was not a frequent lottery player, but was driving home late from work one evening, and heard an announcement on the radio about a $36 million jackpot. Stuck at a traffic light in the right-hand lane, next to a convenience store with a big sign advertising lottery tickets, he thought, "What the heck," and pulled over. He bought five tickets. He won.

He didn't claim his prize for a week. After he did, he immediately took a house at the shore for the summer and moved his family there. He changed his phone number and "disappeared." He remembers sitting with his wife watching the news as reporters from all the major network stations in Philadelphia were literally camped out on the lawn of his vacated house, waiting for him to come home.

During his six-month leave, he called me every so often to see how everyone in the company was doing. One day toward the end of his leave, he called and said, "I miss all my friends at work. My kids ask me what I do, and I don't have an answer for them. I want to come home." So he began to work for us on a part-time basis in one of our locations near his home. His expertise is invaluable and his loyalty is unshakable.

Jake says, "One of the most important things we do is serve as a role model for our kids. Life is hard. You don't just grow up and win the lottery. I want my kids to see me working hard the way I always have. I had to talk to my son's class, with all the other dads, about what I do. I was glad to be able to talk about my work with Rosenbluth."

In terms of applicability to other companies, it's not likely that many employees will win the lottery, and less likely that if they did, they'd be interested in coming back to work. But this example, probably more than most, points out the value in having the type of company where people *want* to work, honoring their choice to leave to focus on their priorities, and nurturing ongoing relationships with them. These are keys to retaining top talent for whatever contributions they are willing to make to your company.

Hollywood and Motherhood

Producing corporate videos, staging major events, all with quality time for family: This is the story of Melinda Rippy Smith. She joined the company in 1983, and ultimately became vice president of marketing. In 1988, she became the mother of twin boys, and remained with the company for several more years. But from the day of their birth, she made it clear that there would come a time when she would leave. She wanted to accomplish *her* goals with the company and help the company reach *its* goals, but eventually she would close that chapter to spend more time at home. That day came in 1993.

We left her alone for about three months; then we couldn't resist asking if she wanted to help us with a few projects. The first was selling advertising space in our global hotel directory, which outlines specially negotiated rates and services for our clients. Melinda sold the first ad in the first directory. The suppliers who advertise respect her experience in matching their business needs to the opportunity.

She works on the project each year for about four months, 15 to 20 hours a week. Very little administration is required. It's a turnkey project for our company and for her. We don't need to set aside a resource for four months a year, and find something meaningful for that person to do the other eight. We don't need to train anyone to do the work. And because she works out of her home, we have no overhead on the project.

In 1996, Melinda helped us create a corporate library we call The Gathering. It's a comfortable place where associates can meet informally, share ideas, and keep in touch with the world. She selected a wide variety of publications in the business, technology, service, and work/life arenas, and set up daily delivery of newspapers from around the world. The Gathering houses information about job opportunities, corporate videos, a TV normally tuned into CNN or the Fox News Channel, and an "idea graffiti board" for sharing ideas and solutions; associates also have access to the Internet there.

Melinda's largest project was staging a companywide meeting of our associates from around the world. The 1997 meeting was attended by more than 4,000 people from some 25 countries, and included a complex lineup of meetings, events, and a trade show.

The project was an enormous undertaking and one that would have drained company resources considerably for over a year, had we elected to manage it completely internally. Melinda initially served as an advisor on the project, building a team of former and current associates to plan and implement it. Ultimately, she assumed overall responsibility for the entire event.

We needed a strong team on the project for an entire year, but how many companies have a team like that just "sitting around?" You'd have to worry about one that did. An ideal solution is a team anchored by former associates with knowledge and experience, but without the long-term overhead commitment.

Project Specialist

Jennifer Howard joined Rosenbluth in 1991 and was drawn to human resources shortly thereafter. Several years later, she left to begin a family, then decided to return to work 27 hours a week. After a year of part-time work, her desire to spend more time with her family, coupled with her lengthy daily commute, led her to the difficult decision to leave the company.

After just two months, she received a call from her former colleagues in human resources, asking her if she could work on a special, short-term project. She quickly found herself with one project after another and has settled happily into her role as an outside project specialist. Jennifer works an average of 15 hours per week, and enjoys the type of work she's doing.

One project was to develop and implement an automated phone-screening system for potential applicants. Using a toll-free number, 24 hours a day, potential applicants can provide us with their basic employment history before sending a resume. It's a very efficient way to begin the recruitment process. Potential applicants call at a time that is most convenient for them. The HR representative receives a detailed report and can listen to the phone screening at any time. This enhances the productivity of our HR staff, who are being called upon for increasingly strategic roles.

The project was ideal to outsource to a former associate who understands the company, its hiring goals, the style of its HR team, and its vision for the future. And piloting and launching this project didn't drain the productivity of the department in the process.

Diverse Projects

What do the virtual future and books have in common? The answer is Diane McFerrin Peters, my coauthor. She has taken on projects to create both. She joined our company in 1987, and over the years headed up new ventures and corporate communications. Even when she told me after seven years that she was leaving to start a family, I was sure it wasn't the end of the story. It wasn't long before she began to work on special projects. And the first request came from me.

Our director of corporate communications was relocating and leaving the company, and I knew it would take some time to find the right person for the job. I asked Diane to mentor the department while I found a leader. She did so for four months, in the office one day each week and accessible by phone the other six. She was hands-off, encouraging the team to assume responsibilities that had been handled by the director. They grew and enriched their jobs, enabling the new director to take on a more strategic role.

Diane's next project was an unusual assignment: to create a place where clients, associates, and suppliers could experiment with, strategize about, and touch the future. It was to be a hands-on research and development lab in which to test products and services, solicit our clients' input, and mold the future accordingly. Called The Continuum, it's a future center, where some of the world's leading companies display their newest products and services for our clients to experience. It features a virtual trip, including experiential visions of the future of travel. Beyond that, it enables visitors to experience the convergence of telecommunications, computing, and consumer electronics. To develop the center, Diane worked with a team of inside associates for eight months, one day per week in the office and the rest of the time from home.

Setting Up an Outsourcing Program

All the projects outlined here demonstrate the beauty of using outside resources: expertise coupled with availability (preserving core resources). These former associates also bring a fresh perspective—they've stepped away from the company, and can look at it more objectively; they have a rested approach, a sprinter's energy. And in some cases, they've been working with other companies on projects, and so bring a breadth of experience. The administration is easy and the talent is among the best. The relationships former associates have built over the years, both inside and outside the company, are irreplaceable benefits. Even if people, departments, or product lines change, these former associates still know how to navigate to find the answers they need. There's no delay in hiring and training. They hit the ground running, and fast.

The administration involved in outsourcing the type of projects discussed here is rather simple, and best if kept flexible. For example, Melinda usually bills her time by the hour, submitting weekly accounts of her time and activities, although on The Gathering she billed a flat fee. Jennifer is administered as a part-time associate; Diane is paid as an independent contractor, and submits her hours and reports monthly. The journals Melinda and Diane provide are excellent blueprints for future projects.

As for our current staff, they're happy to have the help and expertise. Their plates are already overflowing. They know that these are people who *chose* to leave the company. They're not looking for a way in the door as a typical consultant might be. These are people who are interested only in getting the job done.

Melinda said, "Sometimes I work for people who used to work for me. I'm perfectly comfortable with that. When I was with the company, I had one of the nicest offices imaginable. Now, when I am in the office I use whatever cubicle is available, and that's fine with me. All I need is a computer and a phone and I'm happy."

Diane said, "I understand the incredibly fast pace at which this company operates, and I can relate to the feeling of having so many projects you'd like to launch, so many new ideas to explore, and simply not enough time to do them all. I enjoy tackling those projects for people, and still having the time I need with my family. When my daughter or son talks on their toy phone, playing Continuum, or play author on their computer, I get such a kick out of it. And I get tremendous satisfaction from the work, especially the people."

A Growing Trend

Our peers have their own unique approaches to broadening their companies' intellectual capacity. Here are a few of them.

USAA. Since 1991, at USAA, more than 120 retirees have been employed as temporary employees. They have worked as service representatives, underwriters, system analysts, data engineers, and in other consulting roles.

ALAGASCO. Alagasco has had a good deal of success in using former employees for special projects. For example, they've had several pipeline construction projects on which they've used retired employees as consultants. These types of projects work well because they have specific beginning and end times for the retirees, and they provide satisfaction to both the retired and active employees working together.

Another Alagasco project involved the purchase of a municipal gas system in the southern part of their service territory. Alagasco felt there was a great deal of marketing potential in this particular area. To maximize it, they used retired employees, who actually went door-to-door to speak with potential customers.

Alagasco also works with retired employees on a contract basis, to help out on special projects or during peak winter work periods, which they say has been very effective and "fosters the family feeling." Says CEO Mike Warren, "We have worked hard at making retired employees feel a part of the continuing efforts of the company. Our Blue Flame Retiree Clubs are active in each of our seven divisions, and senior management visits each group frequently. We involve retirees in all company outings and celebrations and now include them in the company matching for charitable contributions."

MARY KAY. Mary Kay's very structure is the ultimate in expanding brainpower and utilizing outside resources. It takes both corporate employees and independent beauty consultants to make the company successful. The consultants are entrepreneurs (nearly half a million of them) who aren't linked to the company by the traditional paycheck but rather by the strong value system and culture. Like Rosenbluth, Mary Kay also occasionally calls upon former employees and retired employees to consult on special projects.

NORTHWESTERN MUTUAL LIFE. Like Mary Kay, Northwestern Mutual Life's structure inherently incorporates brainpower outside the head-quarters walls. The company has more than 7,000 independent agents they consider part of the family, and who are very much a part of the structure and processes. And knowledge-sharing is a key component in the company's success.

A feature article on Northwestern Mutual in the January/February edition of *Reputation Management* describes it well: "There is a free flow of information horizontally between related departments—facilitated by an elaborate system of liaison committees—and vertically between senior managers and those at lower levels of the company, with information and ideas flowing in both directions."

Externally, information flows between the home office, agents, and policy owners with the help of some unusual measures by the company. One such program is Northwestern Mutual's Policy owners' Examining Committee. Once a year, five policy owners, elected by the board of trustees, make an independent, unrestricted evaluation of the company's operations, management, and strategic plans. The group reports its findings to the board and then to all policy owners in an unedited section of the annual report.

FEL-PRO. Fel-Pro reminds us of how important it is to share knowledge with our customers. Fel-Pro's president, OE Sales & Marketing, Paul Lehman, says, "Over the past five years, we've increasingly been sending employees (including shop floor workers) to customers' facilities. There, our employees meet their counterparts on the shop floor and see our products being used right on our customers' production lines. It used to be that the only people dealing much with the customer were those in sales and marketing. Now our technical people are there as well. We truly have multiple points of contact with our customers."

GREAT PLAINS SOFTWARE. When it comes to expanding brainpower beyond a company's walls, Great Plains Software is an innovator. They view themselves not as just a company, but as part of a larger virtual organization, including their distribution channels and employees. Value-added resellers, consultants, accounting firms, and the like participate with Great Plains in every step of a cooperative sales and service model, including product development, demand creation, sales, implementation, and ongoing service.

The company recognizes that the strength of these organizations is critical to its success, and rather than fretting about the universal challenges their industry faces, Great Plains has set out to do something about it—on behalf of everyone with whom they work. To answer the needs of this virtual organization, Great Plains launched an initiative called CORE (Center for Organizational Excellence). CORE is an aggressive program designed to address the human resource requirements, professional competencies, and organizational strength needed along their distribution chain, to satisfy current and future demand for their products and services (which outweighs capacity).

CORE follows six strategies: (1) Forecast, recruit, and build human resources throughout the virtual organization; (2) build competencies; (3) foster continuous learning; (4) partner with colleges and universities; (5) foster growth; and (6) create a compelling culture across the virtual organization. Great Plains' goal for CORE is, "To equip our partners better than competitors equip their direct employees."

One of the more creative elements is a cooperative program with colleges and universities in which Great Plains provides the materials that schools need to establish an accounting curriculum. They include free software programs, instruction manuals, technical support, and lesson guides. All the schools have to do is agree to actively use the teaching tools in at least one class for at least one year. More than 100 schools have taken advantage of the program. Schools and students benefit because the tools prepare the students for positions in the industry, and Great Plains has a line to qualified candidates for positions throughout their virtual organization—candidates who are familiar with their products.

This is smart business. A recent report by the Information Technology Association of America estimated that 346,000 positions are currently open in IT companies across the United States. Great Plains notes that several thousand positions are vacant across their channel of partners who distribute and service their software around the world.

Other recruiting programs include a co-op Web recruiting system, which markets job openings collectively for the virtual organization; a recruiting event during Stampede, their annual partner meeting; candidate screening; and a host of other services. In addition, Great Plains offers distance learning and organizational consulting to their partners. Distribution leadership: the next frontier.

Maximizing Brainpower: A Summary

- It's estimated that 50 percent to 90 percent of a company's value is in its intangibles—people, ideas, and customers. To maximize that value, consider a human capital management initiative. A good place to start is to appoint a resource to lead the charge, if not a full-time, dedicated resource, then a short-term or partially dedicated one.

- Companies need to recognize the risk of "losing the recipe" for success. Too often, the best work is not documented thoroughly because we're so busy *doing* the work. This point really hit home for us while we were working on this book. We discovered that the best information about one of the most important events in our company's history was locked inside the memories of those who participated.

- When setting up an initiative to maximize brainpower, it's important to determine whether the focus will be on structural, intellectual assets (such as patents, processes, or trademarks), or human capital. Ours is clearly on the human aspect, though we have found that most companies begin by focusing on the structural, as it's more easily measured.

- The first step in the management of human capital should be to measure your company's brainpower, pinpointing where knowledge is. To do that, consider building a database including basic demographic/ administrative information, background and educational information, work experience, and specific skills. Future enhancements could include adding competency information and more intangible skills. Such a database can be used to identify the right person for a position or special project, to measure bench strength for succession planning, or for training and performance management.

- The second step is a prioritization process. Ours includes the creation of "time budgets" by each department of the company; a meeting of top officers to review those budgets, streamline, outsource, and prioritize the actions; the study of trends and the determination to act upon them.

- The third step in human capital maximization should be to incorporate client needs into the process. We do so through extensive planning sessions with our client companies, during which we become immersed in each customer's strategic objectives. This ensures we are prepared to support those objectives. We also look for trends across accounts, to tell us where we need to be in the years to come.

- The fourth step is a method to forecast the potential impact of emerging trends. This can be done by a small, strategic team that meets monthly. Their contribution is thought. A follow-up team takes tactical action.

- Consider a support tool to encourage continuity planning. Our Career Enhancement Guide is a PC-based tool (which is also available in binder form) available to all associates. It includes our company's core competencies, an overview of each area of the company, self-assessment tools, career options, resume and interviewing tips, and a directory of resources for informational interviews.

- Critical talent pools can be an effective way to meet the growing demands of companies. A centralized talent pool of associates who contract out to departments throughout a company can offer just-in-time resources with virtually no learning curve. A good way to venture into this area might be a phased approach. We have a small pool of floating administrative assistants, which is proving to be successful. A critical talent pool can also be a barometer of up-and-coming skill sets, and can offer the opportunity for those in the pool to keep their valued skills fresh through continual use.

- The ultimate goal of human capital management is to leverage the assets of your company, continually realigning resources and brokering intellectual assets across the organization, according to corporate priorities.

- To add to your company's knowledge assets, consider using former top performers for special projects. They have a proven track record, they know your company, and there's no learning curve and no overhead. To attract them, have the type of company where people *want* to work. Honor their choice to leave to focus on other priorities. Nurture ongoing relationships with them, and make it clear they're welcome back at any time.

- There are any number of projects for which pinch hitters are ideal, including short-term projects (like our Gathering); comprehensive, specialized projects (The Continuum and our companywide meeting); pilot projects (our automated phone-screening trial); recurring projects (our hotel directory advertising program); temporary leadership roles (taking the panic out of executive searches).

- Keep the administration of these programs simple and flexible. We let these associates structure their arrangements however is best for them, within reason. Flexibility adds to the attractiveness of the opportunity and keeps things casual. That's part of what makes it work.

- Encourage these associates to help you build your network of potential talent by recommending peers who are qualified and available for projects.

5

Addicted to Learning

My educational experience peaked in kindergarten. My kindergarten teacher, Jane Norman, set my expectations high, and they were never really met after her. What I remember about that year was how much fun learning was, and I couldn't wait to learn for a lifetime. She taught me to hunger for knowledge and to develop my own learning style.

Recently, she was profiled in TV Guide. I caught up with her and we reviewed her career since that time. I was in her first class, and after four years, she left teaching to put her talents to work in television. She believes the best teachers are entertainers, as they teach in such a way that students hardly realize they are learning. Not only are they learning, they are retaining more of what they learn because the learning is fun. She says learning is best when it's "magical, mystical, and fun, and that goes for school and for work."

Jane Norman went on to start a children's television show called Pixanne, *which ran for nine years in Philadelphia, followed by runs in New York and Boston. It later became nationally syndicated. She says she essentially put her class on TV, teaching the same lessons in the same style she used to teach me. Any class fun enough to hold television viewers' attention for over a decade is the kind of class we'd all like to be a part of.*

Besides making learning fun, Jane Norman had an amazing skill for being able to spot individual talents and for encouraging their development. Even, in her words, "if it meant being different." She said I had a mind of my own and a different way of looking at things at that early age. I think that's reflected in my approach to business today.

She shared two stories about students from my class that I think companies can learn from. The first is of a girl named Terry, who would come to school each day dressed in her "Sunday best" from head to toe. She showed signs of tremendous artistic promise, but seldom joined in art projects for fear of messing up her clothes. Jane Norman sent a note home to her mother asking her to send Terry to school in her grubbiest playclothes for a while to see if it made a difference. It did, and the difference was huge. She turned out to be an amazing artist, whose talents had been squelched by restrictive clothing. Companies place similar restraints on their people with restrictive environments. But in companies where employees are given the chance to try, and perhaps fail, people's talents blossom.

The second lesson involved Billy, whom Jane Norman recognized from her first encounters with him as having a gift for music. She called his mother and suggested that Billy have music lessons. Recently, Jane and her husband traveled to San Francisco and heard Billy play piano professionally.

Sometimes all we need is recognition of our individual potential and the encouragement to develop it. A mistake so many companies make is pigeonholing their people into the roles for which they were hired, not recognizing potential beyond them, nor providing the opportunity and resources to develop that potential.

Jane Norman says of teaching and business, "It's all the same. If you allow for and encourage individual growth and development, and utilize the strengths of each person, everyone benefits, be it in a classroom or a company. People love to utilize their strengths; it motivates them. By drawing not just on experience but on interests, you ensure the full participation of everyone." How do you learn what those interests are? "By listening, by watching, and by caring."

Learning can be a fragile thing. It needs to be cultivated and individualized, to take into account individual needs and interests. This is difficult to do in schools and in companies; nevertheless, it is possible and it must be done.

Learning is also persistent. It will occur spontaneously, whether organized or not. This notion was discussed in an essay by our director of human capital and general manager of learning and development, which appeared in *Learning Organizations* (Productivity Press, 1995). They explained, "Sometimes learning takes on a life of its own, bursting openly and happily out of control, spreading like wildfire. At other times learning is forced underground, where it becomes dark, secretive, and destructive. Lunchroom conversations may tell more about the *real* lessons learned in some companies than a hundred formal meetings may ever reveal." Companies need to recognize the power of learning, and turn every learning opportunity into positive growth.

Southwest Airlines: Making Learning Fun

Southwest Airlines subscribes to the principle that learning is most effective when it's fun, and that belief is written all over the company's training catalog. The cover is decorated with cartoon drawings. At the top is a brain surrounded by question marks, and a person pointing to a chalkboard, which says, "This is your brain." Below that is a brain surrounded by atoms, rockets, keys, dollar signs, airplanes, engineering wheels, lightning bolts, and other images that speak to enlightenment and creativity. The caption reads, "This is your brain working at Southwest Airlines."

Inside are courses on everything from financial planning and how to run a profitable airline to Customer Care and Harmony 101, all taught at Southwest's University for People. The beginning of the booklet reads, "And now, an important message from Herb Kelleher, Chairman, President and CEO of Southwest Airlines . . ." On the next page is a picture of Herb in jeans and a Harley T-shirt, with baseball cap on backward, sunglasses, arms in the air, and a big smile on his face. The caption: "Knowledge is good."

Kicking up Dust

Having a great staff isn't a constant; it's a continuum. People must be cared for if they are to remain. They must be given ongoing opportunity to grow if they are to remain *the best*. Our company has long placed a strong emphasis on individual growth and development, but over the past five years, that emphasis has shifted dramatically from *training* to *learning*, and there is a marked difference. Training's focus is more activity-based; with learning, the focus is on results.

We made the change at the most peculiar of times. It was the fall of 1992, when we learned that we would be included among the top 10 companies in *The 100 Best Companies to Work for in America*. Another pleasant surprise came when we heard we would also be recognized in the book as having one of the "Top 10 Training Programs in America." Most companies would ride on that for the next 10 or 20 years. They'd keep everything in the training department exactly as it was—afraid to dust for fear of ruining a good thing. But we're a very contrarian company, so we did mess with a good thing—in order to make it a great thing. In between notification of inclusion in the book and the book's actual release, we completely redesigned our training department and overhauled our entire approach to learning.

Our director of training said, "Admittedly, it felt strange dismantling a department while it was being cited for excellence. But awards focus on the past [and] our sights were set on the future." So the dismantling and rebuilding began with a fury. In the coming pages of this chapter, we'll share the reasons why we made such a drastic change, the steps we took to implement it, the structure of the new design, and some of the important training programs we've implemented since the redesign.

Why?

The training redesign caused such a stir that companies across the country began to inquire about it. Our director of training released a white paper entitled "Creating a Learning Organization: Changing the Tires on a Moving Vehicle," which explained the reasons behind the change and some of the steps taken to achieve it. As he described the process: "At the time of our decision, the training department was traditionally structured, and control was centralized. The department was organized into teams of training specialists, program design specialists, and training coordinators. We offered a full menu of courses, many of which were regularly scheduled at 1 of 10 training sites around the country. Other training was customized and delivered on a 'just-in-time' basis.

"While the quality of training was strong, there were a number of signs that foreshadowed the need for change. Serving a highly decentralized company, we were unable to meet everyone's training needs precisely when they needed it most. Transfer of training was another major concern.

"Our training specialists, organized around the type of training as opposed to the client base, went wherever the next training request took them, with little opportunity to follow up with past trainees. Many associates had to fly to one of our training sites, causing both inconvenience and the loss of a productive associate for more time than was really necessary. In addition, the cost of training was growing at a steadily rapid pace.

"At the same time, we came to a number of conclusions about individual and organizational learning: We realized (1) that most real learning takes place in settings other than a classroom; (2) that a substantial percentage of classroom learning results in little, if any, behavior change back in the workplace; and (3) that many leaders who request training, in response to a problem they're facing, misdiagnose the source of the problem (often a faulty process, a leadership issue, etc.) and incorrectly apply a training solution."

Our associates continually display creativity and guts, but this redesign ranks near the top. To do it, our training team sat down and essentially created a design that would put themselves out of their jobs, if implemented according to plan.

The Results

The redesign of our company and individual departments, such as learning and development, were important steps in the growth of our organization. We shifted from a "paternalistic" environment to one of the higher level of personal responsibility that comes with friendship—that is, a truly balanced relationship. But the process wasn't easy or without its share of pain. There was some resistance to such a major change, both within the training organization and elsewhere in the company. But it was clearly the right thing to do, and because it was, it was relatively quickly embraced.

The results exceeded our highest expectations. During the first year alone, the training redesign saved the company an estimated $1.4 million. The hard-cost reduction came primarily from downsizing the department by nearly a third, closing most of our 10 training centers, and lowering T&E costs by reducing the need to travel to centralized classroom programs. Many of the people affected were redeployed into the business units either in leadership positions or as "leaders in learning," which we'll explain shortly. These associates have been able to put their knowledge to work in the field, sharing their experience in facilitating learning.

Our new training approach is a study in efficiency. The old structure called for 42 people to train 2,500 associates. Today, we have 35 people training more than 5,000 associates, and the quality of the learning has *improved*. Because training is individualized, associates attend only the training they need, as opposed to having all associates in a given position attend a training program, thereby incurring unnecessary T&E and draining productivity. The introduction of self-paced programs has cut the time necessary to complete training as well.

The financial benefits were significant, and continue today, but the impact doesn't stop there. The new design enables customized learning, tailored to the business unit and to the individuals within it. Individuals can now learn exactly what they need to learn, when they need to learn it, and in the style they learn best. It's a far more time-efficient and cost-effective method.

These customized solutions are rarely highly technical. Often the simple solutions are the most effective. For example, in our San Francisco office, associates posted their individual learning goals on flipcharts in the conference room. During the following weeks, people put a note next to a learning need they can help with. Notes such as "I can practice Spanish with you every Tuesday at lunch," or "Feel free to sit with me while I work on some international faring—I can show you what you need to know." Associates were taking responsibility for their own development and the success of the business, and were learning, teaching, and sharing.

Clients are thrilled with the new design, because it answers their specific needs, *immediately*. Rather than waiting for a training need to be recognized, a program created, and associates scheduled to travel to a centralized location to attend the training session, the learning required to meet client needs can be accomplished on the spot. This design enables us to be fast and focused, two imperatives as we meet the future. Our speed of learning has continued to accelerate since implementing our redesign. We can spot the need for change and accomplish it immediately, which is exactly what is called for to meet our constantly changing needs as we grow around the world.

The How of It

The training team met to design the future. (All areas of the company do this on a regular basis.) Around this time, the entire company was moving to our farm structure, which you read about earlier. The new business unit structure created a collection of entrepreneurial groups organized around clients. Our training team knew that this more highly customized level of service would require vastly different training support.

The change they came up with was so profound, they renamed their department Learning and Development. This has become commonplace today, but at the time it was an unusual move. The new name reflected the change in emphasis from feeding training programs to the company to teaching business units and the individuals within them how to meet their individualized learning needs.

The team began by mapping out the change, and educating each level of leadership on the benefits and details of the new design. Helping leaders to understand the importance of taking ownership of their own learning needs was critical. It was equally important to communicate the change throughout the organization, making people aware that learning takes place not just in a classroom environment, but, most important, on the job. Our associates needed to be *aware* that they were learning, so that their experiences could be replicated for themselves and for their fellow associates.

Creating the right infrastructure to support this type of learning was important. Let's look at it the right way: from the front line back, beginning with individual learning approaches and continuing with corporate support programs.

LEADERS IN LEARNING: TRAINING "AT HOME." To help us ensure that each individual's training needs were addressed, we created a critical new role called "leaders in learning." These are front-line people who volunteer to train their fellow associates. They act as liaisons between our learning and development organization and the business unit in which they work.

To begin with, they help assess the training needs in their location. For example, they might assess the technical capabilities of associates in their office who make corporate travel reservations (a core process for us). They would determine who needs support with which aspect. The idea answers the question "Why train everyone in all 10 functions when one person may just need help with part of one function, and someone else might need a refresher on another function?" By assessing and coaching to specific gaps in skills or knowledge, the learning process can be integrated into the flow of work. It's less disruptive, and significantly more productive.

Beyond addressing technical skills, our leaders in learning research, develop, and facilitate courses on subjects such as ergonomics or time management. They determine how to best make learning part of daily life in their unit, make their fellow associates aware of internal and external course offerings, serve as on-site trainers, and help set up peer coaching.

Our leaders in learning are in place in 100 percent of our business units and in most of our centralized service centers (support functions, like accounting, communications, and sales). There are more than 130 associates in this role throughout the company, supported by a leader in learning program manager, who is part of the learning and development organization.

Some leaders in learning fulfill the role on a part-time basis and some on a full-time basis. Normally, they spend about 20 percent of their time coaching on learning issues and 80 percent in their traditional revenue-producing roles. To be fair to the leaders in learning, it's critical to establish, up-front, their exact responsibilities, so they aren't pulled in two directions. This includes specific time commitments and reporting lines for each role they play.

Most leaders in learning are front-line associates who work frequently with clients for example, travel service associates who assist callers with corporate travel reservations. They bring real-world experience to their role as leaders in learning, which ensures that the learning taking place has direct application to what's important to our clients.

An important aspect of the leader in learning role is that it brings the learning process home, to the field. Each associate sees his or her learning coach on a daily basis, and they work alongside each other. They know that the issues important to their business unit, its clients, and associates are at the foundation of the learning in which they will participate.

The learning process is peer-based as opposed to hierarchical. Illustrating that, a recent issue of our leader in learning newsletter, *Outside the Box*, gave some valuable advice. It recommended that new leaders in learning approach their role as one of *sharing* rather than *teaching*. The learning process is a two-way street, and information is much richer when presented in this way.

The leader in learning role is offered to all associates through a listing posted in each business unit, as either a full-time position or as additional responsibilities to one's current position, depending upon the needs and resources of that particular unit. Some business units have many leaders in learning, and others have only one, depending upon the size of the unit. Interested candidates apply for the role and are interviewed by business unit leaders. An overview of recommended skills and interviewing techniques is provided to the business unit leaders by learning and development, to help them find the best candidates.

Once selected, each leader in learning attends a three-day introduction to training program. These are held regionally, and are highly customized according to the developmental needs of those participating. Each class holds from 6 to 15 people. Following this program, the leaders in learning attend individual courses on a variety of subjects, as needed.

Today, there is a certification process for leaders in learning, but when the role was initiated that wasn't the case. We wanted to avoid assembling a mini-training department, dismantling the centralized one and replacing it with a decentralized one. However, we learned the hard way that some standardization in the learning process was important, and that we needed an infrastructure in place to encourage the sharing of ideas.

For certification, candidates select a topic from a series of one-hour modules offered by Learning and Development, including, for example, listening skills, handling challenging clients, communication skills, and others. The one-hour courses are offered in a ready-to-teach format. The candidate watches a live or videotaped presentation of his or her selected course, conducted by someone in learning and development.

The candidate then teaches that course to a live audience within his or her business unit. He or she is observed and evaluated by the leader in learning program manager, who provides feedback, and recommends either certification or continued development. The evaluation takes into consideration both understanding of content and presentation/training skills ability.

Mary Kay: The Best Teach the Rest

Similar to Rosenbluth's Leader in Learning program, but with a slightly different flavor, is Mary Kay's approach in using first-line exemplary performers as trainers. Mary Kay's motto for training the "Mary Kay way" among its independent sales force is "The best teach the rest." This approach is also followed by employees. Longtime employees routinely share personal anecdotes about Mary Kay Ash and the company with newer employees. Storytelling is used formally and informally to keep the culture alive, convey company traditions, and impart "the Mary Kay way."

Rarely does a leader in learning candidate require additional development, and it's not because the process is easy. It's because most possess strong skills. At our companywide meeting in 1997, two leaders in learning presented seminars to their fellow associates and clients from around the world, in a lineup that included professional speakers and seasoned staff from learning and development.

In addition to the training provided to the leaders in learning, they are given support guides and training materials for their programs. Most important, they have built a close network with one another. Leaders in learning from around the world regularly call upon each other for solutions and support. A special voice mail network connects them, in all our locations. They regularly share ideas over the network and call for solutions to challenges. They also have their own newsletter, and they meet once or twice a year face to face. This provides a support network and a best-practices forum.

To further support the leaders in learning, we created a team of internal "learning consultants" who report to the director of learning and development in a temporary capacity. Today, human resources consultants fill that role, meeting both HR and learning needs. They work very closely with each of the general managers of the business units or centralized service centers to which they are assigned. Together, they design strategies to meet the specific needs of the unit.

The white paper on our training redesign made an important point about these consultants: "To be successful, they had to know and understand every aspect of the businesses they supported. They needed to take that giant leap from responsive service provider to strategic partner."

The strategic nature of this type of relationship enables our human resources and learning and development departments to provide an unparalleled level of service to the business units, because they are intimately involved and in tune with the goals and day-to-day operations of that particular unit. In the typical corporation, the usual role of these departments is reduced to that of putting out fires. In this design, they can anticipate the needs of each unit and meet those needs immediately.

According to our corporate design, the focus is on/the business units and their service to our clients. The supporting departments are keenly aware that their roles are those of support. Strategic pairing of members of those departments with the business units ensures that the focus remains on the clients and those who directly serve them, and not on functional roles within the company.

A FLEXIBLE CURRICULUM. With a decentralized structure in place for our learning organization, we then set out to create the right tools to support individual learning. The starting point is the Individual Development Plan, or IDP. Every year, each associate creates his or her own learning plan for the year, which is approved by their leader. All learning objectives must support the company's strategic objectives as well as individual development needs.

The plan incorporates learning objectives for improvement in the associates' current position, as well as objectives to help them advance in the career path they desire. Each IDP includes action steps, completion criteria, time frames, and resources required.

The IDP not only personalizes the learning process to each individual, it also emphasizes the personal responsibility that comes along with that type of opportunity. While IDPs are technically optional, they are well on their way to becoming unanimous. Many leaders believe so strongly in them that they have made them mandatory within their areas. I have asked all of my direct reports to develop IDPs for themselves and I follow one for myself as well.

The IDP is one of the most effective ways to ensure the entire company keeps moving ahead, because each individual is growing simultaneously. Copies of all IDPs throughout each business unit are consolidated and studied to look for trends in the learning needs of the associates. If everyone seems to be looking to develop the same skills, that signals the need for new programs and/or for hiring expertise in that area.

The learning objectives in the IDPs are arrived at through performance measures and reviews, 360-degree reviews, career goals, and knowledge and skill self-assessment tools. A skill profile has been developed for each position in the company. This enables associates to gauge their skills against what's required for their current position and those to which they aspire.

Learning needs are addressed both by individual solutions and by companywide curriculum offerings. Once individuals have a road map of where they need to go, a wide variety of vehicles is provided for them to get there, allowing people to learn as they learn best.

Some training programs still take place in a classroom setting. Many are offered in self-study modules, either computer- or workbook-based. Associates can learn at their own pace, and in the time frame that fits their schedule. A variety of programs have been reformatted into "user-friendly" modules, which can be taught easily on-site by associates with limited experience. Whatever the format, the content is key, and we'd like to share a few program highlights with you.

Orientation. For all of the changes in our approach to training, two things have remained very much the same: our steadfast commitment to learning and our orientation program. Nearly a decade ago, we created an orientation program that remains a hallmark of our company's culture, and it has changed remarkably little over the years. We explained it in detail in our last book, *The Customer Comes Second,* so we won't revisit it here in detail, except to discuss why it hasn't changed much, and the ways in which it *has* changed.

Orientation hasn't changed for the simple reason that it is rooted in our core beliefs, and those will never change. We bring our new associates together for their first two days with the company. We devote the first day to our philosophies and values and the second to service. We let our new associates know that they come first. The leadership of the company is there to serve them as they serve our clients. They learn how important service is, and how high our clients' expectations are. They also begin to realize that they can expect to form deep friendships when they commit to a lot of hard work.

We use unusual and memorable ways to get these points across, and we always end the session with a high tea, served to them by the top officers of the company. That's our orientation in a nutshell, and we don't expect it will change much in the future.

Mary Kay: Building a Base of Understanding

Mary Kay's new employee orientation program is a three-day course for all new, full-time employees. Participants interact with senior management, sales consultants, tenured employees, and each other, to build a base understanding of all facets of the business. Mary Kay Ash's life, vision, and values are examined in depth. All new employees tour facilities, including manufacturing, R&D, an automated distribution center; they even have the chance to participate in an actual skin care class. The program includes a strong focus on teamwork and customer service skills.

What has changed about Rosenbluth's orientation is that the program used to be three days; now it is two. Day 2 used to be devoted to an introductory course in quality. But we learned over the years that quality is best taught and applied when it is part of the daily operations—a way of life, rather than a separate subject.

A few years ago, during an evaluation of our orientation, we made an interesting discovery. We asked people, some time after they had attended orientation, if they were using quality tools on a daily basis. Most of them said they weren't, and we were alarmed because we had devoted an entire day per new associate to teach it. To test the validity of the evaluation, we asked the question in another way. We asked whether they were using agendas, flowcharts, brainstorming, measurements, process flowcharts, fishbone diagrams, and other specific quality tools on a daily basis. To this they answered yes. It's interesting to note that our original objective was to make quality a way of life. It seems we succeeded. Our associates didn't recognize quality as a separate program to be trotted out on special occasions. They regarded it as just the way we do business every day.

We also heard from orientation participants that they found the day-long quality training session to be dry, overwhelming, and, even worse, unmemorable. So we phased it out, and now just include a brief talk to let new associates know they'll be learning quality the most effective way— as part of their daily work. Best of all, this change gives us more time to talk over tea.

**Beth Israel Deaconess Medical Center:
The Power of Preceptorships**

At Beth Israel Deaconess, all new employees attend the company's orientation program. Following orientation, many clinical departments have a very structured, follow-on program during which practices and organizational values are shared. For example, within nursing is a six-week "preceptorship," in which the new nurse is mentored by a highly experienced colleague.

To ensure that quality is very much a part of our daily life, we incorporate it into all of our leadership learning programs. We discuss the importance of measurement and of using quality tools to make good business decisions. One highlight is an intense five-day program on the use of our fully automated Corporate Operations Standards Manual. Using point-and-click technology, our leaders have hundreds of quality tools and checklists available to assess and evaluate their business units.

In our development of the second generation of quality at our company, we have continually shifted responsibility from headquarters to the field. In the past, we conducted mass training by a staff of more than a dozen. Today, two associates serve as consultants to the field to help leaders reach maximum effectiveness.

Quality isn't about charts and graphs. It begins and ends with people. That's why we continually talk about how to involve associates in the quality process, and how to inspire them to embrace quality as a way of life. Our approach to quality is creative. We don't care what people call it, as long as they practice it; and they do. Our quality team has been called upon to share their expertise with companies far and wide, and one of their favorite stories shows just how unusual our approach to quality is. Actually, it shows just how unusual our company is.

One of our vice presidents was invited to speak to a major global car rental company about our approach. Our quality group tries to make the science of quality fun, and they decided to take a risk and use a theme they often use with internal groups: The Wizard of Oz. They chose it because most people can relate to it, and the different characters offer lessons in overcoming intimidation and rising to the occasion.

They rented Cowardly Lion, Tin Man, Scarecrow, and Dorothy costumes, and even brought along a dog as Toto. Our vice president gave a very effective, hard-hitting presentation. The content was exceptional, and very well received by the audience, but they just weren't ready for the theatrics.

When the members of her quality team walked on stage to act out certain points, they were met not with smiles or laughter, but with blank stares and some uncomfortable fidgeting. They said they all felt like Toto by the time they left the stage, with their tails between their legs. They were able to laugh at themselves but decided to take a more conservative approach for external presentations.

Show 'Em the Ropes. Starting out on the right foot is a must, but the steps following that first one are just as important. Our orientation is something our associates remember throughout their careers, and while we're proud of that, we found that back in the business units, people needed further orientation.

To meet that need, we created a program that we call LEAP, for Leader Education and Acclimation Program. It was originally designed for new leaders, but we felt everyone would benefit from it, so we expanded it to include all associates in all business units. It teaches new associates more about the company, their specific business unit, and our industry.

LEAP is an extension of our orientation process in each associate's home work site. It is highly customized to the specific business unit or department in which the associate will work. Some modules are standard and others are unit-specific. Standard components include familiarization with our industry and with company departments. A seminar, explaining the dynamics of our industry, its unique language, and other intricacies, is taught either live or via videotape. An overview of the various departments within the company, what expertise they offer and how to best access the expertise and services they offer, is also presented both live and on tape.

The more customized aspects of LEAP clue in associates on how things work within their business unit, from where the coffee is and how to make copies to the specific daily operations and responsibilities of their unit. This part of the program is usually taught through a buddy system that pairs each new associate with a peer in his or her unit. The buddy has a checklist of everything the new associate needs to know to be able to work efficiently and comfortably.

My coauthor, Diane, tells a story about her first days with our company a decade ago that illustrates why we need a program like LEAP. At that time, we had no orientation program at all. She joined a very busy department, and on her first day, she drafted a press release that needed to go out that same day. After finishing the release, she went to the copy machine only to find someone using it. She worked on other projects, returning every half hour or so, only to find the same person using the machine. Exasperated on her eighth visit, she asked if he could let her know when he was finished, so she could get her release copied and sent. He responded that making copies was his responsibility. They both got a kick out of the whole thing. But lost productivity and frustration are no laughing matter.

Shortly thereafter, our orientation program was born, and associates, new and veteran alike, went through it. But it is not designed to teach day-to-day operations on a local level. That is the responsibility of the individual business units, through LEAP. A checklist of action items is provided to each business unit to help them create and implement their own LEAP program. The list includes suggested items to be completed prior to the new associate arriving, and during his or her first few weeks.

For example, prior to the new associate's first day, their office buddy should be assigned and be prepared to greet them upon arrival. An introduction memo should be circulated prior to their arrival. The buddy prepares the new associate's workstation with a customized nameplate, office supplies, and goody bags filled with things like lunch coupons, "cheat sheets" to introduce coworkers, and other special treats.

During the first week, new associates meet with the members of their immediate team and are introduced to the vice president over their department. They participate in a week-long scavenger hunt designed to facilitate interaction and introduction throughout the business unit.

During the second week, new associates meet with their leader to review any questions they might have and to ensure they are comfortable in their new "home." Then they begin to create their Individual Development Plan.

The LEAP concept grew out of our new approach to learning. Unlike the recent past, when we offered only the initial orientation for all associates, we now offer an orientation that is later reinforced and built upon at the local level by peers. This maximizes the use of resources, builds friendships throughout the company, and results in stronger, more targeted learning.

All of our training programs are available to all associates in the company. To encourage participation, we publish a monthly schedule of all learning programs across the country, including the date and location of the program, along with a description, information on who should attend, and a contact for enrollment. Across every page is written "All classes, including restricted registration, are available to ALL associates for auditing or participation upon approval of facilitator. Your leader must preapprove time out of the office and expense connected with your class." We want to make sure that all associates fully understand that they are welcome to learn whatever they feel they would benefit from. That broadens the horizons of our company and the individuals it comprises.

Learning at Other Companies

Learning is a strength at all of our peers from *The 100 Best*. Here are some innovative program ideas.

MARY KAY. One of the most interesting learning programs at Mary Kay is the assimilation of individuals and teams. It's similar, in some respects, to what we do in our LEAP program as well as our leadership programs (which you'll read about in the next chapter). At Mary Kay, assimilations are required globally for all new director-level and higher positions, during which new leaders meet tenured employees from all areas of the company. Mary Kay's Human Resources Department works closely with all the departments in the company when putting together assimilation schedules. It's not unusual for an assimilation schedule to last 2 or 3 weeks and include 20 to 30 meetings.

Another type of assimilation is required for newly hired or recently promoted managers. Human resources facilitates a meeting of everyone who will report to the new leader, providing an opportunity to ask questions. Then HR compiles a list of those questions, and presents it to the new leader, who answers the questions in a follow-up session with the group. Questions range from "What is your favorite food?" to "What is your strategic vision for the department?"

ALAGASCO. Alagasco introduces its employees to all areas of the company in an off-site program called Alabama Gas Corporation University, or AGCU, which has been in place for a decade and is one of the company's most popular. All officers of the company make presentations during this 3-day program.

Employees favor the team-building aspects, such as the series of outdoor experiential exercises that cap off the event. CEO Mike Warren says, "Class photos are a highlight at this event, as employees become very close with their classmates. A real sense of friendship and camaraderie develops during this learning experience."

All Alagasco employees attend AGCU, and each session of 25 represents a cross-section of the company—management, union employees, clerks, and so on. They have so far conducted more than 20 sessions, and more than 500 employees are now AGCU graduates.

LANDS' END. Lands' End's orientation for temporary staff is a comprehensive and interactive program that explains how the company began, how it has grown, and where it is today. Each new employee is given a *Welcome to Lands' End* booklet at the time of hire, which outlines Lands' End's eight principles of doing business. It is then used through the first two hours of orientation, and referred to throughout.

For salaried staff, orientation encompasses the same welcome booklet, but also includes a walking tour and explanation of Lands' End's history, one-to-one talks about the company, and a program called Internal Seminar Series (ISS). ISS, a 10-week program that covers the fundamentals of each area of the company, is designed to pass on knowledge of the business to all professional staff. Participants also work on a project to acquire customers. A lot of great ideas have come from this part of the program. For example, one class initiated a corporate sales catalog, which is now one of Lands' End's specialty businesses.

USAA. USAA's one-stop service environment is a big part of its reputation for world-class service, and it takes a great deal of training to make it a reality. All new USAA Property & Casualty customer contact employees (approximately 1,000 per year) attend a 380-hour course that reinforces the company's culture and provides the basis for its service. The course combines technical skills (e.g., insurance contracts), nontechnical skills (e.g., empathy, critical thinking), and business principles (e.g., operating expense ratios and key result areas).

The curriculum for this program is event-driven, meaning that the learning is measured through the presentation of actual job occurrences and the skills required to accomplish those events. Ultimately, live phone calls from customers are introduced into the classroom, and at the conclusion of training, the instructor team accompanies the students to the workplace and assists in their assimilation into the workforce. All students are required to successfully complete four performance-based tests with an 85 percent average.

USAA's in-house training organization is composed of 370 people (260 at the home office in San Antonio, Texas, and 120 spread across four regional training units). According to Senior Vice President, Human Resources, Bill Tracy, the beauty of this approach is consistency. He says, "Our members cannot tell if USAA employees were trained in Colorado Springs, Tampa, or San Antonio, as they all receive essentially the same curriculum from highly trained instructors."

When it comes to external education opportunities, USAA offers up-front payment and direct billing in its tuition reimbursement program. Corporate support (from the CEO down) also motivates employees to further their education, as seen in the results. More than 30 percent of USAA's employees participate in the program, compared with a national average of 6 percent. And it has been worth the investment, because 97 percent of the more than 2,000 employees who have completed their college degrees or professional designations as part of the program since 1991 are still actively employed at USAA.

FEL-PRO. Fel-Pro's technical certification program for employees is rigorous. They launched it in 1996, in conjunction with Northern Illinois University. Classes are taught by university professors, but are held on-site at the company. Employees attend on their own time, and they must pass a math qualifying exam to get *into* the course.

The program is designed to prepare Fel-Pro employees for new technologies. It covers such topics as programmable logic controllers, geometric dimensioning and tolerances, blueprint reading, and metallurgy. To give you an idea of how in-depth this training is, just the programmable logic controllers portion is 16 weeks.

According to Fel-Pro's Vice President of Human Resources Arlis McLean, "In the factory of today and the future, people will need to know these things. It parallels the growing role of computers in our everyday lives. Many of the machines found in factories today are controlled by computers, and employees have to fully understand how to use them. People can't just come out of high school and be ready to work here anymore. Factory work is not just muscle; it's brains. And we are not in an industry usually considered high-tech."

BETH ISRAEL DEACONESS MEDICAL CENTER. Beth Israel Deaconess addresses a widespread issue head-on with its Workplace Education Program, which teaches English as a second language as well as basic educational skills. Students are paid for 50 percent of the class time, and an individual plan is created for each employee.

A learning lab is available to students who wish to improve their English, increase their reading or writing skills, prepare for the GED exam, or learn keyboard skills. The lab offers computer-based instruction, one-on-one help, or small group classes moderated by a teacher.

GREAT PLAINS SOFTWARE. Great Plains Software uses a wide spectrum of tools and methods to provide learning opportunities for their employees, customers, and the partners in their virtual organization (as explained in Chapter 4). According to Group Vice President Jodi Uecker-Rust, "Knowledge is transferred in many forms, including classroom, one-on-one, conference attendance, video, computer-based training, and the Internet.

"Our Internet-based training is a new initiative for us. It delivers just-in-time learning opportunities directly to the desktop of our employees and virtual organization. This is in addition to our distance learning offerings, which include videos, workbooks, instructor guides, and teleconferencing. Internet-based training allows us to increase the number of trained professionals by providing unprecedented access to training without travel and timing constraints."

Addicted to Learning: A Summary

- Learning should be entertaining to be memorable. As Jane Norman says, "Learning is best when it's magical, mystical, and fun, and that goes for school and for work."

- Companies should avoid the "Sunday best" syndrome. Just like the student who didn't participate in art projects until she stopped wearing formal clothing and started showing up in playclothes, we never know what someone is capable of until we free them from constraints. Rules, policies (though you need *some*), politics, and fear in the workplace can inhibit creativity and productivity. Loosen the reins and see what's possible.

- Remember, lunchroom and water-cooler conversations often tell more about real lessons learned in companies than do formal meetings. It's a good idea to do frequent reality checks on people's perceptions.

- Consider an emphasis on *learning* as opposed to *training*. Before it was popular to do so, we changed the name of our training department to Learning and Development. But the name is just the beginning; it's the strategic direction that matters.

- Try instituting a very nonhierarchical structure in your learning area. Ours is messy and weblike. It might not look pretty on paper, but it's creative, fast, low-cost, and effective. Above all, it's decentralized and focused on the field, where learning should be its strongest.

- A Leader in Learning Program can be a great way to bring real-world, customized application to your learning programs, while driving down the cost of training. In our program, front-line associates (some on a full-time basis and some in conjunction with other roles) assess the training needs of their operating units, make learning a part of daily work, and serve as on-site trainers. To ensure consistency, our Leader in Learning Program has a rigorous selection process and certification program. A network among leaders in learning around the world generates the sharing of ideas and best practices on the learning front.

- Consider having each employee create and follow an Individual Development Plan to chart their learning goals for the year. It will help individuals to grow in their current positions as well as advance on the career paths they desire. When each individual advances his or her knowledge, companies grow exponentially.

- Offering learning programs in a variety of formats can increase a company's success rate in reaching its associates where they learn best. We offer programs in classroom settings, self-study modules (computer- or workbook-based), user-friendly modules that can be taught on-site by associates with limited experience, and any combination of these formats.

- A memorable orientation program is an important part of starting off on the right foot. Ours brings everyone together for their first two days with the company. We discuss our philosophy, values, and approach to service. We treat our new associates to a high tea served to them by the officers of the company.

- As important as orientation is, to be effective, it must be followed up on a local level with tips for daily operations as well as efforts to make associates feel welcome in their new home. Our follow-up program offers new associates in-depth information about our industry, the company, and their specific operating unit. A buddy system pairs all new associates with a veteran to welcome them and show 'em the ropes.

- All training programs should be open to all associates. We publicize every learning opportunity in the company in a monthly calendar, which features a description of the program and whom to contact in order to attend.

6

We're Not Born into Leadership: We Convert

Companies can't bestow leadership upon people; true leadership is earned with the right attitude, skills, and behavior. But companies can do a lot to ensure that their people maximize their leadership potential. We have for many years offered comprehensive leadership training, although the style and emphasis have changed in recent years. It has, like most of our training programs, become more decentralized and focused on real-world experience than on classroom instruction. When people have the opportunity to *do* what it is they're trying to learn, the learning is significantly more effective.

As with the rest of the company's programs, our leadership training takes a customized approach. Just as our business units are tailored to the needs of their individual clients, the training we offer is tailored to the needs of the individuals participating. We used to offer one leadership program for everyone; now we have several. Our leadership training used to be almost 90 percent classroom-based and 10 percent experiential; today, those numbers are reversed.

When we redesigned our company, we knew we needed to revamp our leadership programs to reflect that new design. We needed faster, stronger programs that would result in a deep lineup of leaders, capable of running their own business, which in effect, was what the new structure created.

Our directive to the learning and development team was: Design and roll out all-new programs within 30 days. The project leader was on vacation at the time, and promptly invited her team of five to join her there for a team meeting. They spent the next few days on the beach, designing the new set of programs in a creative and unencumbered environment. The remainder of the chapter describes the fruits of that meeting.

Internal and External Approach to Leadership

It's imperative to offer those already in your company the opportunity to advance; they must to be able to clearly see that opportunity before them. This is difficult to do when the company is in a rapid growth mode, undergoing intense change, or expanding globally, all of which we have been doing these past few years.

The temptation to hire expertise from the outside, as opposed to honing it from the inside, is strong, and at times that is the right thing to do. But if that's all you do, it's debilitating to those who have been a loyal part of making your company what it is. It can also drastically change the personality of your entire organization in a very short period of time.

Developing bench strength among current associates is a responsibility of every company. It's a commitment companies have to make to their people: to offer them the opportunity to advance and to provide them with the training and tools necessary to follow through. We advocate a combination of preparing current associates for advancement and hiring expertise from the outside. This keeps fresh ideas flowing in from the outside while protecting the company's culture and foundation. To do this, leadership training must be approached from two perspectives: (1) providing leadership skills to those who are steeped in the company but lack specific skills required to advance; and (2) providing training on the company, its culture, focus, and foundation to leaders who join the company from the outside. Let's talk about some programs to achieve those goals.

Preleadership Development Program

All training programs in our company are open to all associates, and our leadership development programs are no exception. The preleadership development program is a great place to start for those interested in pursuing leadership roles. We instituted the program because we noticed a disturbing trend. As our company grew and our products and services became more complex and sophisticated, we saw a widening gap between the skill set at our entry-level positions and what was called for in our leadership roles. No longer was it possible to promote someone solely because he or she was terrific with customers or had been doing an exceptional job in his or her current position. We wanted to be able to do so, as we had for years, but times had changed and we had to change with them.

To develop a program to help us do this, our learning and development crew studied the careers, skills, and strengths of people throughout the company who had successfully made the leap from the front line to key leadership roles, to determine exactly what it takes. Next they put together a program that would help front-line associates build those very skills. All aspects of the program are hands-on, providing real-world opportunities to grow and test these skills.

The program is offered twice a year, and the opportunity is communicated to all associates. The only requirements are that associates be with the company for at least six months and that they attend a one-day seminar, which is conducted on a Saturday. The seminar, entitled Is Leadership Meant for Me?, is held regionally. Travel expenses are paid by the company, but associates must attend on their own time. The program introduces attendees to the demands of a leadership role, after which they can decide if they really want to pursue leadership at that time.

To paint a realistic picture, a panel of vice presidents, directors, and other leaders discuss what leadership is truly like on a day-to-day basis—not always as glamorous as the audience expects. Following the introductory panel, the group jumps into some exercises to simulate a day in the life of a leader. For example, participants are given an "in-box" filled with client letters, memos from senior company leaders, and a host of other documents and phone messages. Then the class breaks into small groups to prioritize the tasks in the box. The groups are given far more than 40 hours' worth of work, and asked to fit it into a week's schedule—a pretty accurate take on what most leaders face today.

The day is a real eye-opener for most who attend. If they're still interested in working toward a leadership role, they proceed with a selection process much like that of a job interview. They submit a letter of interest and a resume to our learning and development team, then go through a formal interview. Internal reference checks are done, followed by a second, more in-depth interview. Not everyone who applies is selected. Usually some 80 to 90 people attend the Saturday seminar. Of those, usually 50 to 60 decide to apply, and around 20 are selected for each class.

One very important component of the program is the feedback provided to those candidates not selected. A representative from learning and development who is involved in the selection process holds a one-to-one meeting with each person not accepted into the program, at the point in the process at which the decision is made. This gives each of them the chance to know where and how they need to develop in order to succeed the next time they apply.

Those who are accepted into the program sign a contract agreeing to spend a certain amount of time per week out of their work schedule (with their leader's approval and support) and a certain amount of their free time working on preleadership projects and studying. The needs of the business unit must come first, so leadership involvement is critical.

The program requires approximately 170 business hours (including class time) and a suggested 110 nonbusiness hours per person over a six-month period. The group meets for a series of two-day workshops held every four to six weeks. Each person develops an action plan that specifies how they will develop their skills and complete the program while continuing to fulfill their current job. They complete another Individual Development Plan (IDP) at the conclusion of the program, to ensure that continual development takes place beyond the course; this is a requirement for "graduation."

Program Plan

There are four major components to the program: (1) a business writing course, (2) a quality project, (3) a presentation, and (4) leadership simulation. We'll briefly describe the first three, and discuss more in depth the part of the program with the most impact: the leadership simulation.

The business writing course is pretty standard, but writing is an important skill because of the communication demands that come with leadership. The quality project calls for participants to identify an area of opportunity within their business unit, collect and analyze data, and recommend a solution. Several of the cases presented by our leadership candidates have saved literally thousands upon thousands of dollars, all while teaching valuable quality and decision-making skills.

For the presentation project, the class breaks into smaller groups to plan, create, and deliver a presentation to the entire group. The presentation is on a department or line of business within the company, for example, telecommunications or corporate communications. This calls for skills in networking, research, and team coordination (team members are spread across the country), and teaches the entire group about the many facets of the company, where to get information, and how to get things done.

LEAD ON. Now for the leadership simulation. This is where we see the greatest impact—where most of the "aha's" take place. We approach the simulation in a variety of ways. At times, the class works together to solve a live business case for the company. They are assigned a project that might otherwise not be pursued in the near-term according to prioritization, but is well worth doing. This provides hands-on leadership experience and the company's "we wish we had the time to . . . " list gets accomplished.

The team is given an important mission, and a safety net as well, so that caution doesn't stand in the way of learning. The team members test and quickly expand their leadership skills under watchful eyes, while completing a very real project.

Sometimes the team is given a task where the project isn't the point, but rather the process or experience. "The tower" is a favorite. We ask the group to break into teams, and to choose a leader for each. Then we give them a pile of stuff (anything lying around the company) and ask them to build a tower. The objective is to build the very "best" tower. Few other instructions are given.

Almost every team does the same thing. They quickly select a leader—usually the bossiest person. Then they proceed to glue, staple, and stack all of the items on top of one another as quickly as possible. But this is not meant to be an exercise in speed. (Sometimes the teams work on these towers over a period of months, learning lessons about leadership along the way.) Usually, the leader dictates how the tower should look, assuming everyone has the same vision of the "best" tower.

As with most group situations, those who are more reserved rarely share their ideas, and assume they wouldn't be heeded anyway if they did. Eventually, the team members realize that each of them has a slightly different view of the goal. Most groups don't recognize for some time that they haven't asked the "client" (the instructor) what his or her goals are for the tower. This is probably the most important message.

The exercise is always tailored to the specific learning needs of the group. One highly competitive group was particularly intent on building the tallest and strongest tower, and that was taking precedence over the leadership lessons. So the instructor asked them to dismantle their tower after they had been working on it over several sessions. She stated that the client had decided they only needed one tower, and that the other group's tower had been chosen. After dismantling the tower, they were free to help the group against whom they had so vigorously competed to finish building their tower. This was a very difficult lesson for the group, but one that mirrors the real world they would face as leaders. They must be willing to change direction and to reprioritize at any moment.

Eventually, team members learn the importance of strategy and planning before jumping in. They learn that no one person possesses all the answers. They understand how important the client's vision is. They come to understand their own style in relating with others, and the strengths and weaknesses that style brings. They begin to understand how much there is to learn.

Another tower-type project was an assignment that sounded simple, but held a world of complexity. We asked a group to create an area outside our headquarters where associates could meet for lunch—kind of a picnic area. Initially, the group thought all they needed was a weed-whacker, some picnic tables, and some flower seeds. But once the exercise began, they ran into obstacles such as city permits, zoning issues, insurance requirements, accessibility and maintenance obstacles, funding questions, and coordination with a host of other civic groups who had their own ideas for that space.

Ultimately, the project was rejected, and while this was a disappointment to the group who worked so hard on it, the lessons they learned were invaluable. And as with all the groups, along with these new skills, they built lasting, rewarding friendships and have continued the learning process far beyond the program.

Following the program, there are no guarantees of placement in a leadership role or advancement of any kind. However, those who complete it gain the competencies necessary to become effective leaders, and the credentials to be considered for leadership positions. The program is built on the recognition that we will be more successful if we work to instill succession planning rather than always going outside to fill a leadership role.

> **The Leadership Track at Lands' End and Beth Israel Deaconess: Putting High-Potential Employees to Work**
>
> Lands' End assigns new high-potential employees to a special group, and then to one of their business units. It's part of the company's Customer Acquisition Training Program. It includes formal training, but the group is given the real business of acquiring new customers, and they focus on that goal.
>
> Beth Israel Deaconess' Leadership Track program is an intensified five-day course focused on problem solving, facilitation of group problem solving, and meeting management. Offered to managers at all levels, participants bring real work issues to use as material for the group problem-solving portion. These mock problem-solving meetings are videotaped, and then debriefed with the group, to further strengthen their skills.

Baptism by Fire

The best way to learn leadership is by living it. While our preleadership program opens the doors to leadership for our front-line associates, we also have a program for those close to being ready to fill key leadership roles, which offers intense experiential learning. The 90-day Accelerated Leadership Development Program (ALDP) includes only three classroom sessions; the rest of the learning takes place in the field.

Participants may take calls at 2:00 A.M. in one of our 24-hour emergency service centers; or they might be assigned to a critical project or to a particularly challenging situation. This may take place in any number of business units around the world. As opportunities arise, those in ALDP are whisked off to business units to capitalize on the unique chance to master the exact set of skills they need.

The program takes our Individual Development Plan (IDP) concept to the extreme. Each experience is tailored to the developmental needs of the individual. They are given meaty roles, and they're expected to successfully manage the situation, measure the effectiveness of their solutions, and produce detailed reports on their approach, steps taken, and results.

Associates are recommended for ALDP by senior leaders in the company. The leader who recommends an associate also takes responsibility for seeing that he or she is successfully placed in the right leadership role at the conclusion of the program. ALDP participants report to a learning and development manager, who monitors their progress and serves as a learning mentor. They meet with her weekly, and are given whatever support they need in order to succeed.

The classroom portion of the program includes one week each at the beginning, midpoint, and end of the three-month period. The first session reviews how critical the core beliefs of the company are—for example, friendship being the cornerstone of our strength. At the conclusion of the first session, they complete a customized learning plan designed to get them where they need to be quickly. The final classroom session includes a detailed report of their experiences and recommendations for the program, so we can all learn from their experience.

As with most of our programs, ALDP is global. We have associates from the United States who spend time in business units abroad, and we have associates from around the world work in the United States to learn from their counterparts here.

There are many success stories from our ALDP program, but one in particular illustrates the concentrated learning that can take place in a program like this. When we redesigned our company, most of the general managers of our newly formed business units came from within the company. Out of the handful that did not was someone who had interviewed with our company over an eight-month period. (That's not unusual when we can see that someone belongs in the company and we're trying to find the right position for them.) The new general manager position was an appropriate career path for him, so we accepted him into the company and placed him in the ALDP program for intensified training. After just three weeks in the program, a tremendous but risky opportunity was presented to the class.

A new account had gotten off to a rocky start. The client had greatly underestimated their travel volume, which meant we were not adequately staffed for those first few weeks. They also didn't have a system in place to bring new locations, acquisitions, and other additional sources of business on board for our service. Most companies give us notice that a new unit will require our service so we can prepare for that volume, but with this particular account, calls would come flooding in from some unexpected location with no warning at all.

It was a very challenging situation. We worked closely with the account to build their processes. In the meantime, we needed to quickly turn our service around with the resources and systems we had in place at the time. Looking for a fresh perspective and an appropriate available resource, the business unit turned to the ALDP program for help.

When the call was given for a volunteer to leave immediately to concentrate on turning the situation around, the first hand to go up was our new associate who had been interviewing with us for eight months. Now with three full weeks with the company under his belt, he rushed off to save one of our prominent accounts. He says, "I called my wife and said, 'I just made either one of the best or worst decisions, and I'm not sure which.'" It turned out to be one of the best, for him, for our client, and for our company.

He says that being a part of a program where intensified learning was the objective and where a safety net meant being able to jump in and try, knowing he would be supported, gave him the courage to volunteer. He says it was the best learning experience of his life. He put everything he learned in those first three weeks of the program immediately to work in the business unit.

More interesting is that he had 19 years of industry experience, and says that for the first time in his career, he was given an opportunity to *do* everything he had learned over those two decades. It was real experience, not just observation or classroom training. He says, "It closed the loop on all the avenues I had been down over those 19 years, and brought it all together." He used every skill he had, and turned the account around significantly in just a week. He stayed for two months, and service continued steadily to improve.

He says, "It was amazing to be entrusted with a major account after only three weeks. And I had total access to any resource in the company, including the CEO and all of the top leaders. It was just like I thought it would be at Rosenbluth, when I wanted to join the company."

Following his stay with that account, he applied for the job of general manager for the Kodak account; he won that role, which he held for a year and a half. He quickly rose to a director position in operations, then went on to global operations. Today, he is a vice president of our company, just four years after joining us in the ALDP program.

He attributes much of his success to the program, saying the design allows employees to chase whatever they need to learn, anywhere in the company. During the program, he had the chance to learn under five different general managers, all with their own styles and strengths. His program mentor is a leader in our quality area, and brought that valuable discipline to his learning experience. The program taught him where to go within and outside the company to get the job done, and that's what it's all about.

USAA: A Tailored Approach for Every Stage of Leadership

USAA's leadership education program covers managers from their initial selection up to and including its executive council, with programs tailored for each level of experience as a leader. For example, the Emerging Leaders program is designed for the new manager the first 90 days of selection. Leadership Concepts and Applications is for the one-to-six-year time frame; Leaders of Leaders is for managers of managers; and on the drawing board are programs for senior executives.

USAA partnered with the University of Virginia to create the Darden Executive Education Program in 1996, specifically to enhance strategic thinking and knowledge of the business, and to develop the leadership skills of managerial employees. All property and casualty managers including VPs and AVPs will attend. In addition, there are follow-on seminars for Darden program graduates.

A Friend in Learning: The Mentoring Program

No matter how sharp the skills that leaders new to the company bring with them, they still have a lot to learn about our unique style. One of the ways we teach them is through a new mentoring program. For new leaders from the outside to work most efficiently within the organization and to gain buyin from company veterans (their new team and peers), it's important that they understand the culture in which they'll be operating. This prevents the annoying "but we did it this way in my old company" syndrome that new leaders often bring with them, along with their share of fresh new ideas.

Because our company's culture of friendship is so important, it demands "teaching." Those who join the company and attempt to trample on our culture find themselves out in a hurry, no matter how seemingly valuable their skills are. Expertise is important, but not at the expense of friendship. Put bluntly, in addition to teaching how to get things done around here, sometimes we're teaching people how not to be jerks. Our culture is one built upon trust and honesty, and from time to time someone from the outside can view such an open environment as an opportunity to move in and take over "the world."

Usually, though, we're helping new leaders "unlearn" skepticism they've assimilated elsewhere. We're teaching them to trust the culture, which to some can seem too good to be true. For a time, a lot of seasoned leaders who join the company wait for the other shoe to drop. That waiting can waste a lot of energy, so we need to make them feel comfortable quickly so they can move beyond that.

To that end, our program matches new leaders from the outside with cultural "mentors" within the company—not necessarily on a peer level with the leader. For example, a new vice president may have a veteran manager as a mentor, to teach what could only be learned through years of experience within Rosenbluth.

For some, the environment takes some getting used to. But the bonds that cement this company are a fortress against our competitors and against any outside factors over which we have no control. Preserving this valuable asset deserves the attention our mentoring program provides.

Mentor Matching

We set some wide parameters around who might be mentors. We decided not to preselect individuals or to call for volunteers, thinking this might limit the number of people who participate. When you preselect, you run the risk of overlooking someone who has a lot to offer but might not be in a highly visible position, or who might be more reserved. And when you call for volunteers, you run the risk that some of your strongest people, who are also likely some of your busiest, might decline. But when faced with an individual opportunity to mentor someone with whom they would be a great match, they will probably make the time to do it. Thus our field of eligible mentors consists of all leaders in the company and all associates who have been with the company for more than five years.

Next we developed a self-assessment survey to determine the strengths and weaknesses of those participating—both our potential mentors and the new leaders joining the company. From the results of the survey, we built a database of our mentors' strengths. We use the database to help us match new leaders with the best mentor for them.

When a new leader joins the company, his or her leader contacts the business unit's designated human resources consultant, who helps determine any particular developmental needs the new leader might have. From this, a set of learning objectives is developed. An appropriate mentor is selected, and once paired, the partners meet to define the program.

Following this first meeting, the mentoring program calls for weekly meetings for at least the first month, to keep the momentum going. Learning and development suggests meetings about every three weeks thereafter. In keeping with our belief in personal responsibility for learning, we ask that the mentee take charge in initiating the meetings, and prepare an agenda that facilitates what he or she desires to learn from his or her mentor.

The program has no defined ending. Most mentor relationships turn into long-term friendships. Many continue in a mentor mode. Each relationship is as unique as the individuals in the program. Three examples will give you an idea of how multifaceted the program is:

- A director in our operations area was mentored by a program manager in our learning and development group. She helped him to custom-design a learning plan for his growth.

- A new general manager for Canada was mentored by our director of finance. He helped her to strengthen her financial savvy in managing the business for that country.

- A director in our supplier relations area was clearly ready for advancement, and felt he needed some outside perspective. We arranged for him to be mentored by a CEO of a major corporation who sits on our company's advisory board. Today, that associate is vice president of Supplier Relations.

Advocacy Skills Program

Client retention is the most important thing we do. It is the ultimate measure of our effectiveness. So while it's natural that we would offer strong learning opportunities in this area, we've found it's not such an easy thing to teach: It's multifaceted and encompasses so much art. Nevertheless, we made the commitment to come up with a program that would strengthen our skills in this area, and it's one that has proven very effective.

Our learning and development team, together with the Richardson Company, developed a course we call Client Retention and Development. Its purpose is to further enhance the client advocacy skills of our people—skills they innately possess but that are too important not to reinforce, refine, and continually sharpen.

The genesis of the client retention course was in recognition of how quickly client needs can change and how vital it is that we be able to anticipate those changing needs and be ready with solutions. Our role is not just to be responsive to client needs, but to be so linked with our clients that we can help define and clarify those needs.

The first key is to be business partners and friends with our clients, which is the case. From that starting point, the seminar teaches our people to research and analyze trends; to fully understand their client's organization, industry, strategic direction, competition, challenges and obstacles, growth areas and opportunities; to evaluate the health of their business, and the outside factors affecting them.

From there, we can determine how we can be of the most help to each of our clients. We get a clear picture of how we're doing and what we can do better. The program helps our people add maximum value to every client interaction and to focus their attention on their clients' needs, as opposed to the products and services we offer. The reality is that the right products and services truly result from this intense client focus.

The program runs for two and a half days, and approximately 250 associates per year complete the course. The classroom portion concentrates on relationship building, precise listening, how to accurately assess things from a client's point of view, and how to continually move from a reactive role to one of strong research, preparation, planning, and targeted, proactive solutions. We move from responding to what clients tell us they need to *knowing* what they need and formulating solution options. We hold this course all over the world, and have found that the trends and issues are universal.

We start by explaining the four basic learning zones: the dead zone, comfort zone, stretch zone, and panic zone. We ask people to move from where most people are (their comfort zone) to where they need to be to bring the most value to our clients (the stretch zone). This is where they are growing, learning, changing—ahead of the curve. Then we begin to build some serious skills.

The course is normally taught to a group whose members span a variety of disciplines within the company, so that we share differing perspectives and expertise. This is particularly important as we move from the traditional classroom portion of the course into business cases.

We present at least 10 case studies, from a wide variety of client profiles and perspectives. Some cases feature interaction with individual clients, and others with teams of clients, to ensure effectiveness in both situations. The "students" discuss the cases, present solutions, and critique themselves and their peers. Each person comes away with an evaluation of his or her strengths and areas to improve, and formulates an action plan for continuous development.

The final day is a special strategy session for live cases. Each person presents his or her most challenging situation, and the rest of the members bring their perspective and expertise to bear on the challenge. This is where the benefit of the diversified group really kicks in. The team analyzes the situation and formulates a plan with specific action steps. A follow-up class two months later reviews the progress each person has made in his or her live case.

I learned just how hands-on and gritty this course was when I popped in with a prospective client (unannounced, as usual) to hear a bit of it. I had heard great things about the program and had been wanting to sit in. I was taken aback.

We walked in at the precise moment when each person in the class listed the biggest obstacles to solving his or her toughest business cases, on charts all over the room. Every obstacle you could imagine was posted everywhere you looked. By the end of class, every obstacle was tackled, but when we entered, all we saw was the patients being brought into intensive care. We didn't get to see them in the recovery room. I knew we didn't have time to stay until the solutions were formulated, so I escorted my visitors out of the room and decided I'd check the timing first before joining the class next time. At least our visitors saw we were facing real issues, head-on.

SAS Institute: Depth and Breadth of Knowledge

SAS Institute's Top Gun training program provides new sales and marketing reps with a solid understanding of the company's business initiatives, core technologies, and ideal customer profile. During the program, participants meet key people at headquarters, attend interactive workshops, and role-play. Finally, each student delivers the Institute's Flagship presentation.

Vice President of North American Sales and Marketing Barrett Joyner says, "Our goal is to ensure Top Gun graduates have a real depth of product and business knowledge so they can understand our customers' business needs and can choose the best software solution for each customer. It's important that they be fluent with both information technology and business unit audiences."

Successful Spin-off

Out of our client retention training program was born a unique program we call Evidence of Value. From analyzing the issues uncovered in the client retention sessions, we came to appreciate the importance of increasing the strategic support we provide to our clients. The pressure our clients face is immense. Their lives are moving at the speed of light. They face challenges from all directions, and are barraged by information from an increasing number of sources. They need someone to break through the clutter, determine true value, and help them seize the greatest opportunities. We believe that someone is us.

To fill that role, we need a deep understanding of our clients, as explained in our discussion of the client retention program. Beyond that, we knew our people needed sharp skills in financial analysis, technology, benchmarking, business planning, and other core areas. Therefore, we created an intense course to provide advancement of those skills through a combination of classroom sessions and on-the-job projects. Using these finely honed skills and tools, we are able to offer our clients quantifiable, objective measurements of potential solutions, products, services, and our service to them.

For example, in the financial analysis portion of the program we teach:

- effective analysis and application of data
- spotting financial trends
- forecasting skills

- creating truly useful account reviews
- redefining data requirements
- increased understanding of global economic issues and their effects on our business and those of our clients

In the technology sessions, we instruct associates in:

- creating process maps
- qualifying where technology will have the greatest impact
- understanding the steps, costs, and resources involved in key processes
- diagnosing the need for reengineering
- recognizing technology's impact on processes

The benchmarking session includes instruction on:

- effective metrics
- comparisons of various benchmarking methods
- limitations of current industry benchmarking
- how to help assess client benchmarking needs
- interpreting benchmarking results for effective action
- effective research techniques
- how to design customized client benchmarking programs

In business planning, we cover:

- how to shift from a short-term mode in addressing pressing issues to a long-term outlook
- the differences between action planning, long-range, and strategic planning
- business plan development skills
- measuring business plan progress
- how to effectively develop a customized business plan for a client

This intensified business course is completed after attending the client retention course. It is a very sophisticated, in-depth study into the vast array of skills required for running a business, which is exactly what our leaders do.

Sometimes, stepping out of context can help us recognize something that is too close to sink in during our day-to-day routines. That was my motivation for a bizarre exercise I conducted recently at a global operations meeting we held at the Rivery, our company's ranch and meeting center.

The event that kicked off the meeting was held in a cattle auction barn. Our general managers from around the world had gathered for some important business and found themselves face to face with cattle. I proceeded, with little explanation, to auction off the cattle, which to the untrained general managers' eyes all appeared to be basically the same. The cattle were, in fact, very different. In a real auction, they would have sold for very different amounts, but to the general managers the differences were transparent. One of the cows was fed grass; the other grain. One was ill and the other pregnant (providing a continuous revenue stream).

At the conclusion of the auction, I gave the city slickers a lesson in cattle. The point I was illustrating was the loss of value upon uneducated buyers. The differences are very real. It is our responsibility to be able to prove, without question, the distinction between what we offer and what others offer. This is the evidence of value.

Converting to Leadership: A Summary

- Check your ratio of classroom programs to experiential programs. At the time of our previous book's release, ours was 90 percent classroom-based and 10 percent experiential. Today, those numbers are reversed, and our results are incredible.

- To balance internal and external leadership, instilling leadership must be approached from two perspectives: (1) providing leadership training to veterans in the company who lack the specific skills to advance, and (2) providing insight on the company to leaders who join from the outside.

- Consider a preleadership program for front-line associates who have leadership promise, to help them be ready for opportunities that may arise. Ours is open to all associates, and is offered twice per year. The rigorous selection process begins with a Saturday seminar to expose them to the responsibilities of leadership. The program requires extensive time, both work and nonwork, and that commitment is detailed in a contract. The curriculum includes a business writing course, a quality project, a presentation, and, most important, a leadership simulation exercise.

- For intensified leadership experience, try a program like our 90-day Accelerated Leadership Development Program. Virtually all of the learning takes place on the job, in the field. The program is highly customized. As opportunities arise, participants go anywhere in the world to pursue the chance to master the exact skill set they need to develop.

- A mentoring program can be a great way to share with leaders from the outside what's important in the company, and how to successfully navigate through the organization. Our mentoring program pairs new leaders with associates, who are not necessarily peers. For example, a veteran manager might mentor a new vice president.

- Consider client or customer retention training. We put together a program to help all of our associates enhance their skill at anticipating the needs of our clients and preparing to meet those needs. The classroom portion covers relationship building, listening, taking the client's point of view, and proactiveness. The course also includes at least 10 case studies from a wide variety of client perspectives, allowing each participant to be actively involved.

- A successful spin-off of our client retention program has been a course we call The Evidence of Value. It covers financial analysis, technology, benchmarking, business planning, and other core areas. By honing our skills in these critical areas, we are able to offer our clients quantifiable, objective measurements of solutions, products, services, and our service to them.

7

Activists for the Internal Environment

A walk through our corporate headquarters in Philadelphia is probably a pretty good introduction to our culture, so we'll take you on a "virtual" tour. As you enter the door to the main lobby, you might just be swept away by our culture—literally. As you walk through them, the front doors create a wind tunnel. What's so culture-oriented about that? The origin. When we bought the building, it had double doors, like most entryways. We removed the inner set to make it feel more like a home than a business. And it does feel more like a home—just a very windy one.

The other visible signs of our culture are a lot more fun. Our cafeteria, with its juke box and big, comfy booths, serves as a gathering spot for meals, socialization, and impromptu meetings. We don't want people to grab their lunch and work in their offices; we want to make it easy for them to visit with each other, share ideas, and build friendships. Creativity flourishes in a relaxed and casual atmosphere. We make it a point to entertain our clients there, as opposed to stuffy restaurants. We want them to be surrounded by our associates, and for our associates to have the opportunity to meet them. We don't believe in executive dining rooms. Our cafeteria is for all of us, like everything else in our organization.

Our Learning and Development area looks like a creative wonderland, with its learning library, interesting murals, and pillars painted like giant Crayolas. (You'll learn more about Crayolas later in this chapter. They play an important role in our company.) The artwork on this floor was all created by children, to remind us of the inherent creativity in us all, which is unfortunately so often squelched over the years.

Then there's The Gathering, our corporate library. When you hear the words "corporate library" they might conjure up images of hard, leather chairs, neat rows of reference books, and bankers' lamps. Not this one. It has overstuffed couches, a casual southwestern style, and is filled with people Net surfing, actively debating solutions, or lounging, feet up, reading newspapers in any number of languages.

We also have an open meeting policy: Every meeting is open to every associate in the company, with few exceptions. The only closed meetings are are those that would betray the confidence of an associate or a client. All other meetings are listed on a bulletin board, and associates from all areas are encouraged to sit in and/or participate. The listing includes the time, location, main contact, and purpose for each meeting. If we limit our ideas to our typical work groups, we miss out on fresh approaches and bigger pictures. We don't want people wondering about what's going on behind closed doors at meetings. We want them in and participating.

Walking through the building, you'll notice the signs on our meeting rooms. We call them Thought Centers because what transpires in them belies the typical image that comes to mind when you hear the word "meeting." There's a Dilbert cartoon we like in which he is walking along, dragging several people who are clinging to him. He says, "Let me get back to you on that." The caption reads, "Always postpone meetings with time-wasting morons." We waste minimal time in our meetings.

Our culture is a unique blend of warmth and friendliness with a hard-driving competitive edge, and our surroundings reflect that dichotomy. One floor below the cozy Gathering is The Continuum, which looks like the helm of a spaceship; its visitors are surrounded by futuristic technologies that span industries.

Across from The Continuum, our Network Operations Center (NOC) showcases our global network on a videowall, where a team of experts track the latest developments in news, weather, and the activity of our clients. It's the "nerve center" of our operations. Daily, hundreds of thousands of calls are electronically directed through the NOC.

The dress code is strictly casual. People need to be comfortable when they're creating. When our company was honored for its humanitarian efforts in 1997 by the National Conference of Christians and Jews, we invited all attending the event to wear "whatever makes you happy." It was quite a departure from the traditional black-tie attire at past conferences.

The visible signs of culture say a lot about a company, and it's a good idea to examine them regularly to make sure they say what you want them to say. Sometimes it takes an objective look from someone outside your company to tell you what their impressions are. And sometimes a look from inside the organization is just what you need—if it's an honest look.

A view from inside our organization led to our current world headquarters. In 1988 our corporate headquarters was a two-story building in Philadelphia, which housed an operations center, a reservations facility, and all of our support departments. Somewhere along the line, we came up with what seemed like a brilliant idea: We'd move all of our top officers to an executive headquarters at the top of a new skyscraper a few blocks away, so they could work more closely together, strategize, and create the future.

It was one of our worst ideas, and we knew it almost as soon as we moved there. We became isolated from our associates, and it hurt productivity because we and our associates at what became the "Ops Center" were beating a path back and forth every day between the two buildings.

Then the rumors started to fly. Almost daily, because we had clients in our offices for meetings, we would bring in lunch. There were no dining facilities, and rather than waste time socializing in restaurants it has always been our style to work over lunch. So it seemed that anytime an associate from our Ops Center came to visit, a catered lunch was being served. The word around the company was that everyone working at our executive headquarters was served free, elaborate lunches every day.

When we began to hear things like that, we began to see how ridiculous the idea had been, though our intentions had been good. We thought we could strategize better as a team if we were all together. But to be together, we didn't need to be separate. As soon as our lease was up, we high-tailed it to a new location where we could *all* be together, and it has made all the difference.

Take a walk through your headquarters, and ask yourself honestly what it tells you about your company, your associates, your executives, your clients. Then ask your front-line people what they think. Ask clients. You'll probably hear some surprising answers.

Well, now our virtual walk-through is over and it's time to get down to the serious business of ingraining a global corporate culture. The power of culture is enormous. It is the foundation of every organization. And that's not always a good thing. A strong, positive culture doesn't happen by accident, and if it isn't given a champion, it will find one by default, one who doesn't necessarily have the time or resources to champion it properly.

Championing Corporate Culture

While reinforcing the culture is every associate's responsibility, we felt naming someone to lead the charge would ensure its success. So in 1996, we made a decision to declare an official champion of corporate culture. We designated a Manager of Culture Development. The role was filled by an associate who had joined the company in 1990 and had worked in a variety of areas, including corporate communications, an area toward which culture issues normally gravitated.

After a year or so, it became evident that the function was imperative, and in fact, warranted a broader range. We expanded the role to that of Director of Cultural Diversity. The change reflected the heightened importance of nurturing our culture as we continue to grow at a rapid pace, as well as the magnitude of taking that culture worldwide, encompassing a vast array of cultures.

The pages ahead describe the ways we perpetuate our culture, while incorporating new people, ideas, and customs. As always, the starting point is to lay the foundation; that is, determining what your culture is and what you want it to be. Beware that what you find may be different from the last time you looked.

Cultures can, and often do, change. We would venture to say that few companies survived the '90s without some significant cultural change. Some aspects should change, for example, to incorporate cultural diversity. Others should not, such as basic values.

To begin to lay the foundation, you must first find the right people, because your selection process and selectors reflect your vision of your culture. Once selected, you have the perfect opportunity to ingrain your culture on their first day of employment.

The lion's share of our new associate orientation is to introduce our culture and welcome people into it. From there, it's up to the company to live up to those expectations and to ensure that they become reality on a day-to-day basis in the workplace. To do that, we have a variety of programs and measurements.

First, we'll outline some of our latest programs that encourage the development of our culture, and then we'll describe how we measure our success. To quote our Director of Cultural Diversity, "Culture is a lot more than just programs. You can have all the 'jeans days' you want, and it won't matter if you don't have the right foundation in place. Credibility is the reason a culture works or doesn't work. It's only sincere if people live it. And to ensure that, companies have to bring in and keep only leaders who believe in it."

Salmon Spirit

In late 1995, during one of our semiannual strategy sessions, our top officers decided we needed to reenergize our culture. In light of our explosive global growth and the intense changes we had undergone, achieving our associate satisfaction goals would require a renewed commitment from all of us.

Our corporate culture is a major differentiator between our company and those with which we compete. Anything that special needs to be nurtured. An associate satisfaction survey just before the meeting (which you'll hear more about later in this chapter) told us that a lot of long-time associates missed "the way things used to be," when we were a much smaller company. But due to our growth, we had scores of new leaders and new associates throughout the company, and not everyone was on the same page. They were reading the same book and were even in the same chapter, but not quite on the same page. Our hearts were in the right place, but, when things got busy, some of the little special touches that made us glad we came to work that day were getting lost in the hustle. We wanted to bring those touches back.

We put together a cross-functional team to come up with ways to make it easier for leaders to support the culture, to recognize their associates, to boost morale, and to just have fun. The team named themselves the Salmon Spirit team. (The salmon is our mascot because we like to be different, to swim upstream, to buck the tide.) The salmon team got to work.

They called for ideas from associates, collected best practices from offices around the world, and came up with ideas of their own. They pooled all of these success stories into a reference manual dubbed *The*

Salmon Spirit Guide, a 50-page, step-by-step guide to planning special events and activities, and distributed it to company leaders worldwide.

In 1996, the first year of the Salmon Spirit initiative, the themes were celebrating success and having fun. In 1997, the themes were self-development and community service.

1996: THE YEAR TO HAVE FUN. We kicked off the 1996 program with four companywide events, celebrated simultaneously in our locations around the world. The activities were supplemented by the aforementioned *Salmon Spirit Guide*.

The first activity enlisted all leaders in the company to express why they appreciate their team. Each leader chose his or her own way to express it, from listing reasons to writing poems to making certificates of appreciation to explaining it in pictures. Then the leaders presented their creations to their teams over lunch or during another group activity. The Salmon Spirit team collected all of the ideas from the leaders and printed a compilation in our associate newsletter.

One leader from the business unit that serves our client Merck said of her team:

Totally committed to our client.

Equally committed to each other.

Always friendly and supportive.

Makes my job easier and a pleasure.

Work together toward common goals.

Offer suggestions for continuous improvement.

Really appreciated for all that they do.

Keep our unit together and strong.

And who says the word "I" doesn't play an important role in teamwork? The general manager of a New Jersey business unit described her team as "Innovative, Invincible, Idealistic, Illustrious, Ingenious, Insightful, Inspiring, Imaginative, Idealistic, Impassioned, Important, Impressive, Independent, Industrious, Inventive, Intuitive, Inimitable, Inquisitive, Inspiring."

The second companywide program was something the team named Fam Day in May. (By way of background: One benefit in our industry is the familiarization trip, or fam trip in travel lingo. Industry suppliers will usually provide discounted or free travel to those in the industry in order to familiarize them with their services, destination, or product. We offer paid time off for our associates to participate in these fam trips plus some spending money for the trip).

Fam Day in May had everyone dressing as the people in their favorite vacation destination do and bringing in show-and-tell items to share with their team. For example, one associate's choice was Mexico, and she brought a tape player with recorded music of a mariachi band she heard while she was there, a sampling of Mexican food for everyone on her team, and photos from her vacation.

Besides being fun, Fam Day in May is a great way to get to know more about team members, and it helps promote a benefit that our people really enjoy. An event like this doesn't have to be connected to fam trips, which are probably available only in our industry. It can celebrate a perk or benefit available in your industry, or you can do a take-off of the theme.

The third companywide event was our Secret Salmon program, not unlike the Secret Santa activities around the holidays. Our version (of course) involves the salmon. On the first day of the event, associates in a department, team, or office draw names. Each day thereafter, associates leave a small gift, such as a mug, discount coupons, or a homemade card, for their secret salmon. They usually do this every day, leading up to the final day, when everyone finds out who their secret buddy is.

The object is for associates to place their gifts on their designated associate's desk without being noticed. They remain anonymous until Secret Salmon Day, when the secret is revealed. Departments normally gather over lunch or breakfast to announce the secret pals, but it can be done after work, or anytime that's convenient.

A program like this is a fun morale booster that gives associates the chance to get to know each other better and feel appreciated. It's easy to administer and the results exceed the effort it takes to implement. Still, there are a few keys to making a program like this work. First, it's important that everyone be included, if they want to participate. We encourage every group to have a back-up plan in the event that someone is out on a given day. It's not much fun to be the only one without a gift on your desk. Offices can keep a small supply of gifts on hand just in case.

It's equally important not to make anyone feel awkward for not joining in. We recognize that religious, social, and economic conditions can preclude people from participating in activities such as this. If they want to, there are other ways they can participate, such as taking pictures during the event, placing gifts for people who are absent, or decorating the office for the final event.

The fourth companywide event of our inaugural Salmon Spirit celebration was our Live Salmon Spirit Out Loud contest. The objective of this event was for all associates to express what Salmon Spirit means to them. We got the most insightful, creative, and heartfelt descriptions of our associates' feelings. This was a program that cost nothing yet was a terrific jump-start to build excitement about the company. It was also a great way to measure whether the word was getting out.

When you ask people to share their feelings, it's imperative that each person's effort be recognized in a personal way. So everyone who participated received a personalized letter and a Live the Spirit T-shirt as a way to thank them. The winning entry from an associate in our London office captured the essence:

Salmon Spirit—Rosenbluth Way

Then

They said we could not make it
When things were tough and
Follow the crowd was the corporate word
Struggle we did as one
Against tide and norm
People first we shout

Play our game he said
The rest will follow
Play we did: technical innovations
and some philosophies and beliefs

Corporate America look
Perhaps we should closely look
They said
A company that is a success story
That must be the "Salmon Spirit"

Now

The playground expanded
The game harder
Rules undefined

but the Spirit the same
Learning we have

People focus is in the air
The rest will follow
Corporate world listen
The Salmon Spirit is coming!

The first year of the Salmon Spirit initiative we held these four companywide events to kick off an ongoing reemphasis on our culture, and we relied on a team of 37 volunteer coordinators to carry it out. In subsequent years, the program evolved to self-implementable modules explained in detail in our *Salmon Spirit Guide*.

The Salmon Spirit Guide has been an invaluable tool for our leaders to keep morale high and our culture thriving in their individual business units. It contains three sections: (1) having fun in the workplace, (2) recipes for celebrating success, and (3) global best practices. The guide is updated annually with new ideas.

The format of the guide is designed to make it as easy as possible for busy leaders to implement the ideas. Each program suggestion includes a set of objectives, a description of the program, steps to implement, lists of what is needed, ways to encourage participation across their team, and helpful hints to enhance the results. These principles can be applied in any company. Here are a few examples.

Associate Welcome. This program can be used to welcome new associates to an office, following a companywide orientation. Or it can be effective when holding a companywide department meeting, such as for operations or accounting. It's a great way to welcome people, break the ice, and build camaraderie.

The person(s) who will be working most closely with the new associate puts together a welcome packet for him or her, which is presented on his or her first day. The welcome can include small gifts such as lunch coupons to local restaurants (with an invitation to join other associates for lunch). It's also a good idea to include "cheat sheets," which introduce other associates in the office (names, job functions, phone extensions, and something interesting about the person). Another helpful practice is to ask everyone to wear nametags or display desktop nameplates until the new person has had a chance to learn everyone's name.

Making new associates feel welcome and comfortable in their new home-away-from-home is essential for strong retention. And the administration required for this program is minimal. Each office can keep a store of the necessary items on hand, or associates can take turns sponsoring a new associate, and submit expenses for reimbursement. As with everything else, it's important to be consistent. Once a program like this is started, it needs to continue and to include everyone.

Salmon Stickers. We use stickers to recognize associates, particularly to express associate-to-associate appreciation. Of course, your company would have another image on your stickers, such as your company's mascot or logo, if you don't have a mascot. We keep an ample supply of them on hand in each location, accessible to everyone. When someone goes above and beyond to help a fellow associate or a client, a colleague will give that person a salmon sticker, usually affixed to a project or document, or on a note posted somewhere visible.

This is a low-cost, easy way to recognize people for their day-to-day contributions to excellence, and that's important because all of those day-to-days add up to the level of service a company stands for.

Activity Days. We encourage leaders to designate one day a month as an "activity day," to foster camaraderie and encourage associates to get to know each other on a more personal level. For example, "baby picture day" (each associate brings in a baby picture for a contest to correctly guess whose picture is whose); "picnic days" (for a departmental picnic, either indoors or out); "dress-up days" (theme-oriented); "picture days" (associates bring photos of their family or pets); and of course, celebrating birthdays and anniversaries with the company.

Activity days are fun. They break the routine, cost nothing, and are an easy way to build or strengthen bonds. To administer activity days, most leaders ask for a volunteer each month to coordinate the effort. *The Salmon Spirit Guide* also recommends that each office photograph the events and keep an office scrapbook to make the fun more lasting.

Associate/Leader Role Switching. This program calls for associates to switch roles with their leader for at least two hours, or more, if possible. It's a great way for everyone to see things from a new perspective, to reacquaint leaders with the daily tasks and processes in their operation, to foster greater understanding of how each role fits into the bigger picture, and to enhance communication.

For it to be successful, front-line associates should outline tasks for the leader to accomplish, such as reports or daily procedures. They should explain the normal steps they take in completing those assignments. Likewise, leaders should prepare an agenda for the associate, including things such as sitting in on, or running, meetings. They must provide manageable activities, and be mindful to include the types of activities that normally fill their days.

If it's more appropriate, the program can be done as a "shadowing" process rather than an exchange, where people join another on the job. Obviously, it needs to be carefully scheduled so as to not negatively affect productivity.

Role switching is not just for associates and their leaders; it can be a great facilitator of teamwork for associates to exchange with, or shadow, their peers. It's also a good idea for those involved to debrief each other following the event, and discuss ideas for process improvement.

Officer Visits. There shouldn't be a need for a program like this, but there is, and it's probably the case with most companies. We're all busier than ever, particularly those who have to integrate travel into their schedules. But as leaders, it's imperative that we take the time to connect with associates throughout our companies. Associates must be able to meet and interact with their company's leaders. It strengthens communication, and it demonstrates that the leadership is listening (hopefully they *are*). An interesting article on listening in the July 10, 1997, issue of *The Wall Street Journal* read, "Overwhelmed by the incessant, intrusive babble of the modern world, the skill of listening has fallen on hard times." One listening expert was quoted as saying, "There's the old joke, the opposite of talking isn't listening, it's waiting to talk."

The way to make this program work is to encourage your officers to take the time to visit local offices when they are in town, when it makes sense. Offices should also extend invitations; they should reserve a time and place for associates to speak with leaders in an open forum, if time permits. If not, they should be encouraged to walk through the office to visit casually with associates. It's also a good idea for the officers to follow their visits with a personal note to the associates, thanking them for the opportunity to meet them.

Open Houses. Holding an internal open house demonstrates how the various departments work together to achieve the company's goals. It also offers an opportunity for people to learn more about other departments, to help them chart their careers. We regularly hold open house events in offices that have more than one department. Each department showcases what they do for both internal and external clients.

As one of the Salmon Spirit kick off events, we held an open house at our world headquarters, in Philadelphia. The building houses hundreds of people, so each of the eight floors took a day to host the rest of the building. Each floor went all-out, and it was great to see such pride and creativity. Some offices have held evening open houses for associates' families. The dedication we ask of our people has a direct impact on their families, and it's nice for them to be able to share what they do with those who support them in their hard work.

Another Salmon Spirit program is our brown bag seminar series, which offers a shared learning experience over lunch, and includes such topics as elegant language, listening skills, serving challenging clients, how to give/receive constructive criticism, and other helpful topics for people's professional and personal lives. There are 12 modules in all, and the courses are taught by our leaders in learning, who have passed a certification process.

There are countless other programs in *The Salmon Spirit Guide*, but these should give you a few ideas of the types of things we do and how easy they can be to implement. In addition to events, ongoing celebration is an important ingredient for a strong and successful culture.

One suggestion from *The Salmon Spirit Guide* is to create an office photo album. All that's needed is a binder, a disposable camera, and a volunteer to take photos and maintain the book. We provided each office with a matching binder for their album. The covers read, "Swimming Upstream: Life at Rosenbluth International." This way the books look similar, so when associates or clients visit various offices, they'll recognize the albums. We also include complimentary letters from clients, the awarding of new accounts, and other key correspondence in the pages of the albums.

Another suggestion is a Wall of Fame on which to display client letters, awards, or other special honors. We place them in a very visible location, for example, a lobby. In larger offices, individual departments have their own walls of fame, in addition to the central one. We always ask clients' permission before displaying their letters, and usually they're happy we plan to showcase it. A program like this is a snap, and it really builds pride in the company.

Finally, at the end of a full year of Salmon Spirit activities, we recap the highlights in a feature article in our internal magazine, *The Associate*. The article, "Salmon Spirit Year in Review," is a way to recognize everyone's support of the initiative and to reemphasize the messages the program sends.

A Celebration Around the World

Other than our Salmon Spirit initiative, probably the most far-reaching method we have of reinforcing our culture is Associate Appreciation Month. For over a decade now, we have designated each August as the month during which to acknowledge how important our associates are. As the kick off memo to leaders from our Director of Cultural Diversity stated, "Associate Appreciation Month is just one more way that we, as leaders and as a company, can 'walk the talk.'"

Every day during August, all around the world, our associates are treated to a line-up of activities and rewards to thank them for their hard work throughout the year. Some activities are centrally planned and implemented companywide, but most are done so on a local level by leaders, with the help of team members who volunteer.

Traditionally, on the first day of August, all associates around the world wear blue and white (our corporate colors). The days that follow include visits by suppliers bearing prizes (free airline tickets, hotel stays, car rentals, etc.) as well as treats (breakfast, ice cream, cookies, etc.). There are theme parties, contests, and yes, lots of dress-up days. For example, a walk through our headquarters on August 4, 1997, would have made you feel as if in a time warp. Everyone wore bell-bottoms, platform shoes, and other disco garb for a '70s day. We showed *The Brady Bunch* in our Thought Theatre. On the 18th, everyone wore western clothes; the movie was *Tombstone*.

During one Associate Appreciation Month, we held a contest to come up with a jingle for the company; entrants had to perform their jingle to be eligible. It was hilarious. We've also conducted a mystery hunt for a disappearing salmon (along the lines of the show *Where in the World Is Carmen San Diego?*) The events always change and they just keep getting more outrageous and more fun.

A few years ago, we began a tradition of holding a VP Barbecue. No, our associates do not roast their leaders. Our senior officers prepare (or at least try to) and serve their associates a barbecue lunch in the parking lot of our world headquarters.

Other events have included a Salmon Gram service (associates sent packages of Swedish Fish candy to each other) and Movietime (we turned our

Thought Theatre into a movie theater and showed a movie each week, complete with popcorn). Hal and Diane say, "Two thumbs up for this program."

A program like Associate Appreciation Month can be adapted to work in any company. It can be a day, a week, a month, or even all year long. It can be done on a global, national, local, or even departmental scale. There are plenty of ideas that cost nothing to implement. The point is to just say thank you.

In advance of Associate Appreciation Month, our Director of Cultural Diversity sends out an informational packet to help leaders prepare, complete with a calendar featuring suggested events, instructions on how to approach suppliers for participation, flyers announcing events, and entry forms for companywide contests.

We encourage leaders to send weekly e-mails, voice mails, or some other form of update to their teams to remind them of upcoming activities and to build excitement. One of the nicest traditions is that every leader writes a personal thank-you note to each associate who reports to them, in appreciation for all they do throughout the year.

Mary Kay: A Leader in Recognition

Throughout the year, Mary Kay shows appreciation to employees in formal and informal ways. For example, each spring, the company devotes an entire week to employee appreciation activities at every location. In 1997, the management team served punch and cookies to employees, similar to Rosenbluth's VP Barbecue. Management team members also wrote personal thank-you notes to at least 15 employees outside their division. Employees across the company responded by sending notes of appreciation to coworkers in a Thanks a Billion campaign. Many Mary Kay employees said it was their favorite event of the year.

Mary Kay's culture is evident the other 51 weeks of the year, too. Highlights include the companywide celebration of Mary Kay's birthday in May, and the company's anniversary in September. Employees also exhibit the Mary Kay culture daily by finding humor in answering the inevitable question "Do you drive a pink Cadillac?" (a reward reserved for top independent sales force members).

Every year, halfway through the year and near year-end, I draft a "state of the company" letter to all associates. It recaps the year's accomplishments, previews developments to come, and thanks everyone for their countless contributions to our success. Last year, for the first time, I concluded the letter with a request that they think about what they would do differently if they were CEO of our company.

I didn't get too many responses, nor did I expect many, but the ones I did receive were very insightful. Here's an excerpt from an associate in our marketing group.

"Creative destruction: I arrived at this theory while I was standing in a grove of giant sequoias in California. When I discovered that many of these sequoias were one to two thousand years old, I immediately asked how they were able to live so long and get to be so huge.

"As it turns out, the sequoias have adapted themselves in a remarkable fashion to rule the forest. Fire is a natural component of the ecology of forests. It also results in the demise of all animal and plant life contained within the forest . . . except the giant sequoias. They have a protective bark that is actually fire-retardant, thus saving the tree.

"Equally amazing is that new sequoia seedlings are generated when tiny sequoia pine cones come in contact with extreme heat. Only then do the pine cones open and release seeds for giant sequoias. These seedlings are able to quickly take root and grow due to the newly created fertile conditions, with no competition from other trees or plant life.

"Since creative destruction is an essential part of capitalism as well as democracy, I thought that there might be some opportunity to apply the lessons of a giant sequoia to Rosenbluth's long-term business strategy, and to capitalize on drastic industry shifts. I must also add that I have not yet figured out how to apply these lessons, but thought you might have some ideas."

In addition to asking associates to tell me how they'd improve upon how I do my job, I also ask them to ask me anything they want, in a special column in our internal newsletter, The Associate. *Here are samples from our "Ask Hal" column.*

Q: What do you think was our company's greatest achievement in 1996?
A: Turnover was reduced. In an industry where turnover is so high, it's great to see that Rosenbluth International is clearly doing the right things to retain

our people. Our associates are our greatest asset. Keeping our associates
satisfied will continue to be our company's highest priority.
Q: When will you come visit our offices in Moscow?
A: When they stop exporting vodka, or by the end of the year, whichever
comes first.

Plenty of questions are generated in the United States, but we find that abroad
our associates are a little more shy about asking questions. To make sure we
answer any questions our associates outside the United States may have, we
actively solicit questions from 10 global offices prior to each issue of the column.

Live the Spirit

In this day and age particularly, when we can have an ongoing dialogue
with someone without ever talking with them in real time, it's more
important than ever to occasionally sit down and talk with each other. In
the past, we held a companywide meeting twice a year; as we grew, we
began to hold them once a year.

In 1992, celebrating our company's 100-year anniversary, we gathered
our associates from around the world for what we intended to be the last
companywide meeting. With offices scattered around the world, and thousands of employees, we thought it crazy to try to continue the tradition.
Well, as it turns out, we are crazy. Five years later, on a weekend in August
1997, we brought more than 4,000 associates, clients, and suppliers
together for a companywide meeting. Those attending came from 25 countries, speaking 12 languages. They came to celebrate a corporate culture
that transcends borders and time. It was a weekend for fun, education, and
enjoying the company of each other, our clients, and key suppliers.

Such a meeting is one of the best ways to introduce, ingrain, change,
reinforce, or celebrate a corporate culture. To be sure, it's a logistical
nightmare and a significant investment, but its benefits can be felt for
years following the event.

To coordinate this massive meeting, we utilized a core team of former
associates (as we discussed in Chapter 4, on human capital). They worked
night and day with a team of current associates, and to help us fund it,
we called upon our suppliers. Forty-four companies supported us, making
the dream of gathering all of us together a reality.

We staged some really unusual (even for us) events, for example, our live, life-sized game of Chutes and Ladders. We created a game board that covered the floor of an entire room in the Philadelphia Convention Center. Live associates stood in as game pieces and game show hosts; we had ladders, slides, and oversized dice that were probably two feet wide. Our clients were divided into teams, and the object of the game was to reduce their (fictitious) company's travel expenditures. It was educational, it was fun, and probably they had never before or since done anything quite like it.

We also held client-specific meetings, where all of the associates from around the world who work on a particular account gathered with their client. Many of them had not met face to face after years of working together.

Another highlight was our Global Village, not your typical trade show. In addition to our suppliers, 28 internal departments, lines of business, and even top-secret, strategic future products were exhibited at the event. A work/life booth offered literature and services to help our associates balance the many demands placed on them in their personal and professional lives. A career center encouraged and supported associates in pursuing their career goals.

Measurement: The Key That Opens the Door

Ingraining a culture is essential, but measuring it is key, because people will do what's *in*spected rather than what's *ex*pected. Morale metrics are the single best way to look your culture in the face. Probably the most unusual method we use to measure morale is our Crayola drawings. We send packs of Crayolas and paper to about one hundred people at a time and ask them to draw how they feel about the company. (We introduced this project in our last book, when the program was in its infancy. Since then, we have received drawings from hundreds of associates, clients, and even from strangers who read about the program.)

In recent years we took the program global, and it has been an interesting experience. Some cultures are more accustomed to on-the-edge activities than others. The first time we sent the mailing to our associates in France, we got zero response and we wanted to know why. We always call people who don't respond to the mailing to find out why they don't respond. Their answers range everywhere from, "My kids took the Crayons" (the equivalent of the dog ate my homework) to "I thought I had missed the deadline" (nice try) to "I can't draw" (most of us can't).

The point is not to make anyone feel uncomfortable for not respond-ing. We want to make sure they feel comfortable responding if they would like to. In the case of our associates in France, we got a real lesson in culture. There, apparently, when people are evaluated for insanity, they are commonly asked to draw; their drawings are analyzed as part of the determination process. Understandably, they were hesitant to par-ticipate. After we thoroughly explained the purpose of the exercise, we got a great response.

Most of the drawings we see are positive, but it's the negative ones that present opportunities and call for action. For example, we received some disturbing drawings from our Singapore office with a common theme. One pair of drawings showed a person at a desk with stacks of work, a frown on his face, and a thought bubble that read, "Alone?" The other had the heading "Singapore . . . in the *future*" and it showed people hold-ing hands, smiling, surrounded by words like "support" and "team spirit." At the time, the leadership in that office was more "old school" and didn't subscribe to many of the attitudes that make us unique; this was reflected in the drawings. We now have a new vice president there who is a model of our culture. He's fun and has a great sense of humor. We've also added a quality manager, an HR manager, a trainer, and a project manager in the Singapore office, and things have improved nicely.

Another pair of drawings, from an associate in New York, showed signs of trouble. The first depicted smiling people working in nice surround-ings. The caption read, "Rosenbluth office—Anywhere, USA." The second showed workstations crammed into a tiny space, with notes at the bot-tom reading, "No lunchroom. No conference room. No sales room." The caption read, "Rosenbluth office—New York City." The drawing, from a leader in that office, came with a letter that read, "My drawing reflects recent comments I've heard from my New York City associates. Frankly, not only do I agree with them, but I think it's time to show some action." All of the issues raised fortunately concerned physical space, which can (and must) be fixed relatively easily. We moved our New York City associ-ates to a new office in a different building that is spacious, full of win-dows, and has room for growth. It has the lunchroom, conference room and all of the amenities mentioned as missing in the drawing.

In contrast, one positive drawing from a client, Chevron, showed two people holding hands, with the caption "Partners." The artist attached a letter reading, "Enclosed is my drawing which expresses my feelings toward Rosenbluth. My perception is that we are partners, and [that] I am fortunate to work with such a wonderful company."

An associate in Pittsburgh drew a picture of his house with five people standing in the front yard, holding hands. They were labeled with his name, his wife's name, the names of his two sons, and the last one with "Rosenbluth." The meaning was clear.

An associate in San Francisco drew a salmon swimming upstream (actually, climbing steps) toward his career goal, showing all the steps from his current role to vice president. The caption read, "Welcome to the Rosenbluth Spawning Ranch, where young salmon learn to thrive on chaos appetizers."

Our Crayola drawing project is one of the easiest to implement, and through such a project you can learn more about your company than you could imagine. Send them to clients, too, and if you operate in consumer markets, consider inviting mass audiences to respond. Or, if you have a retail operation, leave some Crayolas and paper out so that people can stop and do a quick drawing. It's a terrific barometer of the perceptions of your internal and external customers.

More Science, Less Art

Measurement can be both an art and a science; if you're more comfortable with the latter consider an Associate Satisfaction Survey. It's certainly more scientific, and extremely powerful in gauging a company's morale. We sent our first one out in 1994, and have done so every year since. Prior to 1994, we used precursors to the survey, such as the two-page Listening to Our Associates form, which was developed in-house and sent to our operations group. We found it was not universal enough, and we wondered about the accuracy of its results, since we had developed it—not our area of expertise.

Survey results can be skewed by subtleties in wording, and we wanted crystal-clear information. So in 1994, we hired an outside firm to develop and administer the first official Associate Satisfaction Survey. Six pages in length, it asks some hard-hitting questions, highlights of which are listed here.

The General Information section includes topics on:

- tenure
- the degree to which associates feel the company is committed to associate satisfaction
- pride in the company

The Communication section includes questions about:

- sources people rely on for information
- the effectiveness of both the channels and the information
- specific areas of information, such as career, competition, general business, changes, industry, and client

The Retention, Selection, and Promotion section looks at:

- career opportunities and support
- flexible work arrangement options
- company growth
- pay and benefits
- satisfaction with leadership, work environment, and company structure
- personal responsibility to plan and pursue career opportunities with the company

The Job Itself section addresses:

- the amount of work expected of associates
- the effective use of their skills and abilities
- understanding priorities, goals, and objectives
- quality of work and job satisfaction
- respect

The Work and Personal Life section addresses:

- fair treatment
- leadership's level of understanding and compassion for life events
- resources available to help manage balance between work and personal lives
- company support of the importance of associates' personal lives

The Leadership section asks associates to rate their immediate leader in such areas as:

- job knowledge
- feedback
- fairness

- people skills
- technical knowledge
- problem solving
- listening
- motivation
- communication
- recognition
- approachability
- openness to ideas

The Industry section asks associates to compare the company to the competition; specifically, it asks about the level of awareness of the industry's effects on our business. The final question of the survey is one of the most important. It asks associates about their confidence that the company will take action in response to the results of the survey. This is critical, because people will only take the time to respond to surveys they feel will effect change. If people don't believe action is forthcoming, surveys can be demotivators, and can cause cynicism.

Which brings us to an important point: accountability. The two keys to this survey are anonymity and accountability. First, anonymity. If people aren't going to be brutally honest, what point is there in asking for their input? Worse, if people tell you what they think you want to hear (for fear of reprisal), then you're acting on false information, and that's more harmful than no information at all. For those reasons, we only ask associates to indicate the country in which they work, and which business unit, support department, or line of business they are in; if they are in a leadership role; and about tenure with the company. And that's all we really need to know.

In a perfect world, every employee in every company would be able to respond honestly without this degree of anonymity. But we don't live in a perfect world, and it's every company's obligation to remove fear from the process, whether that fear is justified or not.

Now we come to accountability. This is key. There's no point in surveying if we're not going to do anything with the results. So we have put a process in place to spur action. The results are compiled by an outside firm, and summary reports are sent to leaders for their areas. Leaders are also given an associate satisfaction action planning workbook, which provides suggestions on how to share the feedback with their team and to create a plan for improvement. It's important to make it as easy as possible for people to act quickly on the results, and the action planning guide and support from our human resource associates do just that.

We recommend that our leaders involve their associates in the planning and improvement processes. Usually, leaders begin by calling their team together to review the results. The group looks at the top 10 areas of opportunity (those with the lowest scores). We encourage them to focus where they can effect change now, and to steer away from major company issues (which are addressed through another process).

The team then prioritizes the issues and discusses next steps. Each plan includes objectives, action steps, completion criteria, person responsible for each step, and due dates. Everyone gets a copy of the action plan and everyone is included in regular updates on progress made. Most important, copies of all action plans must be submitted to each leader's leader within a tight deadline (usually about three weeks). This closes the loop, and ensures that the completion of these action plans is a priority.

Let's face it, as busy as people are these days, it takes this kind of checkpoint to keep us moving ahead. And if it seems like too much, then probably you have too many surveys. Better to complete one per year and see real action from it than to survey a hundred times. The ultimate measure of success in the process is for scores to continue to go up, which means all those action plans are working.

Our survey program has expanded over the years. The first year, we sent the survey to a sample group and conducted focus groups for additional feedback and to evaluate the effectiveness of the survey by comparing the live responses. The second year, we sent the survey to all associates in the United States. In 1996, we polled our associates around the world, asking into which languages they would like us to translate the survey. We hired a firm to translate the survey into seven languages, and as an added precaution, we sent the newly translated versions to associates fluent in both English and their native language, to review the translation for its accuracy.

The firm that developed the survey for us also handles the administration of it. The surveys are sent directly to them; they tabulate the results and produce the reports. The top five issues are singled out for address by the officers of the company. The overall survey results are published in our internal magazine, for all associates to see, and to hold us accountable for improvement as a company.

A View from Every Direction

Almost a decade ago, I began asking the people who report directly to me to review my performance. This vertical review process became a terrific tool, utilized throughout the company. After company leaders reviewed me, they began to ask those who reported to them to review their performance, and the process moved throughout the company.

In 1993, we decided that vertical reviews in either direction were not enough. We needed a complete, multidimensional view of our leadership, because probably nothing has more of an effect on someone's work life than his or her immediate leader. We implemented a 360-degree review process for all of our leaders. It's not a concept we invented, but it's one that we have had a great deal of success with. Each leader (meaning anyone who has at least one associate reporting to him or her) sends the same survey to his or her leader, direct reports, three peers, and three clients. Leaders also complete the form themselves to assess their own leadership capabilities.

The survey asks detailed questions about a variety of leadership issues, and though absolute scores are certainly important, we probably learn more from disconnects than from anything else. For example, if someone scores well on communication skills with his or her associates in the company, but not as well in communicating with clients, it might mean that he or she needs a presentation skills course to improve their confidence.

If a leader is perceived as fair by his or her leader, but not by direct reports, guess whose opinion counts more? The associates' of course. And that leader must regain the trust of his or her associates. There is really no better tool for a company to evaluate its sincerity, consistency, and integrity.

We view this process as a developmental tool, not as a way to expose weaknesses. It takes a high degree of trust to institute a program like this, and we do have that level of trust in our company—although, admittedly, sometimes it's hard for new leaders. But we make it clear to our leaders that this is a chance to improve, that they aren't going to be fired for bad scores (unless those scores don't show some improvement over time). (In isolated cases where serious improvement was needed, we have used interim 360-degree reviews to accelerate the progress toward improvement.) In addition, our HR team offers personalized, confidential help to leaders who need it. For the most part, these steps aren't necessary, and while the process can be uncomfortable at first, it's an important tool. People and companies need to work past their insecurities and just do it.

Anonymity and accountability are critical with the 360-degree reviews. The results are sent to each leader's leader, who sets a meeting to discuss them together. Next, the leader being reviewed meets with his or her team, thanks them for the feedback, and asks for further clarification, or perhaps examples of any issues that might not be clear. From there, each leader formulates an action plan that becomes a part of his or her Individual Development Plan (IDP), discussed in Chapter 5 on learning. These action plans must be formulated within three weeks.

How the 100 Best Measure Morale

While the frequency and methods of morale measurement varied from company to company, the commitment to measurement was universal among our *100 Best* peers. Here are some methods to consider.

LANDS' END. Lands' End conducts a companywide climate survey every three to four years, and they do something interesting to boost participation: They ask employees to come to a meeting to take the survey. During the meeting, they tell everyone that though they're welcome to take the survey home (self-addressed, stamped envelopes are provided), they hope everyone will complete it on the spot. And it works. In 1997, Lands' End had a response rate of over 70 percent—almost unheard of. In addition, they received more than 70 pages of written comments.

Their follow-up is strong too. They hold a companywide meeting to discuss the overall survey results, followed by group meetings to set action plans at the department level. Senior management sets action plans for the company as a whole. Companywide meetings are held to provide updates and progress reports, and results are discussed in a Q&A format in the company's biweekly newsletter.

In addition to taking careful readings on their culture, Lands' End has a number of programs to nurture it. One highlight is a Breakfast with the Executive Group program, during which all new salaried hires meet with company leaders to talk about who Lands' End is and where it's heading. Another is the monthly Founders' Meeting, during which the CEO is available for employees to stop by to pitch ideas or voice concerns.

And according to Kelly Ritchie, vice president of Employee Services, "An ongoing way in which we ingrain our culture is simply using a personal approach in our daily dealings with employees. This extends from a first-name basis no matter who you are to our casual dress and open-door policies."

SAS INSTITUTE. When SAS Institute conducted their employee satisfaction survey, the responses yielded few surprises. For example, 90 percent either agreed or strongly agreed that they were proud of their work. But Kathy Council, vice president of Publications and chair of the Total Quality Management Committee (which administered the survey), says, "It's very easy for a company to believe it knows how its employees feel; the only way to be certain is to ask. While there were no surprises in the results, we want to address those issues that are of concern."

In response to the survey, focus groups were formed to talk about issues raised and to formulate ways to address needs. As the result of this process, two recent changes were made: (1) Management feedback survey results are shared with the manager's manager, allowing them to work as a team to plan for future development opportunities; and (2) the company has a new paid time-off policy for part-time employees.

ERIE INSURANCE. Erie Insurance has two ongoing programs to measure employee attitudes: a biannual communication audit and a monthly Coffee with the President program. For the communication audit, Erie asks employees to respond to 31 statements and provide written comments. The results are compiled for each location. Senior management is responsible for holding feedback sessions with their employees and developing action plans for improvement in their work units.

Each month, Erie randomly selects some 10 people to join the president for coffee, where he gives a brief talk; then the group is free to ask him questions. Erie does this in the field via videoconferencing. They also do this same program monthly with their independent agents.

FEL-PRO. One of the most unique programs at Fel-Pro is the Employees' Forum, in existence for over 45 years now. The forum is a delegation of employees who are elected by their peers in their work group to serve a one-year term. The forum is an opportunity for them to voice views and departmental concerns. The group meets with key managers and executives every six weeks to discuss issues and resolve problems. Often, they solve issues in advance of the Forum on their own. Results of the meeting are published and distributed to all employees in *Forum Notes,* a special newsletter.

Forum delegates have a number of responsibilities, including participating in company committees; meeting new employees; distributing Fel-Pro's publications; surveying workers; meeting with employees before or after work, at lunch, or during breaks to resolve issues; collecting photos for the company's Brag Board; and soliciting contributions for Fel-Pro's annual Crusade of Mercy campaign.

For their contribution, delegates receive a gift and extra vacation days. Probably the best benefit is the chance to develop and demonstrate leadership qualities. A number of delegates have been promoted to leadership positions as a result of their experience on the Forum.

USAA. USAA measures morale primarily through four programs: (1) employee opinion surveys, (2) an online comment system, (3) trained Employee Service Center specialists for confidential consultation, and (4) numerous forums where senior management facilitates discussion.

A corporate-wide opinion survey is given on an 18-to-24-month cycle, and asks questions about morale, policy, programs, and processes, and includes an open comment section. Results are communicated company-wide, through management meetings, the company newsletter, and on the company news station. Each unit also communicates its results and creates action plans for improvement. USAA also conducts 360-degree reviews for its leaders.

An online electronic document system (ODOC-E) is a tool that enables employees to comment spontaneously (and anonymously, if they wish). Of the system, Tim Timmerman, executive director, Member Relations/Feedback, says, "USAA views all feedback as an opportunity and it investigates each employee comment for possible changes or training opportunities."

Common issues that emerge are discussed in a special article in the company newsletter or on the company station. Items for follow-up are routed to the "action agent" for the area involved, who is required to give a response date (the desired turnaround time is two weeks). USAA's Employee Service Center specialists follow up with the individual (or department, if anonymous). They also look for trends, and report them to senior management along with suggested actions.

Senior executives regularly get together with employees for open dialogue. These meetings range from small group settings over breakfast or lunch to "town hall" meetings in the company's auditorium. Senior management fields questions and offers answers, or promises follow-up within a reasonable time frame.

ALAGASCO. Alagasco has a program that offers a direct link to the CEO. Their "Hey Mike" program allows people to make suggestions or ask questions of CEO Mike Warren. To encourage employees to use the system, cards are posted prominently throughout the company. People can take one and jot down what they want to say. The cards go directly to Mike, and they don't have to be signed, though many employees do. Mike Warren says all signed suggestions are guaranteed an answer, though not necessarily the answer the employee would like. There is also an idea voice mail line that goes directly to Gary Youngblood, Alagasco's president and COO, for suggestions, complaints, and general ideas. Mike says, "These are methods of communication that empower employees and give them a direct line to top management."

In addition to the Hey Mike program, Alagasco uses a number of other tools to gauge morale. One is an employee attitude survey conducted every three to four years. In 1995, they used the Great Place to Work Survey, from the Great Place to Work Institute, in San Francisco, created by Amy Lyman and Robert Levering (coauthor of *The 100 Best*). In addition to responses to the survey questions, Alagasco received 88 pages of comments from their employees. When the results of the survey were compiled, Alagasco's vice president of human resources went on a summer-long road show visiting every office and holding employee meetings to discuss the results. Several months later, Mike followed up with meetings of his own, to review progress made and lessons learned.

Culture: Each Is Unique

The cultures at our 100 Best peers are among their greatest strengths.
Here are some highlights.

SOUTHWEST AIRLINES. Southwest Airlines' culture is legendary. They definitely have their own style, and fun is a big part of that style—for employees and for customers. If you've ever flown Southwest, you'll recall that the flight attendants dress casually (one employment ad promotes "the freedom to wear shorts and tennis shoes to work"). They've been known to sing the safety instructions. Three of their planes are painted to look like giant killer whales (to promote Sea World vacations).

The airline has some unique titles, including Executive Vice President of Customers (both internal and external). They call Human Resources the People Department (a name that other companies are beginning to adopt). They always capitalize the words, Employee and Customer. Several years ago, the company threw out their policies and procedures manual, and replaced it with the 88-page *Guidelines for Leaders*, encouraging common sense and good judgment.

Their CEO, Herb Kelleher, is, well . . . *Nuts* (the title of a book about him and Southwest, written by Kevin and Jackie Freiberg). The authors of *The 100 Best* captured it well when they wrote, "He has been known to sing 'Tea for Two' while wearing bloomers and a bonnet at a company picnic (featuring a chili cook-off) in front of 4,000 employees. He regularly helps flight attendants serve drinks and peanuts when he flies. One Easter, he walked the plane's aisle clad in an Easter Bunny outfit; and one St. Patrick's Day, he dressed as a leprechaun. When Southwest started a new route to Sacramento, Kelleher sang a rap song at a press conference with two people in Teenage Mutant Ninja Turtle costumes and two others dressed as tomatoes."

This is not to imply it's all fun and games at Southwest. Their motto is "Operate during the best of times as though they were the worst of times." Southwest has weathered the volatility of the airline industry extremely well. Rita Bailey, director, University for People, says, "The reason we can have fun is that we keep our costs down—we work hard here."

Southwest does an exercise called Gap Gauge to measure the distance between themselves and their competitors. Southwest believes they are still ahead, and still improving, but they want to keep an eye on how fast their competitors improve (which they say has been steadily increasing).

Years ago, Southwest instituted a 10-minute turnaround on their planes (today, it's 20 minutes). At the time, the industry average was 40 minutes. According to Rita, "We did it out of necessity. We were new, and all we had were four planes. We had to sell one, but wanted to maintain our schedule, so we made it work. We could have taken it down to 20 minutes and still have been the fastest by far, but we needed it to be 10, and so it was."

To protect their culture, Southwest has a Culture Committee, which is, according to Kathy Pettit, director of Customers, "a consortium of employees from across our system whose charter it is to foster our Southwest spirit." The committee is chaired by Colleen Barrett, the company's executive vice president of Customers. Among their many other culture tools, Southwest also has a weekly employee newsletter, a monthly magazine (entitled *LUVLines*), and a quarterly video, *"As the Planes Turn."* The Executive Office answers anywhere from 150 to 200 cards and letters from Employees each month. Executives spend quarterly days in the field whereby they work side by side on the front lines; they report receiving tons of feedback in the process.

SAS INSTITUTE. SAS Institute has some progressive employee benefits that go a long way toward boosting morale and encouraging retention. The Institute boasts a turnover rate of less than 4 percent in an industry with an average rate of 16 percent. Here are a few highlights of the company's unique benefits.

SAS Institute offers on-site health care at no cost to employees and their families; childcare on the headquarters campus with teacher-child ratios as low as 1:3 and elder care services including in-home assessments by the Institute's geriatric counselor, care referrals, insurance advice, counseling, relocation services, and an online listing of elder care needs and employees who are willing to volunteer their time to assist.

The Institute's recreation and fitness center for employees and their families has been twice rated best overall by the National Employee Services and Recreation Association. The Wellness Center features unique services such as on-site massage and an Ergonomics Lab where employees can spend a day working while trying a variety of equipment and furniture. On Mondays, fruit is delivered to break rooms; on Wednesdays, it's M&Ms; and on Fridays, it's the breakfast goody—all at no charge to employees.

HEWITT ASSOCIATES. At Hewitt Associates, culture cues are everywhere. One employee said, "I just joined the firm in '96. What I've found to be different are the signs and messages throughout the organization that say everybody's input is valued. Some examples: only round tables (nobody can sit at the head of the table and dictate the discussion); no titles; only announcing owners once a year (I don't necessarily know who is and who isn't an owner—it doesn't determine your value); and nobody has a corner office."

GREAT PLAINS SOFTWARE. Great Plains Software has an extensive line-up of programs and events to celebrate and encourage their culture. Highlights include a "buddy" program, Lunch and Learn events with the CEO, family events (such as a Children's Museum night), and employee fun events (wine and cheese after 5:00 P.M.)

Great Plains' recognition program is impressive. Recognition events occur all the time, including team recognition, quarterly company recognition (President's Awards, etc.), and an annual companywide recognition event, Pioneer Day. Among the awards on Pioneer Day are the Riding Shotgun Award for commitment to partners and the Jesse James Award for innovation.

Like Rosenbluth, Great Plains holds an internal open house event, their annual Info Day, held since 1992. It's a giant trade show, and every team is given display space and accessories. The exhibits are creative but not elaborate, and everyone learns more about each team and its roles, and how they link together to achieve the company's mission.

NORTHWESTERN MUTUAL. Northwestern Mutual Life's Executive Committee drafted the company's credo in 1888, and to this day, no one has been able to produce a credo they like better. It's inscribed in marble in the lobby of the company's headquarters building, and framed copies are displayed in conference rooms. It reads: "The ambition of the Northwestern has been less to be large than to be safe; its aim is to rank first in benefits to policyowners rather than first in size. Valuing quality above quantity, it has preferred to secure its business under certain salutary restrictions and limitations rather than to write a much larger business at the possible sacrifice of those valuable points which have made the Northwestern pre-eminently the policyowner's company." Company spokesperson Sandra Wesley says, "Far from words that everybody sees but nobody pays attention to, the credo has been quoted by all ranks of employees at various times, including a security guard who captured the attention and the admiration of two senior executives from a reinsurance company who visited Northwestern Mutual in 1994. After their visit, they wrote to President James D. Ericson: 'We had an amazing experience the last time we visited your company . . . . During our drive over, we were commenting that Northwestern Mutual is one of the few companies in which the mission statement truly describes the company and how it conducts business. When we arrived, we decided to go to the entrance at which the mission is clearly displayed on the wall. As we were standing by the guard's desk reading the statement, a guard named Jennifer asked if we would like to hear her recite it from memory. We said yes, at which point Jennifer proceeded to recite the entire mission statement. We were incredibly impressed, to say the least.'"

HALLMARK CARDS. Like Northwestern Mutual, Hallmark Cards employees enjoy some long-held traditions, for example, a *daily* employee newsletter (for over 40 years) and the annual holiday tradition of inviting the employees to the executive offices to meet the Hall family (long lines throughout the day speak to its popularity).

Hallmark's CEO Forums have been held for more than a decade. The company's CEO, Irvine Hockaday, meets with groups of 50 employees 10 times a year to hear what's on their minds. To make sure they feel free to be frank, no senior leaders are present.

Corporate Town Hall meetings, initiated in 1995, are held quarterly, with three meetings a day of 400 employees each. Hallmark's top leaders (including the CEO) talk for a half-hour or so, then it's open discussion for another hour. Through the CEO Forum and the Town Hall meetings, more than 5,000 employees per year engage in face-to-face discussion with Hallmark's CEO.

MARY KAY. This Mary Kay story illustrates the power of a caring culture, on a personal level. In the months leading up to Seminar (the largest company event), it became evident that one of the company's independent sales directors had an excellent chance to break the existing sales record of $2 million in annual retail sales in a year. The sales development team assigned to her division knew that there was no further coaching or techniques they could provide her. But they could offer encouragement.

During the last months leading up to the year-end close, they sent her a homespun video of corporate rank-and-file staff telling her, "You can do it!" She received a Federal Express shipment of $100 Grand candy bars (20 to total $2 million). In short, she was continually showered with all manner of support.

The numbers were to be tallied early on the morning of July 4. The director was sleeping with her beeper at her family's vacation home when she received a page. A caring emplyee had voluntarily made the trek into the office to learn the results. And instead of leaving a return number, he punched in "$2,000,000" as the message.

When the record-breaking sales director spoke at Seminar, she said it was those small acts of kindness in the home stretch that had made the difference in keeping her focused on her goal.

Do all these things make us a better company?

At Rosenbluth, we don't need proof that all this effort to nourish our culture is worth it. For the last two decades we have put forth a concerted effort and we have seen the difference: Our growth reflects it. Our turnover shows it. Our client retention rates support it. These things work, and we're not the only ones who think so. The examples from the highly successful companies woven throughout this book illustrate it.

Data supports it, too. In his book *A Great Place to Work*, author Robert Levering (coauthor of The *100 Best Companies to Work for in America*) cited a study completed by Franklin Research & Development. The study compared the 100 best companies with the S&P 500 companies. They were measured in terms of earnings per share and stock appreciation. The results showed that over a decade, in terms of earnings per share, the 100 best companies were more than twice as profitable as the average for S&P companies. Comparing stock appreciation, the 100 best grew at three times the rate of the average S&P company.

SHARING THE WEALTH. A company's ability to share the richness of its culture outside of its "walls" is an important measure of its success. Making this a better world is a worthwhile investment. According to a 1993 study by The Conference Board and the Points of Light Foundation, 92 percent of American companies encourage their employees to participate in community service.

That same study noted that 77 percent of companies agreed that volunteerism supported their strategic goals. There's more to it than tax deductions and image boosts. The number one reason cited among executives was increased productivity. Having a strong commitment to community helps companies attract better people, and it's great for morale.

Those who volunteer find it a great stress reliever; in fact, studies have shown they are 10 times more likely to have better health. They learn new skills through their volunteer work, and report finding a better balance between their work and personal lives (particularly if their company supports their volunteer work). All that said, the most important reason is that it is the right thing to do.

The outward-in approach we take in running our company is the one we take in supporting philanthropic activities. Our associates come to us with ideas. They are out in communities all over the world. They know which issues are important to them and to our clients. As our director of Cultural Diversity says, "Our associates just care. It doesn't originate in the executive suite, but out in the field. And they know the company will support them."

Because we make it a point to hire caring people, it's natural that they would extend that caring beyond the company. We try to make it easy for them. First, we provide a central point of contact for our associates wishing to enlist the company's support of a program, so they know where to turn when they have an idea or a request.

It's important for companies to have someone clearly designated as the champion. As we discussed earlier in this chapter regarding a champion of corporate culture, if you don't designate someone to champion community support, people will gravitate to someone who doesn't necessarily have the time or expertise. And if the process is fair, all requests should go through a single source. Our corporate contributions coordinator handles all requests (we receive more than 10 a day), which we review on a regular basis. She benchmarks her program with other companies to look for the best approach, to help us make the highest possible impact in terms of support. A majority of what we do is as a "silent partner." We like to support our clients in their philanthropic activities, and of course, we support our associates in theirs.

One showing of support was particularly heartwarming for our company. We have 330 associates in Fargo, North Dakota, site of some of the worst flooding in recent memory. Many of our associates there lost their homes to the raging water and still came to work every day. But they had help. Associates from around the world came to their aid. Scores of associates flew to Fargo to help out with the sandbagging. Donations of money, clothing, toys, and furniture came from our offices everywhere. A number of our clients took up collections of their own, and airline and hotel companies we work with pitched in with money and toiletries. The saying goes, "Charity begins at home." Our associates felt the pain of those in Fargo, and mobilized to help.

Another way we make it easy for our associates to become involved in supporting their communities is our partnership with Cares, a volunteer service organization in 27 cities across the nation. Cares publishes a monthly calendar of projects ranging from community development to environmental, educational, health, homelessness, and senior citizen programs. People can just jump right into the projects of their choice.

Northwestern Mutual: Strong Community Support

The tradition of volunteerism among Northwestern Mutual Life's employees is strong. More than 1,000 Northwestern employees donate 85,000 hours annually to 200 nonprofit organizations. The company recognizes volunteer support in its Employee Community Service

Awards program, and produces an annual brochure to highlight those efforts. For this program, the Northwestern Mutual Foundation donates $10,000 to the nonprofit organization represented by the Most Exceptional Volunteer, and $5,000 to each of the organizations selected by the 10 Outstanding Volunteers

The 1997 winner, Leroy Harmon, is a facility operations coordinator who was honored for his work with a residential treatment center for emotionally disturbed children, as well as for starting a boys' choir, and working in one-on-one mentoring relationships.

Our support of our associates' volunteer activities was given added emphasis in 1997, when we made it one of the two primary points of focus for our Salmon Spirit initiative (community service and self-development). We made people aware of volunteer opportunities and recognized their efforts in a variety of ways, one of which was a booth at our companywide meeting that year, dedicated to recognizing the volunteer efforts of our associates throughout the year, and to promoting awareness of future activities.

One activity we're really excited about is our West Philadelphia Intellicenter. Several years ago, we opened an operation in rural North Dakota (Linton, North Dakota, population about 1,200) to bring some temporary work to farm families during the drought of 1988. We soon came to appreciate the incredible quality of work there. We made it a permanent operation, and expanded the activities to include accounting, travel reservations, and client care. Soon, we opened a center in Fargo, North Dakota, to which we route calls from around the world. We named it an Intellicenter to signify that it combines the best in people, technology, and telecommunications.Now we have four Intellicenters in the United States, with plans for centers in smaller communities abroad. In 1998, we will open an Intellicenter in an empowerment zone just miles from our world headquarters, in the inner-city community of West Philadelphia. There, we will hire and train upward of 100 people from the community to handle overflow reservations for our business and for other industries, such as airlines and car rental companies. We also plan to start a data entry facility to help clients with that need.

The facility will also feature a learning and development center, complete with a resource library, computer rooms (for adults and for children),

Thought Centers for community meetings, and a Thought Theatre, where children and parents can enjoy educational programs. We will have areas for gardening, a playground for children, and sporting facilities for teens. We plan to offer learning programs to help members of the community further their education and help them pursue their career goals. A curriculum is being developed as we write, including math, grammar/reading, computer literacy, career enhancement, and youth programs/tutoring.

Our associates are really behind this, and they are the ones who will make it something truly special. But the support of the company enables them. I encourage every company to build the right support mechanisms to allow their people to contribute as much as they desire to. It's worth the investment.

A SPECIAL STORY. In April 1995, we had a global sales meeting at The Rivery, our company's executive ranch in North Dakota. One evening, we dropped in on a meeting of the local horse club and met the club's treasurer, Jodi Mosset. Jodi has cystic fibrosis, and needed a double lung transplant to survive.

Not only did Jodi face a medical crisis, she had to maneuver a bureaucratic gauntlet as well—being a member of a small community in the most sparsely populated state in the nation doesn't put you at the top of organ waiting lists. After spending the evening in her company, we became compelled to find a solution for her. At the next morning's meeting, we set out as a team to find a way to help. We held a brainstorming session and agreed to dedicate time each day to focus on a solution.

It wasn't long before leads began to pour in from associates across the nation. One had a former college roommate who had become a specialist in the disease. Another had a friend who had lived in North Dakota and who was a successful double-lung transplant. This gave Jodi someone to talk to who understood how she felt, what she faced, and could give her hope.

All the leads were steps toward the answer, but an associate in our Memphis office found the ultimate solution. He called a friend, a former hospital administrator, who had a friend, who headed a pediatric pulmonary department for a hospital with an aggressive transplant program. They put Jodi on the list. When the day arrived, our associates really threw themselves into the effort; Jodi and her family were given air tickets for the trip; they were met at their connections, escorted to the next flights, and provided with snacks, reading materials, and good wishes.

On September 16, 1995, Jodi got her much-deserved lungs, and now has a bright future. The solution was born in a culture where people are determined to make a difference. It's not every day we can help save a life, but we can make the lives we touch better, and that's an amazing way to do business.

Our Memphis associate's compassion, resourcefulness, and dedication were rewarded with the company's salmon pin, our highest honor, presented at our global leaders' meeting in December 1995, just eight months after he had met Jodi for the first time.

BE&K: Putting Experience to Work in the Community

BE&K enlists the help of employees who have retired from the company to support community efforts. (Like Rosenbluth, they also utilize retirees for special projects.) According to Vice President Carolyn Morgan, "Having a pool of retirees with years of experience allows the company to offer their service to many community projects. For example, a retired project manager is leading the renovation of the YWCA. The YW has childcare for low-income and homeless children, apartments for disabled and low-income women, and many other services for women and children in our community."

Activists for the Internal Environment: A Summary

- Try an open meeting policy. A visibly posted schedule of all meetings will let everyone know which meetings might be of interest to them. Only meetings that involve personnel issues or other confidential information should be closed. You'll find the open exchange of ideas and broad input to be invaluable. Not only will it promote internal learning and cross-functionality, it will foster trust among your associates.

- Consider a casual dress policy (if you don't already have one). When we had only occasional "casual days" we noticed people were more productive and creative, because they felt comfortable and relaxed. Now, it's the reverse; if a client is visiting who might object, we declare a "business dress" day.

- Take a walk through and a hard look at your offices (especially your headquarters) to check out your culture. You might want to take someone along who will be really honest—probably someone from outside the company. We bet you'll find some surprises.

- If you don't have an official champion for your company's culture, consider appointing one. The care of a culture is everyone's responsibility, but if a champion isn't designated, things are likely to slip through the cracks.

- A program to reenergize a company's culture can boost morale and teamwork, and is a good way to nurture what's special about the company, and ensure it doesn't fade. Our Salmon Spirit initiative was launched with a series of companywide events, supplemented by a field guide of do-it-yourself program ideas. Each year, the program takes on two new themes to keep it fresh (i.e., celebrating success, professional development, or community service).

- A personal welcome on someone's first day can go a long way to bringing that person into your culture. Following any orientation you may have, new associates should be welcomed by their team, too. A welcome packet with such things as lunch coupons and cheat sheets of everyone's names is always appreciated, as is a designee to show him or her the ropes.

- A role-switching or shadowing program, either between leaders and associates or among peers, can be a very effective facilitator of communication and teamwork, and can generate great process improvement ideas.

- Consider an "officer visit" program that encourages leaders to visit your offices when they travel. It might sound like a natural, but it seldom happens in most companies. If the officers send thank-you notes following their visits, all the better.

- In locations with several departments, think about having an internal open house. It can be very informative and improve operations when various departments showcase what they do. Where we've held them, families have often been invited; they support the dedication we ask of our associates, and deserve to see what's worth working so hard for.

- "Brown bag" seminars on general topics (for example, listening skills and elegant language) can be a low-cost way to impart skills that are helpful to associates in both their professional and personal lives. We also include non-work-related topics to enhance our associates' balance between work and family.

- Set aside a special time each year (or more often) to thank your people for all they do to help your company succeed. Our Associate Appreciation Month is a tradition that our people look forward to each year. Volunteers can coordinate the activities, and suppliers can participate, offering prizes or other shows of appreciation.

- An event where officers serve associates can be refreshing and fun. Our VP Barbecue each year sends an important message: Associates come first! As noted previously, the officers also serve new associates high tea during our orientation program.

- Consider producing a "state of the company" letter for your associates once or twice per year, to update them on how the company is doing, how the competition is stacking up, and to highlight top developments and preview things to come. If you're not a CEO, consider doing one for your department or work team.

- A question-and-answer column in your internal publication or via other communication vehicles (i.e., e-mail, voice mail) can be a very effective way to announce new products or services, squelch rumors, and otherwise answer any questions your associates might have. To be sure the Q&A is representative of what's on the minds of your associate base, you might have to actively solicit questions from a variety of locations.

- A companywide meeting is one of the best ways to ignite a company's spirit, strengthen bonds with clients, and boost effectiveness. It's a logistical nightmare and a significant investment, but using outside resources and asking suppliers to participate can lessen the burden. It's worth the effort. The lasting effects are immeasurable.

- An unusual way to measure morale is to ask people (associates and clients) to draw their impressions of the organization. Provide them with Crayolas and paper. You'll find that the pictures uncover issues that would never come out in traditional survey mechanisms. We've learned immeasurably from them. Be sure to explain why you're doing it (especially outside the United States) and that all drawings will be held in confidence.

- A more scientific way to measure morale is to conduct a hard-hitting survey addressing all the major components of morale. The survey should be worded and administered by an outside firm for which that is a specialty. Anonymity and accountability should be part of the process. If translating for distribution outside your country, be sure not only to use an expert translation firm, but also to double-check the translations with your associates abroad. Publish the results internally, along with regular updates on progress made or action taken as a result of the survey.

- A 360-degree review process (where leaders are reviewed by their leaders, peers, people reporting to them, and clients) can provide a multidimensional look at who's guiding your company. From the process, each leader should create an action plan to improve on their areas of weakness.

- Support the volunteer efforts of your associates. It's the right thing to do, and it improves productivity and strengthens morale. Make it easy and fair, by providing a central point of contact for requests, ideas, and questions. And don't forget to recognize and celebrate the efforts of your associates.

8

One World, One Company

Our journey to becoming a global company has been interesting. The most important discovery we have made is that for all the talk of cultural differences around the world, people are basically the same everywhere you go. They want to do business with people they like, respect, trust, and admire—in a word, with friends.

When several years ago we expanded to the Middle East, I didn't really know what to expect, particularly how Rosenbluth International would be received as a potential business partner by companies in the Arab nations. But I knew from our first meeting with the people of Kanoo Travel (a division of the Yusuf Bin Ahmed Kanoo Group) in Bahrain, that we would forge a special friendship with them.

Their company was very much like our own in many ways: They were founded in 1890 and we were established two years later. Both have always been family-owned businesses, and their commitment to excellence and a caring attitude toward their people mirrored our own. But we had no idea the dimension this relationship would take on over the years.

The depth of this unique friendship is probably best told through a story of loyalty and bravery. During the Gulf War, a number of our clients found themselves faced with trying circumstances, but probably none more than Chevron. During the chaos at the onset of the conflict, some Chevron employees there were not able to get out of Kuwait. The U.S. State Department couldn't provide information, and our stateside friends at Chevron were determined to explore every possible resource to ensure the safety of their associates. They called upon us to help in any way we could, and we immediately called *our friends at Kanoo, in Saudi Arabia. They mobilized a team to reach any and all contacts they had in Kuwait to try to get information on the Chevron executives. Within a matter of days, they were located. What happened next was something only a friend, in the truest sense of the word, might do.*

A team of Kanoo associates assembled to travel into the midst of the war in Kuwait to assist the stranded Chevron executives, whom they had never met. Their mission was to find them, help them depart Kuwait, bring them into Saudi Arabia, then safely on their way home to the United States and their families. Our friends at Kanoo were willing to risk their own safety, possibly even their lives, to protect the safety of people who were important to us.

In the end, the Chevron executives in Kuwait reached safety without the Kanoo team having to travel into the war zone, but the point is, they were ready and willing to do it. Caring can triumph over even war.

Preparing for the Journey

We began our global journey in the late '80s. As with anything, knowing where to start is always a challenge. Like most businesses, we were somewhat intimidated by the myth that cultural boundaries present major obstacles to opening locations abroad. Thus we decided to take a conservative approach to international expansion.

We formed an alliance with companies in key countries where we needed to be able to provide local points of service to our clients traveling abroad. We aligned ourselves with strong service providers who had English-speaking staff on board, so that our clients had a place to turn if they should need anything while abroad. We called our network of companies the Rosenbluth International Alliance (RIA), and it worked just fine for several years. But as time progressed, new opportunities emerged, and we came to realize we had outgrown our initial strategy.

The Implosion

We've always been adamant about uncovering and eradicating conflicts of interest, but by the spring of 1993, we were convinced we had *created* one, though not by design. The RIA was a well-intentioned group of agencies, one per country, aligned to provide service to corporations on a multinational basis. We had invested a lot in the RIA; we had spent six years holding biannual meetings of agency owners in every corner of the world. By night, we feasted on every native dish ever concocted; by day, we convinced each other of our worthiness. We were one happy family. Flags of every nation adorned the tables of our summits. People kissed each other before, during, and after every meeting. Life was good.

And so it continued while client needs were confined to the basics (reissuing tickets, enroute changes, lost luggage assistance, etc.). But then we actually landed a piece of multinational business, and suddenly we needed to coordinate pricing, services, information collection standards, and all of the services we provide for our domestic clients.

A travel management firm is very different from a typical travel agency. The supplier negotiations, reporting tools, and support products and services a management firm provides can drive millions of dollars of cost out of a corporate travel program. But it takes a high degree of expertise and the right tools to do it. The variance among the firms in the RIA became blindingly apparent when we raised the bar.

It quickly became apparent that what we were willing to do for our clients in the states, others viewed as folly. What we were willing to invest in, some of our counterparts weren't. We negotiated favorable rates for our clients with some key airlines, but RIA members had their own relationships with other airlines, and they didn't want to support our choices and lose juicy commission deals from competing carriers. We collected all of our information via one system. The RIA members had their own methods. It was becoming clear that there was nothing aligned about the Rosenbluth International Alliance.

Realizing that an alliance is only as strong as its weakest link, we spent a lot of waking hours at the office in 1993, and did a lot of soul searching. We knew the RIA had to change, but we didn't know into what. One thing we did know was that we had to own it. How else could we be absolutely certain that the business was built around our clients' needs, worldwide?

We scheduled a meeting for spring 1993 in Lisbon. Determined to come out of it with a direction agreeable to most, I decided to leave it up to the membership to help formulate what the new structure would look like. My role was simply to lay it on the table that things had to change. I outlined three critical requirements: (1) capital investment in technology, by all members; (2) common branding under the Rosenbluth International name; (3) Rosenbluth majority equity in strategic countries. These were not popular ideas.

At the beginning of the meeting, I made my announcement, and things quickly deteriorated into a verbal food fight as agency owners tried to steer the organization in a direction suitable to themselves. Breakout sessions more closely resembled playground spats than business forums, and a fist fight almost broke out in one of them. During coffee breaks, danish pastries were flying. We had to ban bagels for fear of someone getting hurt. It was definitely time for a big change.

I left everyone in the lobby bar the first night, marinating in alcohol. I was sure cooler heads would prevail the next morning. Wrong. By noon, a European caucus group cornered me in the hallway to let me know that they were "united as a continent" and that any attempt on my part to control any new structure would be doomed. They said, "Europe stands united." I went up to my room and turned on CNN, which, ironically, was reporting on the fights that had broken out among soccer fans from various European countries following a weekend of tournament play. An interesting reminder that only shared values and priorities will ever truly unite.

Passport to Freedom

It had became apparent that the RIA had outlived its appropriateness. As might have been expected, most of the members could not live with our new requirements. We tried, through a series of meetings, to fully explore any way it could work, but in the end we had to go our separate ways.

So we had to get bold, and we had no time to lose. Our clients had been telling us they wanted our service standards, consolidated information, and leverage with suppliers, worldwide. We had to put a structure in place to be able to offer that. It was déjà vu—we'd been down that road before, domestically. In the '80s, we pioneered U.S. consolidation of corporate travel programs, by implementing the first program. In 1984, we were awarded DuPont's account, nationwide. This created a trend toward single sourcing in our industry, which was extremely successful. Because we believed the trend would evolve to global consolidation, we set out to prepare for the global marketplace. We also believed that the economics of those programs would apply globally. The landscape looked remarkably the same.

U.S. airline deregulation had spawned incredible opportunities for companies to save money on their corporate travel if they worked with a supplier that could make sense of the chaos and shape it into benefit. Airline deregulation was now dawning on multiple continents. Airlines began to move toward multinational negotiations, happy hunting grounds for us. To do what we wanted to do, we had to own and operate our locations around the world—maybe not all at once, but soon.

This scenario has broad application. Companies today are looking for any means available to drive down costs and enhance the productivity of their workforce. Consolidating supplier relationships can help them do both, if they're the right suppliers. As more companies do business around the world, they will seek to consolidate their relationships on a global basis. The steps we took to become a truly global supplier can be followed by any company, in any industry. Whether it makes sense for a company to own and operate its locations, participate in joint ventures, or be part of a consortium, the following steps can be helpful in establishing needs, priorities, and options.

STEP BY STEP. The first thing we did was to spend extensive time with our clients (one to one and in focus groups) to determine their global strategies, needs, and challenges. Next, we met at length with key suppliers to understand the demands they face as they compete globally, to find potential triple-win opportunities. The results of these meetings showed us what was lacking in our industry. From there, we created a charter for our global expansion, which included the following requirements:

- uniform, worldwide service standards
- common point-of-sale and back-room technology
- common global identity and branding
- local country representation
- single point of contact for clients and for suppliers

Later, we polled a broader group of companies by conducting an industry outlook survey (which has become an annual event). We conducted the survey on-site at a major industry trade show, and learned about the attending companies' global priorities. The results confirmed what our charter had addressed.

The few major players in our industry merged, slapping their organizations together, on paper, in an effort to span the globe. We resisted the temptation to merge because we wanted to ensure that we remained fast, flexible, and able to jump on opportunities without being weighed down by bureaucracy and politics. Instead, we set out to accomplish our goal through acquisitions and start-up operations (run by local nationals) in the most strategic countries for our clients.

To begin, we outlined our clients' international business plans and time frames, and overlaid them to get a clear picture of where we needed to be and when. We then constructed a grid of all the countries where we might need to be in the future, and outlined what would be required for us to do business in each of those countries. Prioritization and flexibility are the keys. For example, one company that awarded us its global business required us to be in 60 countries. It didn't make sense to have one-person offices scattered in remote parts of the world, so we continue to do some servicing through joint ventures and servicing agencies. But we do have our own office in every key country.

We also constructed market-by-market client requirements, with time frames, and integrated that information with supplier plans and an intelligence matrix of the marketplace. From that, we created our global implementation plan. Then we were ready to begin the shift from the RIA to equity positions and ownership.

We maintained service relationships with partner companies while we pursued our course. We hired a couple of RIA company owners to join our team. We conducted early expansions into English-speaking countries, simply because they were the easiest, and thus quickest, places for us to do business.

We also quickly accomplished our progression into countries where our key suppliers (particularly our technology suppliers) had a strong presence. They blazed some trails for us. Our technology is a huge global differentiator; we are the only travel management company in the world with a real-time electronically linked global reservations and data collection system. Through it, we can influence supplier market share at the point of sale, instantly, around the world, and that's a commanding tool to use in negotiating on behalf of our clients.

In order for a company to offer its clients the full benefits of global consolidation, it must be able to offer global data and global discounts. The availability of these types of support tools will drive a company's decision regarding owning its own locations or partnering. Since we had a system in place, it made sense for us to venture out on our own, and to draft off of the momentum of our key suppliers.

Looking back, the biggest mistake we made was in trying to take what we had in place and move it to the next level. When we wanted global ownership and branding, we approached the RIA members, seeking to purchase their companies. We did so out of loyalty. But what we really needed was a custom-built solution, a collection of just the right organization in each country to meet our totally new requirements, which is what we ultimately created.

The secret to a successful global strategy is planning, not just for expansion, but for the obsolescence of your short-term plan and the formulation of your next-generation structure. It's certainly worth the effort. Today, we have multinational business originating from all around the world, not just from the United States. And the rate of growth that results is astounding.

So You Want Offices Abroad

We have developed some commonsense steps to global expansion that have worked well for us, and we're happy to share them. We take a three-step approach, which we refer to as "sniff, smell, consume." (Hey, we're being candid here.)

Before deciding to open our own location in any country, we first determine whether we can acquire what we're looking for. In the "presniff" stage, this means identifying driving forces behind our interest in acquiring in that particular location, for example, to leverage existing assets, acquire additional talent, increase market share, add a new line of business, or add incremental cash flow. This drives the direction of our search.

During the "sniff" portion of the process, we meet with the owners of the agencies we are considering investing in or buying. We look over their operating stats, along with the alignment of their business philosophies and practices with our own. We determine whether or not their organization adds value to ours. We try to answer three questions: (1) Will the addition bring us closer to filling our needs? (2) Will the price be fair? (3) What is the potential return on our investment?

If all looks good during "sniff," we move on to "smell," which is more complex. We prepare a letter outlining information we will need before we make a bona fide offer. In the letter, we ask that they be prepared to provide past and current financial status, management's current capabilities, current customer status, value of assets to be acquired, and projected two-year income and cash flow.

We also ask for additional information such as which systems they use and what are the nonrecurring expenses, pending business decisions, employment contracts, intangible assets, ongoing owner interests, and various industry-specific issues.

We lay out the major points of the agreement, and have our legal and tax experts review the information. We carefully validate all assumptions, and set a time frame in which the offer will be valid.

The "smell" step is very painful for companies to respond to. Most of the information is not at their fingertips, so it takes a lot of work to answer, and it should. This is a serious decision for both parties.

If all goes well, we move on to "consume." (Don't let the name put you off—these companies *want* to be purchased.) During this stage, we conduct on-site due diligence. We have a due diligence checklist that includes everything from assets to human resource and learning development capabilities to financial information to background on company leaders. If all is in order, we draw up offer letters and contracts.

In summary, then, the basis of "sniff, smell, consume" is (1) search and sort, (2) build relationships around key issues, (3) discovery and offer process, (4) due diligence and closing. Pretty basic stuff, but each step is necessary, and the more methodical you are about it, the more efficient and effective it will be for everyone. Gut instinct plays a critical part in the decision, too, but it has to be supported by fact.

Blending

Once the acquisition is made, the real work of integrating begins. We send in an HR team to begin the process of importing the company culture, while respecting and being sensitive to the local country's culture and practices. A good source is the American Chamber of Commerce (ACC) in that particular country, to check the local employment practices and issues. Consultants can also provide this information, but the ACC is a less expensive route. The team also goes to local bookstores for reference materials on local employment practices.

We also work with our law firm, which has global partners abroad, to direct us to legal advice in each country. We usually work with them during both the acquisition and implementation phases. We always go by the letter of the law, but typically soften the language a bit to make it fit our style. It's critical to uphold the local laws while achieving consistency with the company's culture and practices, worldwide.

Here are some of the steps our HR team takes:

1. Meet with all of the staff one on one and in small groups.
2. Share best practices (the HR team then shares them globally).

3. Work with local leaders to set up performance review systems, individual development plans, role descriptions, and salary lines (we gradually move toward appropriate pay scales, never reducing anyone's pay).

4. Brief other teams (operations, finance, learning and development, etc.) prior to their visits.

5. Implement Rosenbluth culture assessment tools (e.g., Associate Satisfaction Surveys and 360-degree reviews), which are initially completed around six months after the acquisition, then typically yearly thereafter.

Following these initial steps, the HR team travels the world to assist associates with ongoing recruitment, development, and retention. They pollinate global best practices everywhere they go. For example, it is not common practice in most countries to send response cards, notifying applicants their resumes have been received. But a job search is a very stressful time in most people's lives, and we find the practice is a pleasant surprise for most people. It's well worth the extra effort.

Just as our advance team has a due diligence checklist, each department has its own. It's also a good idea to have a checklist of potential sources for help. Above all, it's critical that everything you're doing makes sense in the country in which you're doing it. Different regions definitely have varying personalities, attitudes, speeds, and degrees of acceptance of American business ideas.

Our general manager of Human Resources (who crisscrosses the globe for most of our international implementations) says, "I've never seen anything so 'blue and white' as our Mexico office" (referring to our company's colors and to that office's eagerness to jump into our culture). Regarding the language barrier issue, she says, "It's not a problem. In fact, it's humbling. Everyone tries so hard to communicate with me. But I can't overestimate the importance of being sensitive to the culture. I always do extensive research before I go. For example, the practice in China of giving and receiving business cards with two hands is very important. I think a lot of people know that, but perhaps not quite as many people realize how important it is to keep the cards on the table, once you receive them. I was at a recent meeting with 20 men in China, and I had all their cards out on the table in front of me. To someone from the United States, it would look like I was playing bingo."

You can't get everything right all the time, so she says her best advice is to keep a sense of humor through it all, and be sincere and respectful. Genuinely good intentions are universal.

No Boundaries

In Chapter 7, on corporate culture, you read the winning entry from the Salmon Spirit contest. We want to tell you more about that here because it illustrates how easy it is to have preconceived notions when doing business in the global arena. The winner of the contest was from our London office, by way of India, which turned out to be the source of an interesting lesson for us.

When we kicked off the Salmon Spirit contest, we wanted to offer a really nice prize to the winner, so we decided to provide two air tickets anywhere in the continental United States. What's wrong with that? We're a *global* company. Offering domestic U.S. tickets assumes that an associate from the United States will win. When we realized what we had done, which wasn't until we selected the winning entry, we were embarrassed. Of course, we changed the prize to be applicable to the winner, and we learned an important lesson. You have to look at things through global eyes, all the time.

In fact, we took a step back and looked at a lot of things. For example, our Salmon Spirit team brought to our attention that *The Salmon Spirit Guide* has a global *section*. Certainly, the information in it is helpful (for example, it includes ideas about how different offices around the world celebrate our company's culture, and about special holidays in each of the countries). But we shouldn't outline what happens in the United States, and then add a global section. All of our global best practices should be together.

It's not "us" and "them" anymore, or "here" and "there." It's us, everywhere. It takes some practice to retrain ourselves to truly think globally, but to be global you have to do it. To facilitate our global thinking, we have a number of support programs in place. Here are a few that should apply to any business. These include global meetings, training, buddy programs, and feedback systems.

Leadership Is Global

In December 1995, we held our first global leaders meeting at our headquarters in Philadelphia. It was an important event for our company, and a program we recommend to any organization with international locations. We had grown so fast, and had recently recovered from our redesign into business units, so we needed to step back and address some fundamentals as a leadership team.

The first day, we discussed our approach to leadership, and shared best leadership practices. One highlight was a "values clarification" seminar, led by our learning and development group. We asked each of the leaders from around the world to rank, in order of personal importance to them, some core values like trust, people focus, client focus, teamwork, excellence, sharing, growth, and social responsibility. Then we asked them to rank those same values according to how they felt the company prioritized them, as evidenced by its actions.

Their rankings told us a lot about our company's values and how they align with our leaders' values. Values alignment is critical to the success of any organization, and it can't be assumed; it must be measured and nurtured. Values guide everything everyone does, and they transcend nationality, race, religion, gender, age, and every other possible distinction.

We did some additional exercises: "Values voting" called for yes or no answers to values-based questions; in a "forced choice" exercise, participants made tough choices between two values; in the "values continuum" exercise, leaders placed their values somewhere on a sliding scale. All phases were marked by lively group discussions.

On the second day of our meeting, we held a "leaders' orientation." We discussed ways our company's culture could be integrated with the diverse cultures that make up our company. We talked about ways to best network across countries, and share ideas and expertise. We drove home the point that as leaders, we are cultural ambassadors.

The group identified areas needing improvement, and talked about how to overcome obstacles like time zones, language barriers, and differences in customs. They suggested how to improve global communications, and based on their ideas, we provided everyone with time zone maps and fact sheets on each country's operations. We created a who's who directory to inform people where to turn for help at our headquarters and in each country. We came up with lists of things that needed to be done, and areas where we were duplicating efforts.

At the end of the two-day program, we held an international high tea, which the senior officers served to our global leaders. And we had some lengthy, open discussion. The meeting was a turning point in our transition from a national to a global company.

Variety Is the Spice of Life

We introduced our views on diversity in Chapter 3. But diversity is also an overriding *global* issue. Some of our most interesting programs are designed to help us celebrate the variety in our cultures, whether it be that of two associates sitting alongside each other in the United States or halfway across the world from each other.

One program, called Bridging Cultural Differences, includes discussions about different cultural continuums, individual cultural programming, cross-cultural hooks, and other elements of understanding and celebrating our differences. The day begins with an exercise that assesses the group's comfort and knowledge of diversity, and gauges cultural fluency.

The facilitator draws a wheel divided into the various levels of diversity knowledge. The first group is "those who know" (well versed in cultural diversity). The second group is "those who know but don't know they know" (picked up cultural awareness without even realizing it, for example, from living abroad). The third group is "those who know they don't know" (have a lot to learn, but at least realize it—and that's most of us). The fourth group is "those who don't know" (don't even realize how little they know). The fifth group is "those who think they know, but don't" (Archie Bunker comes to mind). The class talks about the dangers of being in the last two groups. The key is not to know it all, but to be aware of how much there is to learn.

Two of the most interesting parts of the course are the prework required and a "synthetic cultures" exercise, developed by Paul Pedersen and Fred Jandt at Syracuse University. The prework is designed to get everyone thinking about issues they have faced, are facing, or anticipate they might face in the future. Learning programs are most beneficial when they relate directly to our everyday work. The precourse assignments take time and effort, but they strengthen the results significantly.

The synthetic cultures exercise allows participants to examine and role-play four hypothetical cultures, which is useful in demonstrating how real-world cultures contrast with one another. They also show how each culture represents elements found in other cultures, to some extent. The various characteristics are just emphasized differently in various regions. By examining and role-playing the synthetic cultures, participants are able to experience first-hand how challenging cross-cultural interactions can be. It helps them to understand and begin to develop skills that will help them engage in effective cross-cultural communication.

The synthetic cultures are named Alpha, Beta, Gamma, and Delta. Each represents just one element of real-life cultures. For example, the Alpha culture is described as "high-power distance." This is a soft-spoken, polite, often hierarchical, somewhat restrained culture. The Beta culture is described as "strong uncertainty avoidance." Members are verbal and sometimes loud, animated, and often impulsive. The Gamma culture is "highly individualistic," characterized as somewhat self-centered, defensive, and competitive. The Delta culture is "traditionally highly masculine," a loud, critical, argumentative, physical, and macho bunch—Type A personalities.

For each of the synthetic cultures, a number of characteristics are examined, such as language, behavior signals, barriers, stereotypes, gender roles, and even how they handle stress. The group discusses and role-plays how to mediate conflict between the different cultures, in every possible combination. Here is how it works: Each participant in the course selects one synthetic culture (because they closely identify with it, because it contrasts with their viewpoint, or for any other reason). The class organizes in small groups according to the culture they selected.

Once grouped, teams begin to immerse themselves in the synthetic culture they now represent. While in the role, the groups determine how they will address difficulties they might have with other groups because of differences in their cultures. The groups meet for formal "negotiations" to discuss possible solutions. Participants typically are able to role-play three to four synthetic cultures during the exercise, all the while building understanding, skills, and experience.

This is a comprehensive exercise of what we're called upon to do (though much more subtly) on a day-to-day basis as a global organization. We highly recommend an exercise like this one to any company, whether they do business abroad, have clients who do, or simply because their associates have varying backgrounds, viewpoints, and styles.

The Buddy System

A program we call Global Twinning pairs U.S. locations with those abroad for two-way learning. The U.S. general manager teams up with a country manager to become an "expert" on his or her partner's country, to learn how business is conducted there and about the company's local operation. At the same time, the country manager learns more about the U.S.-originated culture and standards.

The program makes the world a smaller place, not unlike having a "pen pal" as a kid. "Buddies" share experiences, ideas, and challenges. Most of the correspondence is via phone, e-mail, or voice mail, though from time to time, the pairs meet face to face. This is a low-cost, high-impact way to further mesh the organization.

Communication between the two offices occurs at all levels, not just GM to GM. The initial focus is on achieving consistent operational standards and processes, but the business units get to know each other on a personal level, too. They generate biographies of their group, including information on the associates and their clients. They also enjoy joint celebrations.

Global Feedback

To have global consistency, you need a universal culture, one flexible enough to accommodate the local nuances, but with the standards and tools necessary to transcend borders. We mentioned earlier that when our HR team goes to a new global location, they implement culture measurement tools, such as our associate satisfaction survey and 360-degree reviews. Measuring associate satisfaction is quite a new concept abroad; it's more widely understood in some locations than in others. For that reason, our HR team spends a lot of time talking about the reasons and the benefits behind such programs. Careful, honest explanation is the key to successful implementation.

All of our measurement tools have taken root successfully abroad (even our crazy Crayola mailings). But we have found the Associate Satisfaction Survey to be the most comprehensive measurement tool we have. We explained how we administer the survey in Chapter 7, but there's something special we do with the survey from a global perspective. In addition to the typical breakdowns of information (i.e., department comparisons, top strengths, top developmental areas), we also include a country-by-country comparison, which then is provided to each country manager. From it, they can see where their particular country rates in associate satisfaction, as compared to other parts of the world. This helps us ensure global consistency.

Friendship Makes the World Go Around

Our lives have all changed dramatically because of our shift to a global organization. As our CFO says, "We're moving at a much faster pace. We don't have the luxury of weeks of contemplating things. Global expansion is highly strategic to our customers, and sometimes they tell us at the last minute about an immediate global need. We have to move quickly. We have to always be looking at the world and where there are possibilities. We're all operating on a 24-hour basis. I have e-mail and a fax machine at home, and work almost as many nights as I do days. In an emerging environment, you have to, to do business around the world."

One constant is friendship, and our friendships are much richer because we have them everywhere. I recently visited our offices in China to say hello to my associates and to formalize a number of pending agreements with Chinese companies.

Before heading to Asia, our learning and development team held a refresher course about cultural do's and don'ts. After all, we were going to meet with a number of Chinese ministers while in Beijing and Shanghai, and we didn't want to look or act like total buffoons.

We practiced eating gummy bears with chopsticks, we learned how to give and receive business cards with two hands, and we memorized when and where to bow. After a couple of hours of instruction, we felt confident enough to venture to the airport and begin the trek.

Our first stop was in Hong Kong, where after spending time visiting our two offices, we embarked for our first meeting, with the executives with whom we planned to joint-venture in China. Not only were the owners of this multinational conglomerate present, but so were leaders of another company from Beijing.

Upon arrival, we exchanged business cards in the appropriate ritual, and then sat down for cocktails prior to a formal banquet in our honor. This wasn't our first meeting, so most of us felt pretty comfortable. We moved on to dinner and the exchange of toasts to each other's companies. Things seemed to be going pretty well.

Leaving nothing to chance, I had practiced my chopstick dexterity on the flight over and felt relatively confident to use them at dinner. We all sat down, and a welcome toast was made in our honor. A few minutes later, remembering my training, I returned the favor and thanked our hosts. I hadn't really noticed that my wine glass was being replenished every sip or two, and that I was feeling mighty comfortable. The first course was jelly fish and seaweed (I'm not sure which was which), and no faux pas had occurred. Laughter filled the room. Things couldn't have been going better. A couple of courses into the meal, I proposed another toast. What I didn't realize was that my chopstick skill had been impaired by my wine consumption, and more food had gone on my suit and tie than into my mouth. During my toast, my colleagues looked as if they were about to burst out laughing, but I disregarded it because our gracious hosts didn't let on. I sat back down to face the next course.

It was composed of large chunks of something I couldn't figure out how to cut with chopsticks, and I just shoved the whole thing in my mouth. Wrong move. I heard a loud crunch. A bone in the middle of whatever it was had broken a temporary crown my dentist had fitted me with a few days earlier. Before I could formulate a plan, the bone and crown pieces came flying out, onto my plate.

Everyone was hysterical with laughter; even our hosts couldn't contain themselves any longer. After I toweled off and recovered my composure, the senior executive from Beijing stood up, raised his glass, and said, "Friends before business." The next day, we signed a letter of intent to do business in Beijing.

Other Global Experiences

As companies expand globally, much can be learned through shared experiences. Here are some practices from our *100 Best* peers.

MARY KAY. We asked our friends at Mary Kay, "What has been the most difficult challenge for your company in the past five years?" They answered, "Transitioning from a U.S. corporation with some international subsidiaries to a rapidly expanding global corporation. All corporate support groups have been charged with the task of integrating international work into the company and developing systems to support a growing global business."

Mary Kay places a high priority on attracting and retaining employees with international experience and making sure they understand and embrace the company's values. President of International Tim Wentworth says, "No matter how many miles our subsidiaries are from our world headquarters, the culture must emulate what we have right here in Dallas. We have found that in the places where we have the right leadership—people with a Mary Kay heart—we will always succeed."

One way Mary Kay ensures a consistent culture worldwide is through an international assimilation program, in which key new employees from international locations travel to Dallas for an intense two-to-three-week program to learn the Mary Kay culture. During the program, the visiting employees tour headquarters and meet with departments across the company. Likewise, Mary Kay offers a Global Awareness Program to its U.S. employees to teach them about the 26 countries where it has subsidiaries.

By mid-1997 more than 50 international assimilations had taken place at Mary Kay. One participant, the new general manager of Mary Kay Czech Republic, came up with a suggestion that illustrated the effectiveness of the program. The company planned to open its Czech Republic operation on September 1, 1997, but the new GM suggested they postpone until September 13—not because she wasn't ready, but because that's the much-celebrated company anniversary. The folks at headquarters hadn't thought of it, but their new leader abroad had.

Tim Wentworth uses four interlocking rings to represent the model the company strives to emulate in transitioning to a global organization. Each ring represents a region of the world (the United States, the Americas, Europe, Asia-Pacific). The center point of the overlapping rings represents the company's goal of sharing learning across all regions through what he calls "globalizing thought leadership functions."

Mary Kay assembled a cross-functional, cross-geographic team to develop its New Market Model, to determine where the company opens new subsidiaries. Over a six-month period, the team talked with 100 employees across the organization to seek best practices for opening a new market, and the key characteristics for success. The team developed an analytical model for opening new markets that the company now uses to make solid decisions about its international expansion.

The company has been highly successful in instilling enthusiasm worldwide. Mary Kay Ash, the founder, had a memorable experience when she visited Germany shortly after the fall of the Berlin Wall. At a sales event, one of the newly free East German independent beauty consultants came across the stage to meet her. The consultant took the microphone and said, "First we get freedom. Then we get Mary Kay!"

HEWITT ASSOCIATES. Hewitt Associates also places a high priority on its global culture. One associate told us, "I've had the opportunity to visit other offices around the world—mostly while on vacation. No matter where I've visited, I've always had a sense of 'belonging' the minute I walked into the office. Our vision for the future is that we will be celebrated and recognized around the world as the global service provider of choice for our clients, *and* as the global employer of choice."

ERIE INSURANCE. Erie Insurance demonstrates that companies need to think and act globally, even if they have no international locations. Claims adjuster Leslie Bush submitted a suggestion that the company subscribe to Language Line, a call-in translation service offered by AT&T. She says, "This country is a melting pot, and I believe we owe superior customer service to all our customers, not just those who can speak English." By using the product, Erie employees can now converse with customers in 140 different languages, through three-way conference calls.

BE&K. The key to success reported by most of the companies we talked with seems to be total company involvement in global expansion, not just participation by a global team. For example, the folks at BE&K told us, "Within the past five years, BE&K has gone from a company working solely in North America to one that currently has work in 13 countries. With this expansion, a different mind-set is necessary. Every department within the company has played a part."

One World, One Company: A Summary

- There are many avenues to consider when planning international expansion. A phased approach worked well for us. We formed an alliance with partner companies abroad until we were awarded truly multinational business. That called for a different set of requirements, and we stepped up to the challenge by shifting to our own international locations.

- Beware the inherent conflicts of interest in partnership agreements. Although they can serve many purposes, those who participate in them must be fully aware of their limitations; for example, standards (of excellence, of service, of systems, etc.) are not universal. Each company must know which standards are critical, and make decisions about partnerships accordingly.

- To determine where you need to be for the future, plan the obsolescence of your current strategy today, so you're ready to act when the time comes. Start by asking yourself, "To fully take advantage of the global marketplace, what would my company ultimately have to look like?" Be willing to face the truth when it's time to move on to your next strategy.

- To determine what the future looks like, meet extensively with your clients to understand their global business strategies, then do the same

with key suppliers. There may be some opportunities to piggyback successfully on their efforts, and vice versa.

- Look for opportunities within your industry to encourage global consolidation on the part of your clients. But be confident that you're in
the winning position before you recommend single sourcing. If you
are, the sky's the limit.

- When looking for partners or for acquisition opportunities abroad,
make your search process a tough one. It might be painful for prospects,
but it should be. If you're painstakingly thorough up-front, it will save a
lot of grief on the back end. Send your decision-making and implementation teams in with detailed due diligence checklists, and also have lists
of potential resources for help and advice, should they need it.

- Gathering all your leaders from around the world can be a very enlight-
ening undertaking. It's a great opportunity to ingrain worldwide standards, culture, and direction. It's also a good gauge of consistency.

- Training in cultural diversity is critical for doing business successfully
in the United States, and especially if you plan to expand internationally. No one can know it all, but everyone should at least be aware of
their level of knowledge.

- A global twinning program, to pair U.S. offices with their counterparts
overseas, can be a great way to share best practices, bridge cultural gaps,
and foster consistency.

- Gathering feedback on a global basis is critical, but challenging. A great
deal of explanation is needed to ensure everyone feels comfortable in
responding. The United States is far more accustomed to feedback than
many other countries.

- Don't believe that culture and language barriers are obstacles to doing
business abroad. Cultural sensitivity is really important, but people the
world over just want to do business with people they like and trust—
with friends.

9

Mind Meld

We hope you have found some helpful ideas in these pages. We've certainly learned a lot from the input of our 100 best partners. In the opening chapter, we summed up the overriding issues we think companies face today and in the future; to close, we submit a few quotations we think capture the essence of how the best companies in America are facing these issues.

The approaches of the 15 companies in this book are so similar that these comments could have come from any one of the companies. They speak to our key concerns of change, growth, competition, globalization, design, personal responsibility, the tough HR market, and unwavering values.

"Today we do twice as much business in just one week as we did in the entire year of 1972. This explosive growth and our expanding business directions put new and different demands on our work environment and our people. Our continued success is closely tied to our ability to assess and adapt our work environment to embrace these new realities, while nurturing our unique, successful way of conducting business."

—Dale Gifford, CEO
  Hewitt Associates

"My advice to all of us is really an admonition: To remember that our core values relating to the worth and contributions of our people are key to our success now and in the future. To expect them to be nimble and creative in the face of constant challenges requires a commitment from our organizations' leaders to all employees that we will not give up our values in the process of change."

—Laura Avakian, Senior VP, Human Resources
Beth Israel Deaconess Medical Center

"Always remember that the business of business is not business or money. The business of business is *people*, and if your Employees—*your* people—are not happy, not feeling that they are valued nor that their work is noble, they will not be inclined to ensure that your Customers are well served."

—Herb Kelleher, CEO, Chairman, President
Southwest Airlines

"If you treat employees as if they make a difference to the company, they *will* make a difference to the company."

—Dr. Jim Goodnight, President
SAS Institute Inc.

"Our unique culture is our competitive advantage. The challenge is how we reinforce the company culture as we grow worldwide. This is what made our company successful in the past and will be the key to our future. We are building cornerstones to ensure the culture remains the same for years to come."

—Kelly Ritchie, VP, Employee Services
Lands' End

"In every sector of the corporate world, increasing competition will take its toll. It is employees who will solve the competitive problems—employees who are happy on the job, act like owners, and support the company at every opportunity. The hard part is that you have to do it every day and literally thousands of times each day—and the rules keep changing."

"The companies that will thrive in the coming decade will be those that practice strategic visioning versus those that rely just on strategic planning. They will be flexible, and make things happen in spite of a variety of obstacles. The truly successful companies will be in an ongoing 'virtual reality' experience."

—Mike Warren, CEO
Alagasco

Friendship and business are not too different, and the basic rules of friendship we learned as kids will apply forever. The true leaders will be companies whose people can laugh and cry, and where a smile can reach completely around the world. Companies whose leaders hurt when their people hurt, and rejoice in their happiness. Companies built on friendship. Friends help each other succeed, whether in a boardroom or on a ball field. True friendship is not defined by barriers. Friends can be associates, clients, and suppliers from any continent in the world. A friend knows no race, no religion, no boundaries. Companies of friends will not let each other down.

Time is a currency of the future. What we used to accomplish in two years, we now do in two weeks. What used to take us two weeks now takes only two hours. But there is a second currency of the future. It's the currency of friendship, and we can mint as much of it as we like. Through friendship, we gain time, speed, and productivity. Through friendship, we gain strength, happiness, and success.

Friendship can break down barriers. Barriers to peace, barriers to performance, and barriers to perfection. Friendship is the true enabler of the future. I am happy, my friend, to have shared our company's beliefs and practices with you.

A story about syndicated sports columnist Red Smith is a pretty good take on how we feel about this book. It seems a young would-be sportswriter said to him, "There's really nothing to sports writing, is there?" Red Smith replied, "You're right. There's nothing to it. Just sit down at a typewriter with a blank sheet of paper and slit open a vein."

We've tried to share our company's heart and soul with you, and our friends from the *100 Best* have done the same. We hope you have enjoyed what we've written.

We'd love to hear your ideas. We can be reached at:

Care to Compete?
c/o Rosenbluth International
2401 Walnut Street
Philadelphia, PA 19103
(215) 977-4000
E-mail: goodcompany@rosenbluth.com

Index